BMF

BMF

THE RISE AND FALL OF BIG MEECH AND THE BLACK MAFIA FAMILY

MARA SHALHOUP

ST. MARTIN'S PRESS NEW YORK

Insert photographs copyright © Ben Rose/BenRosePhotography.com

Black Mafia Family Tree by Brooke Hatfield

Photos for Black Mafia Family Tree courtesy Atlanta Police Department; DeKalb County, Georgia, jail; Fulton County, Georgia, jail; Spartanburg County, South Carolina, jail; U.S. Marshals Service

www.stmartins.com

Library of Congress Cataloging-in-Publication Data

Shalhoup, Mara.
    BMF : the rise and fall of Big Meech and the Black Mafia Family / Mara Shalhoup. — 1st ed.
        p. cm.
    ISBN 978-0-312-38393-0
    1. Flenory, Big Meech.   2. Black Mafia Family.   3. Drug dealers—United States—Biography.   4. Drug traffic—United States.   I. Title.
    HV5805.F53S53 2010
    364.1092—dc22
    [B]

                                                                            2009040090

First Edition: March 2010

10 9 8 7 6 5 4 3 2 1

CONTENTS

ACKNOWLEDGMENTS

This book would not have been possible without the support of Ken Edelstein, who guided me through the infancy of its research. I'm also indebted to my fellow journalists Scott Freeman and Shaila Dewan, my husband, Todd, and my parents, Diane and Alfie, for their generous insights and critical feedback. I owe a huge dose of gratitude to the investigators who helped me bridge the narrative's gaps, to the attorneys who shared their insider knowledge of various criminal cases, to Rasheed McWilliams for noticing my early coverage of the Black Mafia Family, to my amazing agent, John T. "Ike" Williams, for listening to Rasheed, and to my ever-patient editor, Monique Patterson. Lastly, thanks to Tammy Cowins for keeping me in the loop—and to Big Meech for his willingness to sit down and talk.

CAST OF CHARACTERS

BLACK MAFIA FAMILY AND ASSOCIATES

(See insert for the BMF family tree)

Demetrius "Big Meech" Flenory

Terry "Southwest T" Flenory

Charles "Pops" Flenory

Chad "J-Bo" ("Junior Boss") Brown

Fleming "Ill" Daniels

Barima "Bleu DaVinci" McKnight

Eric "Slim" Bivens

Benjamin "Blank" Johnson

Arnold "A.R." Boyd

Wayne "Wayniac" Joyner

Omari "O-Dog" McCree

William "Doc" Marshall

Jacob "the Jeweler" Arabo

Jerry "J-Rock" Davis

Tremayne "Kiki" Graham

Scott King

Eric "Mookie" Rivera

Ernest "E" Watkins

Ulysses "Hack" Hackett

Jay "Young Jeezy" Jenkins

Radric "Gucci Mane" Davis

INVESTIGATORS

Bryant "Bubba" Burns

Marc Cooper

Jack Harvey

Rand Csehy

Rolando Betancourt

BMF

PROLOGUE: MARCH 2008

As bad as they wanted me, there was no winning.
—DEMETRIUS "BIG MEECH" FLENORY

The most notorious inmate ever to set foot in the St. Clair County, Michigan, jail is reclined on a ledge just off the hallway that leads to his cell. His hair, unwound hours earlier from the braids he usually wears, is pushed back from his face, falling to his shoulders in kinky waves. He's saddled with a few extra pounds, but that's to be expected. He's been locked up in this suburban facility, an hour north of Detroit and just across the water from Ontario, for three Michigan winters. That's countless days stuck in a coop where you can't be let outside, not even to exercise, not even for an hour, unless the thermostat creeps above 40 degrees. Fat chance of breaking 40 in February, or even in March. He's actually looking forward to prison, hopefully somewhere down South where it's warm.

Still, he's not complaining. They've been good to him here. He's polite and well mannered, and that's earned him certain privileges. When visitors come in from out of town—a guest list that he claims has included rap superstars Akon and Young Jeezy (Snoop Dogg tried to come, but got snowed out)—the deputies go out of their way to accommodate them. To the inmate, preferential treatment is nothing new. On the outside, he was used to getting what he wanted. Jail is no different.

Knee propped up, back pressed against the cement wall, he leans into the glass partition. There's no chair on his side, and though a guard just announced over the loudspeaker to please refrain from sitting on the ledge, he's sitting on it anyway. So he has no choice but to look down at me. It's not a patronizing gesture, but one that brings to mind his unshakable pride, his famed largesse, his ability, even now, to salvage some of the grandeur to which he'd grown accustomed.

I ask about one of his other reputed traits, one that paints him in a less generous light—or, as a federal informant once put it, his street rep as "a vengeful killer who threatens people." He kind of chuckles and takes pause, as if bemused by the question. "I'll put it to you like this," he says, leaning in closer, casual and friendly. "If trouble comes to me, then I'm going to deal with it."

That kind of stuff—petty stuff, stuff that got blown out of proportion—used to happen all the time, he says. There'd be jealousy over girls, or people thinking their crew is better than his crew, and so forth. "Some guys make a fool of themselves," he continues. "Then, before they know it, they look up and there's a bunch of us. We just handle the problem the best way we know how." Again, he claims, that's only when people come asking for it. He'd prefer to keep things civil. "I'm more old-school, more family oriented," he says. "I don't believe in airing differences in public places."

It's a reasonable explanation, from a seemingly reasonable man. But it's not hard to glimpse the darkness behind the facade. He offers it up every now and then. It slips from behind that transformative smile, peeks around a pair of otherwise warm and engaging eyes. Those eyes narrow when I bring up a murder charge filed against one of his closest crew members. It's the only violent allegation to hit his

ONE CHAOS

They have a lot of money. They have a lot of drugs.
You don't know what you're getting yourself into.
—MYSTERY 911 CALLER

Demetrius "Big Meech" Flenory didn't just walk into the club. He arrived.

He usually arrived under the watch of bodyguards. Every now and then, he arrived with a hundred or so hangers-on. And on those nights when egos were bruised or the wrong woman got involved, he arrived with trouble. It was hard to compete with a presence so huge, not to mention one that could drop fifty thousand dollars on a single bar tab. And so sometimes, his arrival was cause for others in the club to bolt.

The first sign he was coming: the cars. They coasted to the curb like supermodels down a runway. Bentleys and H2s, Lambos and Porsches. And, when the crowd swelled to full ranks, tour buses. Under the marquees of clubs from Midtown Atlanta to South Beach Miami, the streetlights bounced off the million-dollar motorcade, and it was blinding.

Next, the crew. Meech liked to treat all of them as family. "Everybody moves like brothers," he used to tell them. "Everybody moves as one." But as with any entourage, there was a definite hierarchy. Pushing into the crowd (if that were possible), you'd first find the guys who hover on the fringes, moving forward with a menacing sway. Go deeper, and the vibe would start to change. Guards would come down. Egos would edge up. Keep going, and you'd encounter a steady calm. The aura was one of undisputed confidence and quiet control. That was when you knew you'd hit Meech.

Tall and broad, with the posture of a prizefighter and the swagger of a big cat, Meech could cause the climate in a room to change. "All Meech did was walk in the spot," one woman would later recall, "and panties got moist." His pale bronze skin exaggerated the depth of his ink-black eyes. A movie star's mole rested just below his left temple, at the tapered edge of an arched eyebrow. The aquiline curve of his nose offset his high, chiseled cheekbones. And a pencil-thick mustache and goatee framed a pout that barely turned up at the corners, giving the impression that, even at his most serious, he was about to break into a grin.

Waxing eloquent in his velvety drawl, bedecked with enough diamonds to stock a jeweler's counter, Meech was the center of attention at all the best clubs and the biggest parties, and that's where he intended to stay. He kept the company of rappers and moguls, models and athletes, and, most important, a group of men whom he employed and indulged. He fed the crew six-hundred-dollar bottles of champagne and top-notch ecstasy. He took care of them, lifted them up, behaved as their friend and benefactor. They, in turn, would honor and protect him. He was perhaps more comfortable with the arrangement than he should have been. It was easy for him to forget that there were some things he couldn't control. And one of those things would take place on November 11, 2003. It proved to be "the big one," the very event that Meech—as well as the jittery residents of Atlanta's swankiest neighborhood—had long feared. Though for different reasons.

With its sparkling glass towers and Italianate architecture, its foie gras–obsessed menus and Versace shopping bags, Buckhead is the epicenter of Atlanta's wealth, an Upper East Side with an abundance of parking lots. But by dint of its upscale offerings, the neighborhood—situated a few miles north of downtown and split down the middle by the city's iconic thoroughfare, Peachtree Street—had begun to attract a crowd that made the resident blue bloods cringe: professional sports and music stars, and those who wanted to party with them. And a growing number of that crowd was black. For decades, Atlanta had boasted a thriving African-American middle class. The majority-black city suffered its share of racial tension, but more so than in other places, blacks and whites in Atlanta had benefited from an era of prosperity and, for the most part, the appearance of goodwill. The culture clash in Buckhead was a sharp departure from that.

Historically the provenance of sensible Southern ladies and old-moneyed men, Buckead morphed in the mid 1980s into a debaucher-ous entertainment district populated by a mostly white, notoriously rowdy crowd. Then, by the late '90s, Buckhead changed again, earn-ing an identity as the nightlife district of Atlanta's nationally renowned hip-hop scene. Clubs that formerly catered to frat boys and bachelor-ette parties switched formats to rap and crunk nights. All too often, the partying got out of hand. And the hip-hop scene was easy to blame. The most notable meltdown was the post–Super Bowl stab-bings for which Baltimore Ravens' linebacker Ray Lewis was arrested for murder—and, after the case against him fell apart midtrial, walked away from with a misdemeanor. (The outcome of the case exempli-fied a growing trend of witnesses becoming unable to remember who shot or stabbed whom.) That was three years earlier, outside Cobalt Lounge.

About a block away, near the intersection of Peachtree and Paces

Ferry roads in the heart of Buckhead, a nightclub of similar glitz was earning its name. Chaos was one of the "it" clubs. Shaquille O'Neal and Eminem had partied there. And Monday's hip-hop night was the club's biggest draw. Hundreds of people would pass through Chaos's plate-glass doors on what, for other clubs, was the slowest day of the week. At Chaos, the only thing slow about Mondays was the line.

On that particular Monday in November 2003, you couldn't walk across the club's lacquered wood floors, you couldn't lean against its exposed brick walls or grab a seat on its minimalist leather sofas without catching sight of one of Meech's guys. As usual, Meech's crew was everywhere. Anthony Jones must have known that. Yet Jones, better known in hip-hop circles as "Wolf"—and more important, as Wolf Who Is Sean "P. Diddy" Combs's Former Bodyguard—did something that stood a good chance of starting an all-out war.

Wolf was no stranger to conflict, and as a professional bodyguard, he didn't go out of his way to avoid it, either. He'd been convicted in 1991 for the attempted murder of a New York cop, and he spent two years in prison. Two years after his release, he witnessed an Atlanta club shooting that defined the clash of East and West Coast hip-hop. A crew from L.A., including Death Row Records founder Marion "Suge" Knight, was pouring out of West Peachtree Street's swanky Platinum club—only to come face-to-face with the arriving entourage of Knight's biggest rival, Sean (then "Puff Daddy") Combs, CEO of New York's Bad Boy Entertainment. In the ensuing brawl, a record exec in Knight's camp was shot several times. Weeks later, he died. Six years passed before the long-dormant investigation was resuscitated—with Wolf as the prime suspect.

Wolf also was hanging out at a Times Square nightclub in 1999 when, once again, gunshots rang out. This time, the fight started when a club-goer threw a fistful of bills in Combs's face. After fleeing the scene with Combs, Combs's then-girlfriend Jennifer Lopez, and his rapper-protégé Jamal "Shyne" Barrow, Wolf was arrested on a weapons charge—which he later beat. Shyne didn't fare so well. He was convicted of assault and reckless endangerment and was sentenced to ten years in prison.

Soon thereafter, Wolf relinquished his post as Combs's most coveted muscle, and he came to Atlanta to start over. He wanted to make a name for himself as a hip-hop promoter. He became well known in the local club scene as a big spender and, on occasion, a big pain in the ass. Wolf, with a build reminiscent of a brick wall and a villain-styled widow's peak, was a tough guy. He was a tough guy who would talk himself out of bad situation when he could. But when all else failed, he wasn't exactly quick to back down. The problem was, Big Meech wasn't the type of guy anyone should stand up to for long.

Among Meech's distinguishing characteristics was his insistence that every guy in his crew be given his own bottle of Cristal or Perrier-Jouët at the club—even when the numbers grew to fifty or more. It was one of the obvious ways Meech built allegiances, but it wasn't the only way. People were drawn to him not against their will, exactly, but because his aura of wealth, power, and generosity was impossible to resist. And once inside his circle, his followers rarely left. Sure, there were VIP rooms and beautiful girls and all kinds of money to be spent on whatever luxury you could possibly imagine. But more important, there was Big Meech in the middle of it, his hand resting on your shoulder like the father you never had, the one who let you drive the car your real father could never afford, the one who took you everywhere with him, wherever the business was. This management style served Meech well. His crew's loyalty was like armor. It very nearly made him invincible. And November 11, 2003, was no exception.

In Meech's eyes, he and Wolf were friends. A local celebrity photographer had snapped a picture of the two men just a couple of months earlier, each with an arm draped around the other's neck, wearing glazed-over but friendly smirks. In those early morning hours at Club Chaos, however, any semblance of camaraderie between them vanished. It started when Wolf got rough with his ex-girlfriend. She wasn't just any ex-girlfriend. She was an ex-girlfriend hanging out with Meech's crew. Wolf made it clear he didn't want her keeping that particular company, and he knew enough about the crew to know his objections, once they turned violent, wouldn't be tolerated. Still, Wolf wouldn't let up. Enraged by his ex's refusal to bow to his demand, and with a rapt audience looking on, Wolf grabbed her by the neck.

Meech didn't miss a beat. He stepped in and told Wolf to back off. And for a while, he did. Wolf actually retreated. But Meech had a feeling that Wolf was still angry. And he thought it had less to do with the girl than with a theory he'd hatched: that Wolf was jealous of what Meech describes as a close friendship with Combs. Both Meech and his brother claimed to be tight with the New York music magnate. And it seemed to Meech that Wolf didn't want him on that turf, either.

An hour later, Wolf stepped back into the picture. He went straight for his ex. He started roughing her up again. That time, Meech didn't even have a chance to react. Club security swooped in, and Wolf was tossed out.

It would seem that with Wolf's exit, the night's trouble would have come to a close. Meech and his boys went back to doing what they were known for doing—ingesting an obscene amount of champagne and spending an even more obscene amount of cash. It was only 1:30 A.M., after all, and the bar wouldn't close for another two and a half hours.

Wolf, banished from the cozy confines of the club, stepped into the cool November night and headed toward the parking lot behind the building. He hooked up with his friend, Lamont "Riz" Girdy, whom he'd known since they were kids growing up in the Bronx. He found a comfortable place to lean, up against Meech's Cadillac. And he began to wait.

•　　•　　•

For the past two years, since the spring of 2001, agents of the U.S. Drug Enforcement Administration had been keeping watch on a big white house tucked away in a quiet suburb twenty miles outside Atlanta. Beyond the tall iron gate that kept onlookers at bay—and a front door that admitted select guests into the modern, marble-floored, 4,800-square-foot expanse—agents believed they'd find something they were desperately chasing: evidence to boost their ongoing investigation into Demetrius "Big Meech" Flenory. The problem, however, was getting inside.

The DEA first identified Meech as a suspected drug trafficker in the early '90s. But back then, he was only a peripheral figure. He didn't register as a major player until 1997. That's when special agent Jack Harvey, out of the DEA's Atlanta office, picked up on him. Harvey had been with the DEA since 1984, and he was a good fit for any long, tedious, drug detail. With his pale freckled skin and gentle demeanor, he was unassuming as far as DEA agents go. But underneath his placid exterior, Harvey was an intense and passionate investigator. He had the smarts and the patience to build a case that can take down a kingpin. And after he picked up on Meech in the late '90s, he began to follow him like a shadow.

At the same time that Harvey was tailing Meech in Atlanta, the DEA office in Detroit was developing leads on both Meech and his younger brother, Terry "Southwest T" Flenory. The Flenory brothers had grown up in southwest Detroit, in the downtrodden suburbs of Ecorse and River Rouge, and Michigan investigators had linked the brothers to several Detroit drug traffickers. Many of them belonged to a gang called the Puritan Avenue Boys, or "PA Boys" for short. The PA Boys were a ruthless old-school cocaine crew headquartered along Puritan Avenue in the northwest sector of the Motor City. And with the help of a wiretap investigation and confidential informants, the DEA was closing in on several of its top members. Through that investigation, the agents were beginning to realize that the Flenory brothers, though not members of the PA Boys themselves, had a drug organization of their own. And that organization would warrant some serious attention.

Harvey kept in regular touch with the agents in Detroit. He also began to track several Detroit-born gangsters who, like Meech, had relocated to Atlanta. He built relationships with more than a half dozen confidential informants who slipped him bits and pieces of Meech's history (or at least his myth) in both Atlanta and Detroit. And with each of those tips, the picture of Meech grew more formidable.

One story Harvey heard involved the unfortunate fate of a Detroit drug dealer named Dennis Kingsley Walker. In 1994, Walker had been arrested by the DEA in Atlanta on cocaine conspiracy charges. After pleading guilty, he cut a deal with the feds in exchange for providing information on one of his co-defendants, Tony Valentine. As a result, Walker served only three years of his five-year prison sentence. He was released from a federal halfway house on October 30, 1997. And one of his first stops was the bar at the downtown Atlanta Westin, the second tallest hotel in the western hemisphere.

After chatting up several women and downing a few drinks, Walker left the shimmering glass tower. He drove his Nissan Maxima north on Interstate 85, pulling off near Buckhead. On the exit ramp, a car slowed alongside his. One of the car's windows rolled down. Somebody took aim with a .40-caliber Glock. In a flash, Walker's Nissan was sprayed with bullets. He was killed instantly.

The following January, confidential informants were helping the DEA gather information on who might have murdered Walker. Agents taped a wire to the chest of one such informant, who managed to capture a key conversation: An acquaintance claimed that a man called Meechie gunned down Walker because Walker had assisted the feds in their case against Valentine. Meech immediately became the prime suspect in the murder. But the DEA's trail went cold. Despite an intensive investigation, authorities couldn't come up with enough evidence to make an arrest.

A year later, another confidential informant sat down with the DEA. The first thing he did was pick a picture of Meech out of a lineup. He then shared several things he claimed to know about the man in the photo. The man used fake names, and he'd probably never get a driver's license with his real one. He often walked around with large wads of cash, but didn't have a job. He was known to carry a handgun, sometimes two. He was aware that the DEA was following him, and he wasn't happy about it. Lastly, one of his associates was a notorious Detroit drug dealer and PA Boys enforcer named Thelmon "T-Stuck" Stuckey.

The government already had a thick file on Stuckey. And the more Harvey learned about the flashy old-fashioned gangster, the more parallels could be drawn between him and Meech. For years, Stuckey had split his time between Atlanta and Detroit. Like Meech, Stuckey also had an interest in hip-hop. (He was a producer for the Detroit rap label Puritan Records.) And according to a federal informant, Stuckey had a violent distaste for snitches.

Yet Stuckey was far more audacious than Meech ever was. He once had the audacity to call the police to his Atlanta home after it was burglarized—an unusual move for a drug dealer, even before taking into account the items he reported stolen. Stuckey told police the thieves had made off with a wardrobe that would have made legendary Harlem gangster Frank Lucas proud, including eighteen pairs of five-hundred-dollar alligator shoes and a robust collection of men's fur coats.

A year after the Atlanta burglary, Stuckey found himself in a dangerous confrontation with several Detroit police officers—a confrontation that culminated in him pulling off an amazing feat. The officers claimed that Stuckey fired at them with an AK-47 assault rifle and that he was wounded by return fire. Stuckey was indicted for attempted murder. But he beat that rap. He then turned around and sued the police department for inflicting his injuries. He walked away with a $150,000 settlement.

But perhaps the most outlandish of all Stuckey's escapades stemmed from his relationship with Ricardo "Slick" Darbins, a dirty Detroit cop turned drug dealer. Darbins was fired from the police force after he was caught on a wiretap discussing a cocaine purchase. Stuckey, who was one of Darbins's drug associates, began pressuring the former cop to kill one of the informants in the case. So Stuckey and Darbins drove to a record store where the informant was hanging out. Stuckey hung back in the pickup truck as Darbins went inside and cornered the informant. He fired at him, but missed.

Three days later, Stuckey, who was angry about Darbins's bad aim, decided Slick was too sloppy to do business with. Stuckey drove Darbins over to a fellow drug dealer's house. Once Darbins and the dealer got comfortable watching TV, Stuckey stormed into the room and shot Darbins four times with his .40-caliber Glock. For good measure, Stuckey stood over the body and squeezed off four more rounds. He then leaned over the fresh corpse, kissed it on the cheek, and said, "I love you and I'm going to take care of your family, but you talked too much."

To help dispose of the body, Stuckey had called a "cleanup man," who arrived with rope, gloves, and a roll of plastic. The men wrapped the body in blankets and plastic, tied it with the rope, and dropped it in the trunk of Stuckey's '91 Caprice Classic. They drove to an alley, where Darbins was unceremoniously dumped.

It took six years for authorities to catch up with Stuckey. The DEA got a tip that he was shacking up with a friend in Atlanta, and a team of agents went to the apartment to take him down. It was special agent Harvey who finally managed to arrest him. Amid Stuckey's possessions, Harvey found a piece of paper scrawled with some rap lyrics—lyrics that a prosecutor later would describe as highly autobiographical: "I expose those who knows; fill they bodys wit holes; rap em up in a blankit; dump they bodys on the rode."

The drug dealer who lived in the house where Slick Darbins was killed later turned on Stuckey and testified against him in court.

Stuckey was sentenced to life in federal prison for the murder. With that, his association with Meech ended. But Thelmon Stuckey wouldn't be the last of the Puritan Avenue Boys linked to the Flenory brothers. And the association would come in handy when investigators began building their case against Meech's crew.

From the time Harvey got the tip that Meech was an associate of Stuckey's, two more years passed before he got his next major break. In the summer of 2001, an informant told the DEA that a man named Meechie was living in a huge white house off Evans Mill Road in Lithonia, about twenty miles southeast of Atlanta.

A few days later, on August 15, 2001, Harvey went to check out the house. The sleek, minimalist mansion sat at the corner of Evans Mill Road and Belair Lake Drive, the first in a row of massive homes behind an iron gate that read: BELAIR ESTATES. Over the next few months, Harvey made a habit of driving by the house. Usually, there were high-end sports cars and SUVs parked in the driveway. But toward the end of 2001, it appeared the occupants had up and left.

A year and a half later, the DEA connected with one of its informants—the one who'd heard that it was Meechie who gunned down Dennis Kingsley Walker. Meech was back in Atlanta, the informant said. In fact, Meech would be throwing himself a birthday party that Sunday at the "White House"—the nickname the Flenory brothers had assigned the Lithonia mansion. Meech was planning the event as an after-party for a more formal affair at Sean "P. Diddy" Combs's Buckhead restaurant, Justin's. The grandiose invitations to the Justin's party were printed on the cases of promo CDs, the front of which read, "MEECH'S Harem! A Birthday Celebration of Mass Proportions!" The inside liner promised a party "Fit for a King." And the back of the case teased, "You're invited to indulge in the . . . Mysterious. A Birthday Celebration for a Unique Man!"

At 1:30 A.M. on June 23, 2003, agent Harvey drove over to the

White House to check out the event. Cars lined both sides of Evans Mill Road. Guests couldn't park too close to the house, because the gate at Belair Lake Drive was locked. Partygoers came and went through a small door next to the gate. Surveying the scene from the road, Harvey noticed that groups of people were milling around outside, and the grounds, which included a pool and hot tub, were more lit up than they'd been during past drive-bys. The following afternoon, a confidential informant who'd been at the party gave Harvey a detailed account of the goings-on inside. Meech had surrounded himself with a group of men who were dressed as he was, in knee-length T-shirts printed with the letters BMF. The letters also were tattooed on Meech's left biceps. He wore his hair in braids, huge diamonds in his ears, a large gold ring on his pinkie finger, and a heavy platinum necklace. His ensemble was complete with a hefty blunt, from which he took deep, intoxicating drags.

The guest also told the DEA that in the master bedroom, there was a gun, possibly a .45, lying in plain view.

Investigators jumped at the possibility that there could be drugs and weapons inside the White House. After running a title search on the property, investigators learned the home belonged, at least on paper, to a woman named Tonesa Welch. And DEA files showed that Tonesa was the longtime girlfriend of Meech's younger brother, Terry Flenory. Terry's name, incidentally, had shown up in twenty-two DEA case files dating back to 1990. And, like Meech, he was believed to be a major cocaine trafficker with ties to Atlanta, L.A., Detroit, and St. Louis. Records also showed that Tonesa lived not in Atlanta but in L.A., most likely with Terry. It was a fair assumption, then, that Meech resided at the White House. And investigators hoped to make that connection in their application for a search warrant.

The application was filed on June 25, 2003, two days after the birthday party, and it was filled with the information supplied by the informants: Meech's alleged role in the 1997 highway shooting of

Walker, his reputed association with the Detroit gangster Thelmon Stuckey—even his blinged-out attire at the birthday party two nights before. To top it all off, there was the informant's description of the blunt and the gun.

But the judge didn't bite, nor did he give a reason for refusing the search. The warrant was simply denied, and for a while, the deflated investigators gave up on it. Then, six months later, there arose a more pressing reason to get inside the White House.

Sometime after 4 A.M. on November 11, 2003, club owner Brian Alt was running the night's totals. Mondays at Chaos were good money. Customers were known to spend big on hip-hop night. But those nights also carried a cost. Mondays had gotten so wild that, unlike other nights of the week, Chaos patrons had to pass through a metal detector.

Still, there'd been only a little bit of trouble at the club that night. Three hours earlier, Alt's security team had given him a heads-up that Wolf, a club regular, had gotten aggressive with a woman. Alt was surprised. Earlier that night, Wolf had been bragging to him about his kid and acting the perfect gentleman. Contrary to his violent reputation, Wolf came across to Alt as soft-spoken and articulate, so he took it upon himself to settle the commotion Wolf had caused. He told Wolf it would be better if he left. And Wolf left without a fight.

Three hours later, the night appeared to be winding down without a hitch—until one of Alt's employees came running in shortly after last call, saying something bad had gone down outside. Alt raced out of the club, toward the back parking lot. As he rounded the corner near the club's rear stairway, he passed Wolf's ex-girlfriend, who was running away from the parking lot with tears streaming down her face. Alt feared the worst, and when he got to the parking lot, he found it.

One of his bartenders, a security guard, and two off-duty medics were trying to keep the two men on the ground alive. For one of the two, it was too late. Wolf's friend Riz, who had come to Wolf's aid, was dead. A gun lay at his side.

Wolf, however, was still alert. He'd been shot in the chest but was holding on. While waiting for the ambulance, Alt stuck by his side, imploring Wolf to stay awake, to stay with him. Because sleep might mean there's no waking up.

As Wolf lay bleeding on the asphalt, a car was speeding up GA 400, carrying two other men wounded in the gun battle. They were on their way to North Fulton Regional Hospital. One of them would later claim that after the first shots rang out, he turned and ran and didn't see a thing—a version of events that would be supported, in part, by the fact that he'd been shot in the ass.

On the other side of Atlanta, at Grady Memorial Hospital downtown, Wolf was rushed into the emergency room. Grady's trauma team is one of the country's most adept when it comes to such wrenching injuries as car accidents and shootings, of which Atlanta has no shortage. For Wolf, however, there was little the surgeons could do. Even a wall of bricks can't stand up to several high-caliber bullets. Wolf had walked away from other conflicts, but not this one. Within minutes, he was dead, too.

By the time Atlanta homicide detective Marc Cooper pulled into the club's parking lot, the crime scene had been roped off. His fellow officers were trying to corral as many witnesses as they could, and those patrons unfortunate enough not to have fled were trapped at the scene. No one was allowed to leave. The problem was that none of the people in the crowd claimed to know anything about the gun battle—despite the fact that close to forty rounds had been fired from several weapons.

Detective Cooper's lumbering frame, closely shaven head and matter-of-fact Southern monotone can get him wrongly mistaken for a good old boy. But the detective is a far cry from the stereotypical

Deep South lawman. Within minutes, he realized this was no run-of-the-mill club shooting. The strange silence among so many witnesses in such a public place was something he hadn't encountered before. In the next two years, however, after visiting two more crime scenes with ties to this one, Cooper would become more familiar with the phenomenon.

While the swarm of Atlanta cops combed through Chaos's parking lot to cobble together what bits of evidence they could—a shell casing, a bullet fragment, a few drops of blood—Investigator J. K. Brown fielded the night's first significant clue. It was a phone call. The woman on the line had been transferred to Brown's cell phone after first dialing 911. She said she was calling because she knew who one of the shooters was. She claimed to have seen him reach into the waistband of his pants and pull a pistol. By her estimation, he fired at least seven times. She said that as she ran, she heard more shots. "They have a lot of money," the woman told Brown. "They have a lot of drugs. You don't know what you're getting yourself into." The shooter, she claimed, went by "Meechie."

A second significant clue came a few hours later, when police learned that two men had shown up with gunshot wounds at North Fulton Regional Hospital. One of them had been shot in the foot, the other in the buttock. Atlanta officers picked up both men from the emergency room that morning. They were transported to police headquarters at City Hall East. Seated in separate interrogation rooms, they were asked about their possible involvement in the Chaos killings. After interviewing the man with the foot injury—a lumbering, pale-eyed, and heavily tattooed twenty-seven-year-old named Ameen "Bull" Hight—police decided not to charge him. Instead, they arrested his friend, who said little during the interview and maintained a steady cool, for the murders of Anthony "Wolf" Jones and Lamont "Riz" Girdy. Big Meech was in big trouble.

The only thing Meech did say about the Chaos incident was that he had nothing to do with the murders, that he turned and ran, that he saw nothing. Investigators, hoping to learn more about their suspect, then asked a simple question: Where do you live? "All over," he told them. He had girlfriends he stayed with, he said. Nothing permanent.

Yet the DEA had a pretty compelling argument that Meech lived in a big white house off Evans Mill Road. And it seemed he didn't want them to find whatever was inside.

In light of the Chaos shootings, investigators now had a more specific goal in their application for a search warrant: find the murder weapon used to kill two men in a Buckhead parking lot. The first time around, when investigators initially filed their application, the judge didn't feel there was enough to go forward. Now, things were different. With a few new paragraphs about the double-homicide to flesh out the application, the judge signed off.

On November 17, 2003, a search team led by special agent Harvey filed into the White House, no-knock warrant in hand. In the closet of the master bedroom, the team found the sole occupant of the house, a Haitian immigrant and associate of Meech's brother named Innocent Guerville. Investigators snapped a photo of Innocent and eventually let him go. Then, moving from room to room, the investigators took note of the residence's gaudy splendor. The house was outfitted with $170,000 in marble alone and nearly $50,000 in modern furniture, most of it from an ultraslick Buckhead home store, Huff Furniture and Design. Then there was the rather eccentric assortment of art. The walls of the master bedroom and office were hung with three framed photographs of Al Pacino, lifted from various scenes in *Scarface*; two photos of infamous Gambino family mob boss John Gotti (including one with an encased cigar and bullets); a portrait of slain rapper Tupac Shakur; and, rounding out the collection, a photo of Tupac's archnemesis, fellow deceased rapper Christopher "Notorious B.I.G." Wallace.

The master bedroom turned up other curious items: a police scanner, a stack of fifty CDs titled *Meech's Harem* (including the invitation to his birthday party five months earlier), a fifteen-thousand-dollar medallion that spelled BMF 4 LIFE in white gold, and a loaded 9mm machine gun in the nightstand.

Moving on to the guest bedrooms, the search team found two more handguns (a .40-caliber semiautomatic and a .45), another BMF pendant, and a red spiral-bound notebook. The notebook was filled with scribblings that investigators were all but certain pertained to the drug trade. There were columns titled "airline ticket," "car notes," "money owed," "money paid," "first run," "cali run," "2 nights," "cellular phones."

The notebook also was littered with nicknames that were familiar to one member of the search team, Atlanta police detective Bryant "Bubba" Burns. The detective had seen the names recently, in paperwork pulled from a seemingly unrelated crime scene. And he was about to make a stunning connection.

Like DEA special agent Jack Harvey, Burns was a good match for the intense investigation he was about to undertake. He'd been raised on Atlanta's forgotten West Side, in the shadow of the public housing behemoth Perry Homes and the virtually open-air drug market called "the Bluff." He'd come of age with one ear trained to the police scanner, an obsession handed down from his father, who wasn't a cop but always wished he'd been. It was almost as if Burns's friendly, breathless banter, punctuated by bursts of excitable laughter and grave protestations of the bad guys he chased down, was lifted straight from those crackling airwaves.

For the past year, Burns, a newly appointed member of the APD's organized crime unit, had been working undercover to infiltrate a white-collar crime ring. A purported luxury rental-car company called XQuisite Empire had been using the identities of straw borrowers to purchase BMWs, Jaguars, and Range Rovers for suspected drug dealers. Two months before the Chaos killings, Burns got a major break in the XQuisite investigation. On the night of September 7,

2003, XQuisite's owner, William "Doc" Marshall, called 911 to report that he'd just shot and killed a home invader. When police arrived at the Midtown Atlanta town house, they found that it was outfitted with a peculiar feature. The home had a room-sized safe. If that wasn't strange enough, in a tight passageway flanking the safe there sat a single shoe and a lone kilo of cocaine.

Detectives figured that somebody had been in a big hurry to empty the contents of the safe—such a hurry, in fact, that when his shoe slipped off, he kept on running. The detectives also concluded that the home was a drug safe house. At one point, they figured, the vault likely had sheltered a small fortune in cocaine. And the town house was probably targeted by burglars because the attackers—a crew that targeted coke dealers—knew they'd find drugs inside.

Detective Burns obtained a search warrant for the property, to see if he might find any records pertaining to XQuisite Empire and its owner, Doc Marshall. When he carried out the search, Burns found what he was looking for—and more. The day after the burglary-gone-bad, Burns removed several boxes of documents that divulged intricate details of XQuisite's inner workings, including the names and phone numbers of its employees, a list of cars that had been diverted from straw borrowers to suspected drug dealers, and ledgers that listed the colorful nicknames of the company's shadier clients.

Two months later, after stepping inside the White House, detective Burns was surprised to find paperwork with strong similarities to the XQuisite files. In the White House, Burns discovered documentation for nineteen vehicles (including several limos) and applications for nearly as many cell phones. Many of the cars and phones listed in the White House ledger were registered to the names and aliases of XQuisite's employees. And the mysterious nicknames of XQuisite's clients matched some of the nicknames jotted in the red spiral-bound notebook: E, Country, Cuzo, Wetback. It appeared that XQuisite was funneling cars and phones to the Flenory brothers' associates. Now that Burns had established the link between XQuisite's owner,

Doc Marshall, and the murder suspect Demetrius "Big Meech" Flenory, both his and Harvey's investigations were going to get a lot more interesting.

Something else about the phone numbers listed in the White House paperwork struck investigators: about a half dozen of the numbers had been in regular contact with numbers under wiretap surveillance in Detroit, where DEA agents were building a case against the Puritan Avenue Boys. That investigation was about to wrap up. Eight members of the PA Boys, including the crew's leaders, Reginald Dancy and Damonne Brantley, were indicted on cocaine conspiracy charges three days after the White House search. Meech was not part of that investigation. But his apparent relationship with the PA Boys would help bolster the DEA's suspicion that Meech and his brother Terry were big-time cocaine traffickers.

Rounding out their search of the White House, investigators found a photo in the office that showed the Flenory brothers posing with the PA Boys kingpin Brantley in front of Atlanta's hip-hop mega-venue, Club 112. Also in the office, investigators found an electric money-counter, several bags of rubber bands, and a stack of business cards with the name Terry Flenory and the company 404 Motorsports. One of the owners of the company, federal agents soon would learn, was Atlanta mayor Shirley Franklin's son-in-law. And as the investigation progressed, his connection to Terry would become more and more obvious.

What investigators didn't find, however, was anything connecting Meech to the Chaos killings. Of the three guns pulled from the house—the 9 mm, the .40-caliber, and the .45—none tested positive for a match to any of the bullets or casings found in the club's parking lot. The big-picture investigation, into the scope of Meech's suspected drug organization, was taking off. But the murder investigation was sputtering.

•   •   •

Two weeks after the White House search, Meech was granted bond—an unusual move in a double homicide, especially one that had grown so sensational. In the wake of the shootings, well-heeled and well-organized Buckhead residents were angrily calling for a crackdown on the violence in their neighborhood. ("My question is, how many more body bags have to come out of this area," one exasperated resident, Katy Bryant, told the *Atlanta Journal-Constitution*.) The incident was so emotionally charged that, less than two months after it occurred, it was cited as the impetus for Atlanta City Council's decision to roll back bar closing hours citywide.

Basically, the Chaos gun battle wasn't the type of crime the Fulton County DA's Office liked to leave unresolved. But the prosecutors were left with little choice. Their case against Meech was simply too thin. As it turns out, the seemingly strong lead—the woman who spoke on the phone to the investigator—fizzled out. She was quick to provide the name Meechie, but as for her own name, she wouldn't say. She told police she was scared for her life. Even after she agreed to come down to APD headquarters and give a statement, investigators kept her identity a secret. Investigators didn't name her in any of the subsequent court hearings, either—of which there were only a few.

No grand jury would indict a case without a murder weapon, a witness, or a confession. Indeed, the case never made it to the grand jury. The most that could be concluded was that Meech acted in self-defense, if he acted at all. Meech's attorney claimed the charge was bullshit. Two armed men, one of whom had been tossed from the club, fired on Meech and his crew. Meech said he turned and ran—a fact substantiated by his own bullet wound to the derriere. The injury was sufficient foundation for the defense his attorney would raise: that Meech, far from an aggressor, was in fact a victim.

To Big Meech and his crew, to residents of Buckhead, and to other concerned Atlantans, the Chaos investigation appeared to be a battle the police had lost. But while the murder case against Meech had fallen apart, the APD and DEA were able to take what they learned from the White House search and combine it with other information they'd already unearthed. Judging from the breadth of the evidence, investigators were able to see that they were on to something. It was something big. It was something organized. It was something called, formidably enough, the Black Mafia Family.

TWO THE FLENORY BROTHERS

If you haven't heard of us, you soon will.

—UNIDENTIFIED BMF MEMBER

The thirty-mile stretch of highway between Waynesville and Rolla, Missouri, is among the most taxing of all of Interstate 44, which covers 634 miles from northern Texas to central St. Louis. Heading east from Waynesville, the road grows steep and winding, traversing a rugged terrain that includes the town of Devil's Elbow, so-named for the sharp bend in the Big Piney River. It's a country-side both lush and imposing, and the road that runs through it de-mands a driver's attention. Imagine, then, the difficulty of navigating not a mere car along those slow curves, but a lumbering, forty-foot RV. On the afternoon of April 11, 2004, Jabari Hayes was doing just that. And the RV, a 1999 MCI Coach that more closely resembled a tour bus than a vacationer's motorhome, was carrying some precious cargo.

Given the conditions of the road, it was predictable that the vehicle would at some point drift across the fog line that hugs the highway shoulder. The infraction was small enough, but it was sufficient cause for a Phelps County deputy to flash his patrol lights and pull the RV over. Sitting in the motorhome's cab awaiting the deputy's approach, Jabari had reason to believe this was no random traffic stop. Was he being followed by the feds? He couldn't have known for sure. But he was clearly nervous.

The deputy told Jabari to step down from the vehicle and take a seat in the back of his patrol car. He then ran a check on Jabari's license—a license that didn't identify him as Jabari Hayes from Atlanta. Instead, it listed a Nashville address, one that had been chosen for Jabari at random, and a fake name, Kenneth Tory Collins. Jabari had been issued the license just two weeks before, shortly after he'd been pulled over while driving another vehicle. He couldn't risk getting nabbed again, not after he played dumb the last time. So one of his associates had hooked him up with an inside source at the Tennessee driver's license bureau. The woman helped Jabari obtain the seemingly legit ID, just as she had done for his associates countless times before. After he received it, he was told to memorize all its details. He needed to be ready, just in case.

Now the license was being put to the test. The deputy ran a check on it. It came back clean, just as the woman had promised. Then the deputy started asking questions.

"Where are you from?" he asked.

"Tennessee," Jabari called out from the backseat.

"Where are you going?"

"To visit family in St. Louis, for Easter."

"Did you make any stops along the way?"

"Yeah, one in Georgia and another in Texas, to see my cousins."

Having noticed that the motorhome had neither Georgia nor Texas nor Tennessee plates, the deputy asked, "Where did the RV come from?"

"I rented it in Orlando," Jabari said. "But I left the paperwork at home."

"How much did it cost?"

"About four thousand dollars for the month."

"And how are you employed?"

"I own a valet company."

"Okay," the deputy said, switching topics. "Can you tell me why you have three cell phones?"

Drug dealers are often armed with multiple phones, a fact of which Jabari was well aware. And he was as prepared for this question as the others. His response was quick—and under less tense circumstances, might have gotten a chuckle out of his interrogator. "I like to separate my business calls from my personal ones," Jabari said. "Plus, it helps keep my girlfriends from flipping through my call history and finding out about each other."

His attempt to inject humor into the situation appeared not to be working. Soon after, the deputy dropped a loaded question: "Are you transporting any contraband?"

Jabari tried to maintain his cool, but he couldn't help himself. His reaction to the question was physical. Glancing in the rearview mirror, the deputy noticed that Jabari's hands were trembling. Upon closer inspection, he saw a vein in Jabari's neck, beating faster and faster.

"No," Jabari answered.

Three weeks earlier, Jabari had been stopped on the very same highway, heading west from St. Louis. On that occasion, he was behind the wheel of a Lincoln limousine—a limo whose paperwork the DEA had discovered four months prior, in the office of the White House. The name Jabari Hayes also cropped up in paperwork pulled from the house (hence the need for the fake ID). On that occasion, Jabari had been pulled over not by a St. Louis County deputy or a Michigan State Patrol officer, but by the DEA. The agents brought in a dog to sniff the limo. The dog alerted them to the likelihood of something suspicious. And in a secret compartment behind the backseat, agents discovered stacks upon rubber-banded stacks of hundred-dollar bills—totaling more than half a million dollars.

Yet that traffic stop appeared not to dissuade Jabari, who claimed he was delivering the limo to a friend and had no idea where the cash came from. Nor did it dampen the enthusiasm of other couriers who had similar missions to carry out. In the time that elapsed between that past I-44 stop and this one, Missouri cops busted two other men, Christopher "Pig" Triplett and Calvin "Playboy" Sparks, in yet another car, a Volvo C70, whose paperwork had been found in the White House office. What's more, Pig and Playboy were among the thirty-four nicknames listed in the pages of a red spiral-bound notebook discovered in a White House guest bedroom.

Unlike Jabari's earlier bust, Pig and Playboy didn't walk away from theirs. Inside the Volvo, authorities found nine kilos of cocaine. Pig and Playboy—regardless of whether they even knew the coke was in the car—were facing the risk of major drug felony charges.

Now, however, as Jabari sat in the backseat of the deputy's patrol car, hands trembling and heart pounding, his situation went from bad to worse. Another police vehicle arrived. A drug dog was trotted out. The dog circled the RV, promptly sat down, and started to bark. With probable cause established, the deputy climbed inside the hulking motorhome and, a few minutes later, emerged with three suitcases pulled from the master bedroom. Opening them, he discovered the source of Jabari's dread. The suitcases held bundle after bundle of neatly packed, plastic-wrapped bricks of cocaine. In all, there were more than one hundred kilos—or 220 pounds. On the street, that's about $10 million worth of coke.

Once in custody, Jabari was prodded for information by the DEA. He didn't budge, but agents were able to connect the RV to a Florida luxury car dealership, Orlando Exotic Car Rentals, whose owner, Marc "Swift" Whaley, was believed to have supplied BMF with at least ten vehicles—including Meech's silver Lamborghini.

Those three highway busts in the spring of 2004 were not the Black Mafia Family's first. But for them to come in such close succession was alarming. And if BMF's top brass was confident about Jabari's ability to keep his mouth shut, there was less reason to think Christopher "Pig" Triplett would hold his tongue. Perhaps it was just paranoia, but the smaller shipment discovered in the car with Pig and Playboy shook BMF's nerves all the way to the top, to Meech's younger brother and the organization's West Coast boss: Terry "Southwest T" Flenory.

If Meech was BMF's charismatic face, Terry was its quiet genius, a mastermind who maintained a low profile while overseeing the import of thousands of kilos of cocaine from Mexico to Southern California. Terry was cautious, and he was the antithesis of his brother. Overweight and bespectacled, with a lazy eye that drifted off to the periphery, he had a slightly off-putting, discomforting presence. In matters of business, he was direct to the point of being blunt. He also was understated where Meech was over the top, a shrewd and controlling businessman who kept his followers in check by instilling a sense of apprehension and indebtedness. His leadership style was nothing like the brotherly, egalitarian approach that Meech often took.

In the foothills of L.A.'s San Fernando Valley, Terry owned several suburban properties, including a handsome home for him and his longtime girlfriend, Tonesa Welch, and a couple of stash houses for receiving shipments of cocaine. Like Meech, Terry claimed to hobnob with music producers and NFLers, rappers and entertainment moguls, including Baltimore Raven Corey Fuller and Bad Boy Records' P. Diddy. But unlike his brother, Terry managed to live the high life while staying out of the spotlight. Terry's desire for self-preservation stood in direct contrast to Meech's ambition to be *known*. Meech wanted nothing more than to be a credible force in hip-hop, to see his name join the ranks of such luminaries as Death Row Records founder Suge Knight and Def Jam CEO Russell Simmons.

Terry, on the other hand, was more concerned with survival. Above all else, he wanted to protect the world he built.

And so when Pig and Playboy got nabbed on that Missouri highway, and when Playboy's relatives began to suspect that Pig might in fact be a rat, Terry was quick to offer advice—and create the illusion that all was well with the Family. Speaking on the phone to Playboy's brother, Melvin, Terry did some damage control. But first, he lent Melvin his ear. And Melvin apparently needed it. Because he thought for sure that Pig was going to turn on Playboy.

"I just got through talking to Play about five minutes ago," Melvin told Terry. "He said you might not know what's going on. They went to court, and that nigga Pig can't even look him in his face. He said he don't know if the nigga is trying to turn state's evidence or what, but it's not looking right."

Terry was quick to defuse the situation, starting with a disclaimer about the lawyer he'd hired to defend Pig—a lawyer who, Terry claimed, was held to certain standards. "One thing about this attorney that we got," Terry said, "is that if Pig was doing anything wrong, he would have dropped his case. He don't defend government witnesses." Then, as if to validate his claim that everything was in fact fine, Terry told Melvin he was handing the phone over to his brother, Big Meech. What followed, in true Meech fashion, was an honest attempt to assuage Melvin with a healthy dose of pep talk. Meech had a knack for smoothing wrinkles with his even smoother talk, and this occasion was no departure—except that the voice on the line wasn't his. It was an imposter, a close associate of Terry's named Eric "Slim" Bivens.

Terry wanted to give the appearance that he and Meech were in control, jointly and unequivocally. And so Slim put on his best Meech, and he laid it on thick—starting with, "How you doing, sir?"

"I'm doing okay," Melvin said.

"This is, um, Demetrius."

Melvin then reiterated his concern: "Okay, well, let me say just one thing. I talked to Playboy; he just called me. He said something is not right."

Slim knew just what Meech would say. Or at least he hoped he did. "Listen," he said, reasoning with Melvin, "I know—I can guarantee this one hundred percent—that your brother is just going through a process. It's called patience. He's not going to do no more time. I promise you, your brother is going to be acquitted and be home. I know for sure that the guy that he was with is gonna hold up his responsibility."

"But why can't he look him in his face?"

"Let me tell you something, brother," Slim said, slipping deeper into the voice of a seasoned hypnotist. "I'm gonna be real honest. Your brother is sitting up there, a victim of some wasted time. His mind is playing tricks on him. But I know for sure what Pig is going to do in court, because he already told his lawyer that he's gonna hold up one hundred percent to all responsibility. This comin' from the lawyer's mouth." Then he sugared the situation, as Meech surely would have done. "I just put a thousand dollars on your brother's book," he continued. "Probably in the next couple of days, he gonna see a receipt with a thousand dollars. He don't have to eat that jail food. He can call y'all as much as he want to call y'all."

Finally, Slim offered a Meech-worthy explanation of why things might not be going as well as they should: "It's just been a slow process, 'cause of that town that he's in. It's a hick town. It's a prejudiced town. And they fucking with your brother."

"Okay," Melvin said.

"It's just a mind game. Just tell him, it's a mind game."

Melvin's next question was dangled like bait, and Slim bit. "Well, um, how much will it cost if I go fly down there and see him?"

"Look, to get there wouldn't be no more than two hundred dollars," Slim replied. "But what I'll do is, I'm gonna take that out of my own personal money to fly you there, get you a room. You and your mother can go down and see him."

"I don't want Mom to see him."

"Okay, then, whoever wants to go," Slim offered. "'Cause he needs moral support, and we can't go in there ourselves."

Before ending the conversation, Slim threw in one last gracious note in his attempt to capture Meech's congeniality: "You know what?" he said. "Tell your mom we sorry."

Slim knew what he was doing. The velvet-voiced Meech had such a strong reputation for preaching the gospel of family that anyone mimicking him would know to offer the requisite apology to Playboy's mother. Family was important to the Flenorys. And despite Meech and Terry's growing differences, there was no denying that the empire they'd built was a family affair—one that dated back to the years during which they came of age in southwest Detroit.

Charles and Lucille Flenory were twenty-one years old in the spring of 1969, the year they left Cleveland for what they hoped would be a better life. They'd married two years earlier, not long after graduating high school, and the following summer their son Demetrius had been born. Before the arrival of their second son, however, the young couple set their sights on a new home: Detroit. There was bigger industry in the Motor City, with more jobs to offer and better opportunities for Charles. Plus, Detroit in the late '60s was an exciting place, especially if you were young and black. Motown Records and its aptly named Hitsville USA were churning out top-ten records at breakneck speed, from Diana Ross & the Supremes to Stevie Wonder to Marvin Gaye. For Charles, whose love of music bordered on obsession, Detroit was a better fit than Cleveland.

From the time he was thirteen, back in the early '60s, Charles Flenory had prayed he'd one day become a professional musician. But there was no room in his parents' minuscule budget for music lessons, and Charles would be called upon for other, more pressing tasks. His father, a World War II veteran and warehouse worker, had fallen ill when Charles was a teenager. To help support his ailing father, Charles found work in a Cleveland steel factory, and he handed over each of his paychecks to his parents. In his spare time, though—what little he had—he taught himself guitar. He built up his skills until he was good enough to perform in his church's gospel band. And his dream of making and recording music followed him throughout his adult life.

By the time Charles, Lucille, and baby Demetrius had settled in Detroit, a second son, Terry, was on the way. He was followed several years later by a daughter, Nicole. To keep up with his growing family, Charles typically held down two jobs at a time. He forged metal in a foundry, worked maintenance jobs at several local hospitals, was hired on at three of Detroit's auto factories, and took countless odd carpentry jobs, most of them at local churches. Of all the work he did, the carpentry was most rewarding. That's because those jobs brought Charles closer to two of his most consuming passions: god and the sacred steel guitar.

Usually, the strings of the sacred steel guitar are plied and plucked to mimic the wailing voices that belt out the Sunday hymns. It is a soulful, ethereal instrument. In Charles's hands, though, it was slightly different. Charles had a bluesier, more rocking style than the genre typically permits. When Charles played the sacred steel, the sound was gospel meets Hendrix.

While Lucille pressed upon her children the importance of going to church, Charles imparted to them his love of music. He was able to set up a little music studio in the basement of his family's modest home, in a working-class suburb not far from where the majestic Detroit River swallows the puny River Rouge, and the studio fascinated Charles's elder son. Meech wanted to be a part of the music, so Charles encouraged him to learn an instrument. Eventually, father and son began performing together in the church band, Charles on guitar and Meech on drums.

Charles did his best to keep his family afloat, but try as he might, he couldn't lift them out of poverty. Nor could he and Lucille shelter them from the streets. At one point, when Charles had been laid off from one of his jobs, holes slowly began to wear through the bottom of the children's sneakers. There were days when the kids came home from school to find the gas and power turned off. In the worst of the Michigan winters, Meech recalls his father treading out to the power line, secretly restoring the electricity himself. Watching their parents struggle made the Flenory boys want more. And a job at McDonald's, Meech told himself, wasn't going to cut it. He and his brother had other ideas.

To those who knew Meech and Terry, particularly the neighborhood kids who wanted in on what would soon be a bustling cocaine trade, Charles and Lucille seemed especially supportive of their children. Poverty was a way of life in their neighborhood, but devoted parents were more of an anomaly. Even after Charles and Lucille divorced in 1986, after nineteen years of marriage, they remained close to each other and their teenaged children. In fact, the only thing that appeared dubious about the Flenory clan was that the two sons, starting in the late '80s, began running a neighborhood cocaine ring out of their parents' home. The brothers quickly graduated from slinging fifty-dollars bags of crack on the corner to moving as much as two kilos per week.

Benjamin "Blank" Johnson, who met Meech and Terry when he was eight years old and would go on to become a trusted manager in their organization, witnessed the brothers' early years up close. As a teenager, Blank would walk the few blocks from his house on Patricia Street to the Flenorys' home on Edsel several times a week to pick up an eightball—or about an eighth of an ounce—of cocaine. The coke was a front, lent out to him on consignment. He'd turn it around on the street—where it would break down into seven half-gram bags, worth about thirty dollars each—then would pay the Flenorys back, pocketing the profit.

Throughout the years (in Blank's eyes, at least) it was common to see cocaine lying around the Edsel Street house, a blockish two-story structure at the end of a dead-end street, bounded by an I-75 on-ramp and a pollution-cleanup plant. Blank also recalls that Charles Flenory often would be hanging out when Blank picked up his drug order from Terry, and the transactions did not occur behind closed doors. On occasion, Blank would be let in the house, would drop off as much as three thousand dollars for Terry, and would help himself to his biweekly cocaine supply. He knew just where to find it. The brothers' stash was always in the same place: a hole in the wall above the linen closet door, the one between the living room and kitchen.

The brothers were smart about their business, but they weren't untouchable. The game caught up with Meech early, and from then on he managed to make a hobby of getting into—and, more important, out of—trouble. In 1988, at the age of nineteen and about three years after dropping out of tenth grade, Meech was arrested for possession of a bag of weed and carrying a concealed weapon. He was sentenced to high-intensity probation, but he didn't do any time. In fact, over the next two decades, despite being arrested on a dozen occasions on charges ranging from felony firearm possession to murder, he avoided prison altogether. Part of his ability to stay ahead of the law was his veritable menu of aliases, complete with social security numbers and driver's licenses: a Michigan license in the name of Rico Seville (Terry, in a show of brotherly solidarity, had a fake Michigan license in the name of Randy Seville), a Georgia one with the name Ronald Ivory, a California one with the name of Aundrez Carothers, and one from Tennessee identifying him as Ricardo Santos. Meech also went by Roland West—the name he gave when, five months after that marijuana charge at age nineteen, he was arrested again. Like so many times to come, he used the alias to elude detection and avoid violating his parole.

That same year marked another milestone for Meech. In 1988, the first of his two daughters was born. She was called Demetria, after her father. A year later, Meech fathered a second daughter. He wasn't exactly a regular presence in their lives. Before the girls were out of diapers, their father's work would carry him away from Detroit—and into the big leagues.

When Meech left Detroit in 1989 at age nineteen, he already was respected on the streets. Even then, his name meant something. But he needed a change, so he decided to scope out the scene in Atlanta. Geographically, Atlanta was a good choice. The city originally called "Terminus" was once the last stop for four converging railroad lines. A hundred years later, Atlanta had morphed from a railway hub to a highway town, a place where commuters would travel more miles on average than anywhere in the world. The three major highways extending from Atlanta easily led to the Carolinas and, by extension, the rest of the eastern seaboard; to all of Florida, including one of Meech's favorite cities, Miami; and to Texas and, ultimately, California, the two locations where the majority of the country's cocaine arrived from Mexico. Along the way were drug markets in Alabama, Tennessee, Kentucky, and Missouri—places where the cocaine trade wasn't so saturated that the Flenorys couldn't stake a claim.

The brothers were born hustlers, and they each had a distinct style. Meech was restless. He wanted to leave Detroit as soon as he could, to strike out and find exciting new territory. Terry, on the other hand, sat back and plotted his course. He had a slight advantage over his brother: money. In his younger years, a bullet grazed his right eye, and it was common knowledge in the neighborhood that he received a settlement as a result of the shooting. Word on the street was that the doctors messed up his eye even worse while operating on it. As a result, his eye drifted slightly, so that it often was fixed, disconcertedly, on whoever approached him from the right side. Later, Terry used the settlement money to start a sedan service. He recruited friends from the neighborhood as drivers. And his experience in mapping out routes and directing the drivers came in handy for another, more profitable enterprise.

In the early '90s, when he was still in Detroit, Terry began moving larger quantities of dope, and he started cooking the cocaine into crack with the help of hired hands, including his childhood friend, Blank. Eventually, he and Blank were cooking up two kilos per week, the conversion of powder into crack equaling a windfall on the streets; whereas a brick of powder cocaine can net around $100,000 in street sales, the same brick converted to crack can rake in twice as much. By then, Terry was in his early twenties and was still operating out of his parents' home. He was a solid midlevel distributor, with a fleet of vehicles at his disposal. And the mood and scale of the operation were about to change.

Investigators would later believe that, thanks to an older associate by the name of Wayne "Wayniac" Joyner, Terry and Meech were hooked up with a California cocaine source in the mid-1990s, a source who could supply them with Colombian dope delivered straight from Mexico. Through the source, the brothers would import more kilos than they could've possibly dreamed while working the grind of an average inner-city distributor. Thanks to Wayniac and the Mexican connection, the Flenory brothers began to move hundreds—and occasionally over one thousand—bricks of cocaine per month. To keep up with the flow of drugs and cash, the Flenory brothers would have to employ a network of several hundred couriers, distributors, and money-launderers in nearly a dozen states. The brothers, in turn, had the smarts and stamina to manage a network of that size. At least for a while.

There were two prices that the brothers paid for their cocaine, depending on how they worked the payment. When they bought the kilos outright, the brothers paid fourteen thousand dollars apiece. That was called, simply, a *buy*. When they bought the bricks on consignment, a pick-up-now-pay-later arrangement, the price was upped to sixteen thousand dollars. That kind of deal was called a *push*. Regardless of the payment plan, the deal was for pure, uncut cocaine.

And so the next stop for all the bricks was one of several labs that the brothers operated in Detroit and Atlanta.

The labs were set up in inconspicuous locations: a house in the upscale Detroit suburb of Farmington Hills, a nondescript apartment in nearby Southfield, a half-million-dollar town house on the outskirts of Atlanta's Buckhead, and another swanky home across town: the White House. In each of the residences, the room used for the lab would be outfitted with an air-filtration system, to make sure the workers didn't get too much of a contact high. The workers themselves would wear rubber gloves, goggles, and surgical masks. Their task was to break apart each brick of pure cocaine and remove 125 grams (an eighth of its total weight). The weight was then replaced, or "cut," with a filler, or "comeback." Both the cocaine and the filler, typically a liquid additive called Pro Scent, were thrown into a food processor and thoroughly blended. The workers then used spatulas to spoon the mixture into a mold. Finally, a five-ton hydraulic jack pressed the kilo back together. For every seven kilos that were cut, blended, and repressed, a new kilo would be formed out of the grams that had been removed. And all the cut kilos would be nearly 90 percent pure.

It sounds like a lot of work for a little payoff, until you consider that hundreds of kilos were processed every month—at *each* lab. For every one thousand kilos that were cut, an additional 150 kilos were created. And with each kilo selling at a three-thousand-dollar profit (not to mention the pure profit off the 150 newly created kilos), the Flenory brothers cleared roughly $5 million on every one thousand kilos they purchased.

As far as hauling the cocaine shipments from California to the labs, and from the labs to the distributors, that would be a relatively easy, if risky, task. The kilos were transported in cars, vans, and limos that were outfitted with secret deoxygenated compartments, called *traps*. Some of the vehicles had names. Two Lincoln Navigator limos, one black and one gray, were known as "the Tank" and "the Gray

Lady." Depending on the size of the haul and the length of the ride, the drivers of the vehicles were paid between eight thousand and twenty-five thousand dollars per trip. The most lucrative drive was the one from California to either Detroit or Atlanta, particularly if you were driving one of the Navigator limos. The limos could carry up to two hundred kilos, more than any other vehicle, and only the most trusted drivers knew how to access the traps in which the cocaine was secreted away. New drivers, on the other hand, would have to rely on a manager, who'd be waiting on the shipment at the destination. With the Navigator limos, the trick was to simultaneously pull the emergency brake, hit the rear defrost button, and open the moonroof. That would disengage the lock on either the right-hand or left-hand compartment. Other combinations, in other vehicles, required the use of a magnet, which was held up to the dashboard, or the depression of a secret button under the floor mat.

In addition to carrying shipments of pure cocaine from California to the labs, the shipments of "cut" cocaine would have to be picked up at the labs and delivered to distributors not just in Atlanta and Detroit, but also in New York, D.C., Missouri, Florida, the Carolinas, Kentucky, Alabama, and Tennessee. The drivers then collected cash from those distributors and hauled the money back to the labs in Atlanta and Detroit, where it would be counted and paid out to the drivers, distributors, and managers. Finally, what was left of the proceeds would be driven back to California, to purchase the next shipment of cocaine. The drivers would carry as much as $9 million in cash at a time. For hauling cash, they'd be paid considerably less—as little as one thousand dollars—because the risk wasn't nearly so great.

To maintain such an intricate and sophisticated web, the Flenory brothers needed an overarching structure to govern their organization, and a guiding philosophy to steer it. They opted for something a little different from many of their predecessors. Meech and Terry chose not to model their Black Mafia Family after '80s-era drug empires such as the Supreme Team, led by Queens native Kennith "Preme" McGriff, which ruled the streets by instilling fear and creating chaos. Instead, they assumed a more corporate model, with Meech and Terry as semi-benevolent CEOs. And while their organization did resemble an actual Mafia in more than just name, the brothers held to some rather standard business practices, starting with the hierarchy of their staff.

Aside from sharing a few drivers, the brothers employed separate and distinct crews. And they had different philosophies on how crew members should be treated. Meech played the role of magnanimous leader, a friendly and revered godfather—and his second-in-command, a longtime associate out of St. Louis named Chad "J-Bo" (short for "junior boss") Brown, handled the dirty work. J-Bo, whose slick bald head and rotund belly belied a lean cunning, often was found at Meech's side, a literal right-hand man who watched the organization like a hawk and was known to notice a few hundred dollars missing from a stack of five thousand dollars. J-Bo could be counted on to run the ship when Meech was out of town, and he dealt with the day-to-day stuff—most important, overseeing the arrival and departure of cocaine shipments. Meech himself was seldom, if ever, in the same room as the coke. He didn't touch the drugs, he didn't handle the cash, and he didn't give direct orders. Those were J-Bo's jobs. For many of the crew members—from the drivers to the high-ranking managers—the only real interaction they had with Meech was partying with him in the clubs.

Below J-Bo were Meech's top-level managers, Martez "Tito" Byrth, a towering and quiet figure who stayed behind the scenes, and Fleming "Ill" Daniels, a short, sweet-faced, and ill-tempered New Yorker who was likened by other crew members to the actor Joe Pesci. Meech hand-picked Ill because of his work as an enforcer on an East Coast cocaine route, and he was prized for his loyalty and protectiveness. Rounding out Meech's crew were Barima McKnight, a fame-hungry Carson City rapper better known as Bleu DaVinci; Marque

"Baby Bleu" Dixson, a strikingly handsome Californian believed to be Bleu DaVinci's younger brother (the two were not related); Ameen "Bull" Hight, a hulking and pale-eyed manager who'd been shot along with Meech behind Club Chaos; and, in a tier below the others but still a significant player, Omari "O-Dog" McCree, an Atlanta coke dealer from a storied, drug-infested neighborhood called Boulevard. Omari was a confidant of Meech's slender, husky-voiced assistant, who went by the nickname "Yogi"—and a close friend of then-up-and-coming rapper Jay "Young Jeezy" Jenkins.

Terry, like Meech, was generous with his crew. But in other ways, his style was a drastic departure from this brother's. Terry assumed a more direct role in the business. He was known to pop in on the labs to make sure they were humming along, and he often was on hand in various states to receive the cocaine shipments directly. He kept the drivers on their toes, and found ways to make them indebted to the organization. When Terry was in a particularly manipulative mood, for instance, he'd tempt a lower-tier driver with a fancy new car. Then, after the employee accepted it, Terry would make him pay off the vehicle by withholding payments for his various cross-country cash and cocaine runs. "Whatever way he could keep his foot on your neck," one of his high-level managers, Arnold "A.R." Boyd, once remarked.

A.R. was part of Terry's innermost circle, and though he respected his boss, he found fault with him, too. A.R. had started off as Terry's personal driver (the boss hated to fly), and he rose to a managerial position only after his older brother, the Flenorys' childhood friend Benjamin "Blank" Johnson, was locked up on a cocaine charge. With the long-trusted Blank indisposed, A.R. was the natural replacement.

Of Terry's other, numerous employees, Eric "Slim" Bivens was among his favorites. Terry lavished him with perks, such as the time he gave Slim a $200,000 black Bentley coupe for his birthday. Slim also was one of the few of Terry's associates who'd met the Flenroys'

Mexican cocaine connection. The other anointed ones included Derrick "Chipped Tooth" Peguese, who kept watch over Terry's side of the Atlanta operation; William "Trucker" Turner, a manager who helped handle the cocaine when it arrived in California from Mexico; and Marlon Welch, the adult son of Terry's longtime girlfriend, Tonesa.

Below Terry's inner circle were his midlevel managers: Terrance Short, a cousin of the Flenorys who hailed from Texas and went by the obvious moniker "Texas Cuz"; Michael "Freak" Green, a trusted childhood friend of the Flenorys and sometime overseer of the Atlanta White House; and another overseer of the White House, Innocent "50 Cent" Guerville, who resembled the rapper with the same nickname. Terry also oversaw a BMF cell in St. Louis that was manned by Danny "Dog Man" Jones and Deron "Wonnie" Gatling, the latter of whom was friendly with another kingpin, Jerry "J-Rock" Davis, who ran a sister cocaine crew to BMF.

In fact, J-Rock introduced the Flenorys to one of their most important associates, William "Doc" Marshall. Doc, a slightly built and preppily dressed Atlantan who had a knack for pulling guileless young women into the organization's fold (he fathered twelve children by his mid-30s), had started off his lengthy criminal career as a high-end car broker. That's how he met J-Rock. J-Rock needed someone to help him obtain Mercedes, BMWs, and Ferraris, and Doc was a wiz at coming up with people both real and imagined in whose names dozens of vehicles could be titled and paid for, so as to throw the feds off of drug dealers' trails. One day, when Terry Flenory mentioned to his friend J-Rock that he was in need of such a service, J-Rock said he had just the guy.

After meeting Terry, Doc immediately noticed something different about him. Unlike most of the drug dealers Doc did business with, Terry didn't sugarcoat what he did for a living. He was completely up front with Doc about being a drug trafficker. If they were going to do business, Terry told him, he needed to know exactly where Terry was coming from. Another notable thing about Terry was that he wanted far more cars than the other kingpins who relied on Doc's services. So when Terry requested that Doc deal with him exclusively, Doc agreed. Doc had reason to believe that Terry had some serious clout—especially after Terry flashed a few pictures of him taken with P. Diddy.

Doc—at Terry's urging—also started getting cars for Meech and his crew. But, as with everybody else who worked with Meech, Doc didn't do any transactions with the boss himself. Instead, he negotiated with J-Bo. After dealing with the brothers for several years, however, Doc and Meech became closer. And eventually, Doc's job description changed. There came a point when Doc could no longer get cars for the Flenorys, because one of his cars was pulled over, and the cops found twelve kilos inside. That brought too much heat to Doc's company, XQuisite Empire, and to all the cars that he'd brokered over the years.

But because Doc had grown so familiar with the inner workings of both Meech's and Terry's crews—and because he was so good with numbers—he was promoted to a new position: the Flenory brothers' chief financial officer. As CFO, Doc kept track of how the organization was spending its money. He documented outstanding debts that were owed the brothers. And he identified ways in which the brothers could launder and invest tens of millions of dollars in drug proceeds. To that end, Doc helped set up bank accounts into which Meech and Terry's cash could be deposited, by viable sources and in modest amounts, to avoid federal detection. (Doc did, however, bring some unwanted attention to BMF when he shot a home intruder in self-defense—one who'd most likely had his eye on the contents of a room-sized safe in Doc's Atlanta town house.)

Doc also started distributing the Flenory brothers' cocaine to local drug dealers. He typically moved twenty to thirty kilos per month. It was a natural progression, considering the number of drug dealer contacts Doc had acquired in the car business. Doc, like most of the people the Flenorys employed, had a knack for the drug game.

For Doc—and for all the brothers' employees—the rules were simple: Don't speak of the organization to anyone outside the organization. If you get busted, take your own heat. Reckless violence is frowned upon, as it attracts too much of the wrong attention. Loyalty is prized above all else, though you should manage to keep your wits about you, too. And if you can in some way prove your undying devotion to the organization, do it. To that end, the younger and more audacious of the organization's members (almost all of them in Meech's camp) took the crew's motto to the extreme—and to their skin. The tattoo they bore, in thick cursive lettering spanning the length of the forearm, made the point succinct. The letters *BMF* were intertwined with the crew's motto: *Death Before Dishonor.*

One of the first orders of business when dealing with a highly profitable cocaine enterprise is finding something to do with all that cash. It's more problematic than one might think. To buy a house, or even a car, with a pile of money is like sending a letter to the feds asking them to investigate you. Even the type of jewelry the Flenory brothers favored—chunky diamond medallions, weighing in at increasingly astronomic carats—couldn't be purchased outright. Same goes for an Italian leather sofa, or imported marble slabs for a bathroom renovation. All those things cost more than ten thousand dollars, and anytime a consumer pays that much or more in cash, the merchant is required to file a federal Form 8300 that documents the transaction. Rack up enough 8300s, and you're bound to pop up on the IRS's radar—particularly if you have no verifiable income and haven't filed a tax return in a half dozen years, which pretty much described Meech and Terry's situation.

Basically, the Flenorys had to come up with new ways to launder their dirty money. One such scheme that Terry hatched involved the manipulation of the Michigan State Lottery. A cocaine distributor who worked with Terry was friends with a Detroit convenience store owner. At the distributor's urging, the store owner set aside stacks of his shop's winning lotto tickets, typically scratch-offs worth between five thousand and seventy-five thousand dollars a pop. Terry would buy the tickets off the store owner—at the store owner's profit, of course (say, $5,250 for a $5,000 scratch-off). Then, Terry would have various girlfriends, and at least one of his girlfriend's mothers, cash in the tickets. For several years, each of the women claimed between $30,000 and $100,000 in annual lottery winnings. That way, the women appeared to have legitimate incomes—incomes with which they'd buy homes, cars, and jewelry for Terry, the kind of things drug money can't buy.

Of course, the organization couldn't launder all its millions of dollars using the lotto scheme. And so, as any good corporation is inclined to do, BMF diversified. The Flenorys, with the help of CFO Doc Marshall, flooded money into the bank accounts of associates with clean criminal records and legit employment histories. Under the guise of those associates, the brothers invested in real estate, the businesses of friends and family, and, in Meech's case, a hip-hop magazine and record label. The result was that the brothers created jobs, some legal and others not, for several hundred of their nearest acquaintances.

On the one hand, the brothers' cocaine empire capitalized off the affliction of inner-city blacks who, not unlike themselves, were the product of struggling schools and limited opportunities. That could be viewed as a predatory business model. On the other hand, if it wasn't the Flenory brothers doing that line of work, someone else would—perhaps someone not so willing to give back. To Meech, the ends justified the means. It was a warped inversion of the American dream, a Robin Hood mentality tailored to the drug trade, a belief that if you worked hard and beat the system, then funneled some of your cash back into the community, at least some of the system's casualties would benefit from your enterprise.

Yet the Flenory brothers didn't exactly live like paupers so they could give to the poor. They reveled in the kind of decadence enjoyed by the nation's most well compensated chief executives—and, in a way, they fancied themselves a member of that class.

Terry, the more understated of the two CEOs, eventually set up shop with Tonesa in Los Angeles, where the organization's drug shipments arrived from Mexico. Terry was familiar with the lay of the city; even before he moved there, he spent much time in L.A. for business and pleasure. (Some of his California friends assumed he was in the music industry, due in part to the fact that he flew by private jet to parties in Miami and New York, including those hosted by P. Diddy.) Over the course of several years, Terry bought at least three homes in the San Fernando Valley, all of them placed in Tonesa's name, and the houses reflected Terry's growing stature in the City of Angels. First, there was the two-story Italianate stucco, just barely on the wrong side of Ventura Boulevard and strategically located in a small cluster of homes behind a formidable iron gate. The gate allowed the residents to control who came and went, and to enjoy a level of privacy other homes in the area didn't offer. Nobody, including the feds, could watch the house too closely.

Crossing over Ventura to the south, approaching the more posh side of the L.A. suburbs and inching ever closer to the coveted hills, was Terry's handsome split-level, all but obscured by a thicket of well-manicured California flora. (Again, all the better for evading detection—especially considering that the property was monitored by an elaborate system of hidden cameras.) The house was called the Jump, and its long driveway that wrapped around back was perfect for the arrival of limousines, loaded with cocaine, that went undetected by the neighbors. Terry and Tonesa didn't live at the Jump. It was simply a place to meet "the connect."

Something else about the split-level—it just so happened to sit on a cul-de-sac within spitting distance of the home of another major drug dealer, J-Rock. J-Rock's organization, Sin City Mafia, was closely aligned with the Flenorys'. The two drug rings shared the same distributor, two of the same hubs (Atlanta and L.A.), and even a few associates—one of whom, the son-in-law of Atlanta mayor Shirley Franklin, would soon bring some unwanted attention to both crews.

The most impressive of Terry's homes, though, the one that lorded over the others, sat on the most prestigious of L.A. streets, an address from which you could climb no higher: Mulholland Drive. The house was built into the hillside, a modern terra-cotta-roofed structure with a three-car garage and three-sided courtyard. The $2.9 million home, situated at the foot of a descending driveway and tucked safely behind by a security gate, offered a commanding view of the eternal sprawl of the Valley, a repetition of palm-lined and smog-choked streets, soulless chain stores and dingy fast food joints— and, in the midst of it all, a couple of BMF stash houses through which an estimated $270 million in cocaine eventually would flow.

The next stop, for most of the coke, would be Atlanta—a market largely overseen by Meech. In prior years, a crew called the Miami Boys was responsible for most of the cocaine funneled into Atlanta. But in the early '90s, the feds caught up with the crew, and with the Miami Boys extinguished, there was an opening in Atlanta's drug market for a new ruling class. As it was, the city's top-level distributors were buying their coke from various sources, often scrapping with each other over territory and pricing. In the disorder, Meech and Terry saw an opportunity. Rather than strong-arm their way into the trade, as the bloodthirsty Miami Boys had done (and the Supreme Team before them, up in Queens), Meech and Terry entered the market in a businesslike manner; they sat down with Atlanta's major cocaine dealers and offered them a better price: seventeen thousand dollars per kilo. The brothers were able to undercut the competition because they had access to such a vast supply. And so it made sense to move the kilos at a lesser price, even if the profit margin was lower, because it served to choke out all rivals—who, unlike the Flenorys, didn't have nearly so deep a well from which to draw.

And so Atlanta, with its web of highways and its easygoing drug market, turned out to be a good choice for Meech. But Atlanta would become attractive for another reason, too. Less pressing than the business of setting up the drug enterprise, but closer to Meech's heart, was the fact that starting in the late '90s, Atlanta began to blow up on the national hip-hop scene. Rappers were flooding the streets with mixtapes, a phenomenon that allowed music to flow straight to the people—and helped build a quick buzz around new talent. The "tapes," which usually took the form of CD compilations, were played at clubs and on the urban radio stations, were handed out at shows and on street corners, and were sold online and in underground music stores, all without the interference of a major record label. The mixtape culture brought a new immediacy to hip-hop. Artists could keep fans up to date on allegiances and feuds with other rappers. They could respond to each other's attacks and counterattacks with freshly pressed verses, released within days rather than the months it takes a label to press a traditional album. The mixtape culture would soon catapult Atlanta rappers such as Jeezy, T.I., Lil Jon, and Ludacris—as wells as the terms *crunk* and *Dirty South*—to superstardom. It also helped change the face of the city.

In the late '90s, Buckhead's clubs were booming with the bass of homegrown tracks such as OutKast's "Rosa Parks," followed a few years later by Lil Jon & the East Side Boyz' "Get Low." The scene was almost unrecognizable from a few years earlier, when Buckhead, though still debaucherous, was a far whiter place. Ironically, as blacks were enjoying increasingly more influence in the glitziest of all Atlanta neighborhoods, many of the city's traditionally black neighborhoods were hemorrhaging residents. Across Atlanta, an intown renaissance was under way, spurred in large part by the demolition of an eventual dozen public housing projects, all of them torn down to make room for "mixed-income" (read: whiter and wealthier) communities. The two forces—the whitening of intown Atlanta and the darkening of Buckhead—weren't exactly at odds. The influx of young up-and-comers from the suburbs and from far-off states, coupled with Atlanta's soon-to-crest hip-hop wave, was reshaping the city as a more upscale and glamorous place, less like the forlorn Detroit to which the Flenorys were accustomed and more like the sparkling Miami and L.A to which they aspired.

But as the city slowly morphed, forcibly displacing some down-and-out residents, several pockets of urban blight remained. The biggest of them comprised an area called the Bluffs, off the old Bankhead Highway on the West Side. On the east side of the city, the most concentrated center of poverty could be found along a corridor flanking the thoroughfare called, simply, Boulevard. While other intown neighborhoods sprouted independent coffee shops and $400,000 condos, the drug trade flourished in the Bluff and on Boulevard, making the influx of crack and powder cocaine all the easier for the Flenorys to control. And control it they did, from the safe distance of several unassuming stash houses in upscale Atlanta neighborhoods.

For Meech's bigger vision to work, he actually *needed* both Atlantas: the one embodied by Boulevard and the other by Buckhead. Thanks to the cocaine distributors who thrived in the drug districts such as Boulevard, Meech raked in the kind of money that laid the groundwork for another endeavor, one that necessitated his presence in the Buckhead clubs. At first, he cut a shadowy figure there, almost blending into the backdrop except that he struck club-goers as something exotic, a light-skinned, ever-so-slightly thuggish figure with chiseled features and braided hair, watching the crowd with an air of authority. He seemed to always be around, solitary and unassuming and yet, when you look at it in retrospect, most certainly plotting something—and imagining the day, not too far in the future, when the spotlight would be focused on him.

At the same time, Meech was gaining a sinister reputation in some

of the city's seedier corners. Those who knew him, if only peripher-
ally, knew the rumors about his dark side. There was one incident,
back in 1996, when he was arrested at one of the city's most popular
watering holes for both rappers and ballers, a place where new tracks
were dropped to gauge the crowd's reaction and, subsequently, where
many a career took a boost or a nosedive. The scenery wasn't too
shabby, either, depending on your taste. Magic City, directly across
from the downtown Greyhound station, boasts Atlanta's finest selection of buxom all-black strippers, capable of gravity-defying, seemingly unnatural feats. From the finely polished bumpers of H2s and
Lambos in the parking lot to the equally well-buffed curves gracing
the fleet of women inside, Magic City was a place you came to show
off. In 1996, Meech wasn't quite ready to expose the full potential of
his wealth. He hadn't reached full potential yet. But he was able
to prove that he was a badass. One February night, he was taken out
of Magic City in handcuffs, having been accused of throwing a bottle
at another patron and slicing his neck. And still, Meech was allowed
back inside the downtown club.

The Magic City agg assault charge was dropped a month later. It
had been filed under one of Meech's alias, Ronald Ivory, the name on
his Georgia driver's license, and authorities hadn't yet caught on to
the ruse. Two years later, he was arrested again in Atlanta, during the
raid of a suspected drug house; that time he fell back on one of his
earlier, Michigan aliases, Rico Seville. After he was charged with
felony obstruction and misdemeanor marijuana possession (the raid
was pretty much fruitless), he was released. Soon thereafter police
discovered a match between Rico Seville's fingerprints and Ronald
Ivory's, and the DEA helped draw the connection between Rico,
Ronald, and Demetrius "Big Meech" Flenory.

And then, it seemed, Meech disappeared from Atlanta. Over the
next few years, some of the few hints that law enforcement gleaned to
his whereabouts came from confidential informants and a minor arrest. In 2000, he was charged with DUI in L.A., and he identified

himself using a recently issued California driver's license in the name of Aundrez Carothers. Again, his fingerprints gave him away, but not until after he was released. A year later, an informant told agents in Atlanta that Meech was making regular trips across the country in a white van—loaded with up to two hundred kilos of coke. According to that informant, Meech made the trip from L.A. to Detroit, where he'd typically drop off half the load, and then to Atlanta, where he'd deliver the rest. The following year, a third informant heightened the profile on Meech. He told the DEA that the kingpin from Detroit was a vengeful killer who vowed to "whack" anyone who cooperates in an investigation against him. And in 1997, Meech's name was mentioned in connection to the Atlanta drive-by killing of the federal informant Dennis Kingsley Walker.

Meech's low profile didn't last. In 2003, he was back in Atlanta, bigger and more visible than ever. He descended on the strip club circuit with newfound rigor, religiously showing up on Monday nights at Magic City—and purportedly finding himself banned from another club, 24-K, after getting into a fight with one of the dancers. This time around, he was almost always in the company of a large crew, and the crew was throwing around fistfuls of cash. The outings were among the first obvious displays of allegiance to Meech and the mysterious organization he'd created. Wads of dough aside, the crew members weren't exactly difficult to pick out of the crowd. Proof of their affiliation was even less subtle than the blue bandannas favored by Crips, the L.A.-based gang with whom Meech's crew was loosely affiliated, or the red ones worn by rival Bloods. Meech's entourage wore black T-shirts printed with three letters, ones that might have puzzled onlookers at first. Yet within months, in circles not only in Atlanta but also in Detroit, L.A., Miami, and New York, the abbreviation BMF would become synonymous with the Black Mafia Family—as well as with a particular brand of partying that bordered on the absurd.

The letters were not only displayed on members' shirts (or, in some cases, tattooed on their forearms), but were also spelled out in diamonds hanging from their necks on platinum chains. At first, the medallions were modestly sized, perhaps an inch tall and a couple of inches across. (Referring to the diminutive carat count of one of those early chains, one crew member said in a whisper, "BMF.") Over time, however, the medallions grew, as if along an arc drawn by BMF's growing dominance in the cocaine trade. And so Meech and Terry would have to employ a jeweler, one of the world's best—and that would necessitate an increasing number of trips to New York, to the posh Upper East Side shop of celebrity jeweler and self-pronounced "King of Bling," Jacob Arabo.

Long before he had the pleasure of creating diamond-encrusted "Five Time Zone" watches for the likes of David Beckham, or of dressing Christy Turlington in a $180,000 necklace for her wedding to actor Ed Burns, Jacob was a struggling immigrant working in Brooklyn's then-not-so-chic Williamsburg. In his midteens, he'd landed work in a jewelry factory, welding bracelets for $125 a week. He found the work was inspiring, and in his spare time he sketched out jewelry ideas in a notebook he carried with him. Twenty years later, his eye for design had turned him into a multimillionaire— thanks in no small part to the status heaped upon him by rappers who coveted a "Jacob," as his pieces were affectionately called. It was Jay-Z who helped popularize the phrase "Jacob the Jeweler" among the hip-hop set, and others followed suit: "I went to Jacob an hour after I got my advance," Kanye West would later rap. "I just wanted to shine."

His Upper East Side store, Jacob & Co., was designed to look like the inside of a diamond mine (a mine perhaps inhabited by a Rocke-feller), and the walls were hung with autographed photos of Jacob's clientele: Jessica Simpson, P. Diddy, and 50 Cent. In wealth and ap-pearance, Meech and Terry came across no different from a vast number of Jacob's customers. But the Flenorys would stand out in one significant way. Jacob was more than familiar with the federal Form 8300, the one that the IRS requires for any cash transaction totaling more than ten thousand dollars. The vast number of Jacob's pieces exceeded that price—and many of his clients actually carried that much cash. But with Meech and Terry, as with most of the associates who showed up at Jacob & Co. on their behalf, no such forms were filed.

One of those associates, Terry's upper-level manager A.R. Boyd, recalls accompanying his boss during one of his more exorbitant purchases: a $300,000 pinkie ring. Another associate, Slim (the one who impersonated Meech on the phone), traveled with Terry to Jacob's so that Terry could pick up some jewelry for Tonesa. On that occasion, Slim recalls that Jacob's wife, Angela, said she didn't like how Meech and Terry came into the store with large groups of people. So from then on, Terry would meet Jacob in various New York City hotel rooms—where A.R. helped count and pack between $100,000 and $300,000 that Terry was shelling out for Jacob's bling.

Terry and Meech also purchased jewelry with the assistance of friends who actually earned, through legitimate channels, the kind of money that would allow them to shop at Jacob & Co. Damon Thomas, an L.A. music producer who constitutes half the Grammy-nominated production duo the Underdogs, met Terry in 2004. They were introduced by Damon's cousin, who described Terry as the manager of several rappers. A year later, Damon would try to cover up the fact that he helped Terry buy jewelry from Jacob—a decision Damon would come to regret. Similarly, Meech used Swift Whaley, the Orlando auto dealer who procured his silver Lamborghini, as a go-between to buy jewelry from Jacob. In the end, that arrangement didn't work out so well, either.

But for all the hoops the Flenory brothers had to jump through, it was worth it to see those three diamond-studded letters—*BMF*—grow bigger and bigger with each passing pendant. It was an honor to bestow increasingly massive medallions on their most loyal associates. And it was a source of pride to see others gawk at the sparkle that hung from the crew's neck. Most onlookers could only fantasize about the wealth that made such a thing possible.

One of those onlookers was a man hired in the spring of 2003 to remodel the White House. Over a period of six months, the contractor built a granite wall, installed new cabinets and kitchen appliances, and laid a limestone floor in the basement, among other tasks. The bill for his work came to about $200,000, and all of it had been paid by a man called Pops—typically in cash installments between seven thousand and nine thousand dollars.

The contractor soon learned that Pops was Charles Flenory, the father of the man who owned the house. Pops's son, Terry, supposedly was an investor in several Atlanta nightclubs. Thus the explanation for the stacks of bills seemed reasonable enough; after all, nightclub owners had access to large amounts of cash. But the contractor's bank wasn't buying it. He was warned by bank officials that his deposits looked suspicious, as if he or his client was trying to avoid the ten-thousand-dollar reporting requirement.

Soon after the warning, the contractor was witness to other curious goings-on at the White House. Once, he saw several men crashed out on the basement floor, sleeping alongside piles of guns, money, and platinum medallions that spelled BMF. He later asked one of the men what BMF stood for, to which the man replied: "It stands for the Black Mafia Family. If you haven't heard of us, you soon will."

Others who visited the White House in 2003 recall seeing more than just guns, cash, and bling. Throughout the summer, Doc, the Flenory's CFO, stopped by to pick up his weekly shipment of cocaine: ten kilos. High-level manager Freak Green typically oversaw the White House and, by extension, its cache of drugs. But on other occasions, BMF's upper echelon—Slim, Texas Cuz, or Terry himself— would be on hand to dole out the weekly supply. Even A.R., who was fairly new to the organization, was privy to some major transactions at the White House. No one asked him to turn his head when, in the basement of the house, he laid his eyes on a hundred neatly stacked kilos.

A.R. also was close enough to Terry to tag along with him while he checked out an investment opportunity: a car dealership and customization shop called 404 Motorsports. The slick showroom was located on the southern fringe of Buckhead, just north of a seedy row of strip clubs on Cheshire Bridge Road. The business, with its polished floors and $100,000 whips, was impressive—as was its co-owner, Tremayne "Kiki" Graham. Kiki's shop had sold tricked-out rides to mega-producer Jermaine Dupri and Atlanta Brave Andruw Jones. And Kiki, a sinewy, six-foot-five Clemson University graduate, was the equivalent of local royalty. The seemingly gentle and soft-spoken giant was married to the daughter of Atlanta mayor Shirley Franklin.

It appeared that the meeting between Terry and Kiki went well; a week later, Kiki stopped by the White House, and A.R. helped load Terry's investment in 404 Motorsports into the secret compartments in Kiki's customized car. Terry's investment totaled $250,000, broken down into rubber-banded stacks of cash.

Later that year, Terry offered a friend from New York a job at the dealership—not that the friend didn't have other employment opportunities. After all, the man, Darryl "Poppa" Taylor, is the cousin of music mega-producer Sean "P. Diddy" Combs. Terry first met Poppa through Diddy's chief of security, Paul Buford. Terry and Paul were tight, and Paul had impressive credentials of his own. In addition to working as Diddy's personal security (a job that had once belonged to Wolf Jones, whom Meech was accused of killing), Paul also had been the bodyguard of Diddy's most prized rapper, Christopher "Notorious B.I.G." Wallace. But Paul wasn't just a bodyguard. He also distributed cocaine that he got from Terry. And on at least one occasion, a BMF driver delivered sixty thousand dollars from Terry to Paul, who received the money at Diddy's New York record label, Bad Boy Entertainment.

Terry made frequent trips to New York, often to visit Jacob the Jeweler. During one of the trips, Paul set Terry up with a car and chauffeur: Poppa, Diddy's cousin. Poppa was paid two thousand dollars to drive Terry from New York to Detroit. From then on, whenever Terry came to New York, Poppa would drive him around and would supply his crew with vehicles. Poppa picked them up at the airport, drove them to their hotel, took them shopping, dropped them off at parties—whatever the trip entailed. Then, toward the end of 2003 (close to that fateful night when Wolf was shot dead behind Club Chaos), Terry offered Poppa a job in Atlanta. He said he wanted Poppa to work at the car dealership, 404 Motorsports.

Poppa moved his wife and children to Atlanta, but the job at 404 never materialized. Instead, he started driving Terry's vehicles—which, supposedly unbeknownst to him, were packed with cash and cocaine—from Atlanta to St. Louis, Detroit, New York, and L.A. Poppa claimed he first found out that he was transporting cocaine when, upon dropping off a van at Doc Marshall's house, Doc asked him how to "open it."

"Open what?" Poppa asked.

Doc then called Slim to get the combination to the van. Poppa stood by, startled, when Doc revealed a secret compartment stuffed with bricks of cocaine. For months, Poppa had been led to believe that Terry was a car broker and music producer. And yet, even after the truth emerged, Poppa continued to work for him—eventually becoming one of Terry's major distributors in New York.

Wolf's murder didn't appear to seriously dampen the relationship between BMF and Diddy's camp, either. After the shooting, Terry and others in BMF still did business with Poppa and Paul. But while there appeared to be no lingering bad blood between Diddy and the Flenory brothers over the death of Wolf, the killing did put a strain on Meech and Terry's own relationship. After Meech was arrested in November 2003 for the double-homicide, investigators received a long-awaited invitation to dig through the White House. The heat Meech brought to the organization as a result of the warrant quickly drove a wedge between him and Terry—a wedge so deep that the brothers' differences could not be reconciled.

By mid-2004, Terry was fed up. He was back in L.A., chatting on the phone with a family member and letting her know that Meech had failed him. He was saying how he and Meech had always been partners, fifty-fifty. But these days, it was as if Meech was responsible for 100 percent of the organization's grief. The partying, the drugs, the violence, the clamoring for attention—all of it was bad for the Family. It's one thing for Meech's lifestyle to land him in jail; it's something else for it to land Meech *and* Terry in jail. Terry said he wasn't worried about a small charge. He could deal with five years or so. But the way Meech was acting, the feds could come down hard, and that was more than Terry could handle. Terry knew his limitations, and he wasn't shy about sharing them. He confided over the phone: "I can't do no twenty."

But as Terry fumed over his brother's insensitivity to the organization's self-preservation, he appeared unaware of the damage he himself was inflicting. Months earlier, a federal investigation into the BMF cell in St. Louis had culminated in a judge approving a Title III wiretap investigation. After climbing onto several St. Louis numbers linked to suspected drug dealers, investigators caught up with one that had a Detroit area code. It was the cell phone of Benjamin "Blank" Johnson, the Flenory's childhood friend who lived up the street from them and used to help himself to the cocaine stashed in the hole above the linen closet. Johnson's number was turned over to DEA Detroit, which initiated its own wiretap. Through listening to Johnson's calls, the agents were able to jump onto Terry's number— three of Terry's numbers, in fact. To have a wire running on Terry was a major coup.

The Detroit wiretap ran for five months on eight phone numbers, three of them belonging to Terry, one to Johnson, and the others to various BMF associates. Yet the agents never were able to identify a number for Meech, who was more careful about talking on the phone. Terry, for all his caution, was less reserved when it came to phone calls. He didn't speak directly about the drug trade, but agents, reading between the lines, got a pretty clear picture of what was going on. Early in the investigation, they picked up on a call during which Terry, much in the style of a traditional crime boss, offered those reassuring words to Playboy's family. There were other hints, too. For instance, during one call, Terry mentioned his recent purchase of a $200,000 Bentley—and his interest in buying another for $160,000. He spoke of the expense of securing tickets for the Pistons–Lakers playoff game. ("You know what I'm saying—if you going with a group, you going to spend fifty to sixty thousand dollars to sit in the prime seats.")

Bentleys and Lakers playoffs aside, some of the most illuminating conversation had to do with the growing rift between the two brothers. More than most anything else, Terry's complaints about Meech offered insight into BMF—and offered some clues as to why the agents couldn't catch Meech on the line, not even to offer his brother a friendly hello. When the topic of Meech came up on the wire, Terry didn't mince words. "Shit, that crazy motherfucker running around over there, he mad at me," Terry told one associate. "He letting them motherfuckers put shit in his head. He don't even know why he is mad."

Within a month's time, the chasm between brothers was all but complete. And BMF was starting to splinter. While talking with his friend Shep, who'd called from federal prison, Terry offered a final and ominous prognosis of his and his brother's failing relationship. When Shep asked how Meech was doing, Terry told him: "Losing his mind, man. We don't even speak. He lost his mind."

THREE **PUSHING JEEZY**

We comin' in at the top of the game. . . . We don't
need nothing else but to make good music.

–BIG MEECH

nside a windowless Atlanta warehouse, Meech is seated at the head
of a marble slab table, watching the events unfold with untrusting
eyes. A man in a white dress shirt, the only one in the room who's
not wearing all black, starts his spiel. "Yo, Meech," he says excitedly,
leaning into the table, "I got the deal of a lifetime. . . ."

On the expanse of table in front of the CEO, stacks of bills are
piled to generous heights. To his left, his second in command, J-Bo,
maintains a stony silence. Flanking them at the table are two more
men. In the dark, cavernous background, two scantily clad women and
a guy wearing a T-shirt that says FREE MEECH barely make an impression against the shadows.

Meech quickly puts an end to the negotiations.

"Look here, man," he says in a low, raspy drawl. "The deal don't
mean nothing to me, man."

Meech turns to the guy to his right. "I'm not even supposed to be talking to this dude." Turning the other way, to face J-Bo, Meech hollers, "Get Bleu on the phone. Somebody get Bleu on the phone, man."

Bleu DaVinci, the rapper from Carson City and a close friend of Meech, answers the call.

"What up, dude?"

"Bleu, man, this man is interfering with my business," Meech says. His agitation is starting to dissolve into hysteria. "You need to get down here and talk to this man. I don't know why somebody let him in the room to see what's goin' on anyway, man."

"All right," Bleu says. "Just let me, um, run down here and check on that little shipment I was telling you about yesterday, and I'll get down there in a little while. Just give me a minute."

Not long after, Bleu, loaded with chains, his cornrows tucked behind a black bandanna, swaggers into the room, singing, " 'Cause I'm a boss . . . when I'm runnin' . . .'" By then, the man in the white shirt is gone.

Bleu glances up to greet Meech. "What up, man?"

Meech is mumbling to no one in particular about the music, the money, the problem at hand. Motioning to Bleu, he says, "You cannot be havin' that music dude comin' up in here, seein' all this money like this, man. You gotta be able to separate the two. You can't do it. We *cannot* do it, man."

What's going on in the room is not what it seems. Or maybe it is.

The two scenes—Meech calling Bleu and Bleu showing up at the warehouse—are bookends of a $500,000 video for Bleu's 2004 single, "We Still Here." Directed by famed hip-hop videographer Benny Boom, bankrolled by Meech, and with guest appearances by Brooklyn rapper Fabolous, California's E-40, and Bleu's protégé, an equal parts beautiful and frightening teenager called Oowee, the video has all the cinematic appeal of well-done Hollywood. There is a story arc, sophisticated aerial camerawork of downtown Atlanta, a choreo-graphed dance scene, and Meech leaning comfortably against a steel-colored Rolls-Royce Phantom, taking in the dazzling production at hand.

If it seemed ballsy for a major drug-trafficker to finance a video in which he's cast as what appears to be a major drug-trafficker, well, it *was* ballsy. It also wasn't the first time Meech commissioned art that perilously reflected life, and it wouldn't be the last. Somehow, he felt safe presenting himself as a drug lord. He was flaunting it, sure, but flaunting it alone is not a crime. In fact, in this instance, flaunting it was a strategy.

Meech sensed that in order to continue making money, he'd have to come up with a legitimate explanation for where his money was coming from. One way to rake in that kind of cash was through the music business. To Meech, the move was a natural progression, a way to transition from one kind of hustle to another. More than that, it fulfilled a passion. What better way to legitimize your wealth than by doing something you love—and something your father always wanted to do, but couldn't? To Meech, the key to liberating his "family" (both his criminal and blood-related one) was to launch a successful hip-hop label.

As early as 2003, Meech began to direct his resources toward rap-pers he believed stood a chance of stardom. If they succeeded, they would sell enough albums to elevate Meech's name from street lore to national renown. In turn, the artists would need him as much as he needed them. That's because Meech could create for them the illu-sion of wealth, a prerequisite for hip-hop fame. He could deliver the symbols of success—the cars, the jewels, the videos, and so forth—that would boost their notoriety. And if they were to hit it big, so would his newly incorporated record label, BMF Entertainment. It would be the ultimate return on his investment—but only if the feds didn't catch him first.

Meech was so confident about his plan that, even before his label landed a hit (let alone released a full-length album), he publicly spelled out his intentions. By doing so, he hoped to get noticed in an industry where there's no such thing as too much excess. Yet to some, both inside and outside the business, his words were offensive—in part for the assumption that he could buy success. "We comin' in at the top of the game," Meech boasted in a 2004 DVD that chronicled the making of Bleu DaVinci's album. "We got all the cars we want, all the houses we want, all the clothes we want, all the jewelry we want, and all the hos we want. We don't need nothing else but to make good music. That's it. And bring everybody else in with it and create jobs.

"We can do all kinds of things if we start from Bleu DaVinci."

Meech anticipated that Bleu's track "We Still Here" would be the break-out hit for BMF Entertainment, and he spared no expense when the time came to produce and promote Bleu. As the label's CEO and sole financier, Meech could throw as much support as he wanted to at Bleu, his lone artist. "We Still Here" was recorded, along with a handful of other tracks, at Atlanta's Patchwerk studio, whose vocal booths have been graced by Whitney Houston, Cher, Britney Spears, and Snoop Dogg. But according to Patchwerk chief operating officer Curtis Daniels, Bleu booked more time at the studio than any other artist.

In addition to the pricey studio time and glitzy video, Meech lavished other luxuries on Bleu: fancy cars, diamond-studded chains, and parties, parties, parties. The label hosted a listening party for "We Still Here" at Patchwerk, attended by such guests as Goodie Mob front man Big Gipp. Then there was the after-party at the Westin in Buckhead, followed by the after-after-party at a warehouse space downtown.

When it came time to perform—be it for an audience or in front of a camera—Bleu easily fell into the role of the rap superstar he wasn't. In one documentary-style video, he brandished a .357 Magnum that he casually claimed could "blow you back about four feet."

On another occasion, he talked about getting in shape so that he could fire an AK-47 with one hand. On film, he often spoke of himself in the third person, waxing philosophical about "who is Bleu DaVinci?" Basically, he ate it up. He was a goofy showman, one who overacted the part of the sinister gangster with a lighthearted side.

While performing live, it was the same drill. Bleu hammed it up for the camera, and the rest of the BMF crew quickly fell into place. As hundreds of guests thronged the stage at Bleu's after-after-party, he spat his lyrics into the mic while swaying in a mass of VIPs including BMF honchos J-Bo and Fleming "Ill" Daniels, rappers Oowee and Young Jeezy, and, at Jeezy's side, an upper-level BMF distributor named Omari "O-Dog" McCree.

The only one missing was Meech. He was still under house arrest for the Chaos killings, as evidenced by the FREE MEECH shirts that J-Bo and Ill wore on stage. But the boss did make a cameo, of sorts, with the help of a film crew that visited an Atlanta high-rise where he was holed up.

He was dressed in all white—white T-shirt topped by a baggy white tracksuit. He was sporting a huge diamond cross. And because the film was shot in grainy black-and-white, with the camerawork slightly out of focus, the result was a vision of Meech as an ethereal, thuggish angel. "Even though I'm not there," he told the camera, as if speaking from the grave, "I'm not the focus. Bleu DaVinci is the focus. That's what y'all are here for tonight. I wish I could be there tonight—God knows I wish I could be there tonight. But one day soon, I'll be there, with God's blessing."

And so Bleu became the center of attention—the attention of the film crews paid by Meech to follow him, of the club-goers who aspired to BMF's style of partying, and, most important, of the CEO himself. As Meech said from his exile, "All our independent focus is on what Bleu DaVinci gonna do and how he's gonna make it. If he take off, then we take off. If he don't take off, then we don't want to take off. Simple."

Meech's explanation as to why he put everything behind Bleu doubled as a wider, inspirational message to anyone who might be listening. Meech didn't intend merely to lift BMF Entertainment up to the level of "Universal, or Interscope or DreamWorks or Def Jam." He wanted Bleu's ascent to serve as a ghetto Cinderella story. "We want Bleu in the best of everything," Meech told the camera, "show him the best of everything, show him that a person can come from nothing to something and step in this game and keep going. He have everything that he could want right now, and he's still trying to do something to bring other people up with him."

The problem was that in the summer of 2004, it wasn't Bleu who was taking off. All the sparkly bling and fancy cars and state-of-the-art studios in the world couldn't compensate for the one thing Bleu DaVinci lacked: raw talent. Bleu's rhymes were straight gangster rap, and he delivered them with an appropriate dose of animosity: "You can't catch me on no corner pushin' nickels and dimes / I got the bricks flying right out of Buckhead." But despite his air of credibility, Bleu was not coming up with the kind of lyrics that would raise the genre to art—let alone generate any serious radio play. It was as if Bleu were the caricature of another rapper who actually did possess that rare combination of gritty authenticity and transcendent poetry. That rapper was Jeezy.

Jay "Young Jeezy" Jenkins grew up on the outskirts of the history-rich, have-and-have-not middle Georgia city of Macon. Rooted in the rock 'n' roll and R&B sensibilities of the Allman Brothers Band, Otis Redding, and Little Richard, Macon had grown into a hip-hop hub, a farm team to Atlanta's booming rap industry. Like Atlanta, Macon had a strong mixtape culture and some heavyweight hip-hop clubs, allowing young rappers to find fame on the streets before approaching the big leagues. Jeezy, who was known as 'Lil' J' when he first started rapping, quickly established himself in those venues. In his early twenties, he relocated seventy-five miles north to Atlanta, where he fell in with the crowd that hung out along Boulevard. He befriended one of the resident drug dealers, O-Dog, and both the dealer and his hood proved fertile material for the rapper. Jeezy gives shout-outs to O-Dog in several tracks, including his early hit "Air Forces," and the neighborhood serves as a backdrop for a number of other songs. The streets around Boulevard—characterized by brick low-rises sequestered by iron gates and crowds of boys squatting on the lawless corners—were as real to Jeezy as any he'd known in Macon. And he'd known a few.

Meech, who was O-Dog's boss, grew well acquainted with Jeezy—though perhaps a tad too late. Meech was generous with the rapper, paying Atlanta club DJs to play his yet-unheard tracks and lending him cars and jewelry for various video shoots. But Jeezy did not join BMF Entertainment's roster. By the time the label was incorporated in early 2004, Jeezy, who was twenty-six at the time, was running his own company, Corporate Thugz Entertainment, which sold tens of thousands of his mixtapes. He'd also hooked up with Atlanta mixtape gurus DJ Drama and DJ Cannon, who ran the production team Gangsta Grillz and would soon release Jeezy's wildly popular street album, *Trap or Die*. (*Trap* being a synonym for the drug game.) Jeezy also had buy-in from two major labels. Jeezy, along with three other rappers, was part of the collective Boyz N Da Hood, which had inked a deal with P. Diddy's Bad Boy Entertainment. And as a solo artist, Jeezy had just signed with Def Jam.

But as far as Meech and the rest of BMF were concerned, Jeezy was one of them. Jeezy wasn't resisting. Outside the Westin on the night of Bleu's listening party, Jeezy draped an arm around Bleu and declared, "This is my mutherfuckin' homeboy, Bleu DaVinci. It's love, man. It's family, dog."

Meech placed his bets on Bleu because he had to, but it was Jeezy who supplied the soundtrack for BMF's ascent. When Meech and his crew rolled around Atlanta in their Bentleys and Lambos and Ferraris and Maybachs, Jeezy's tracks were pumping through their speakers. That was back when few outsiders would've recognized the rapper's

smaller loads and handed them over to the distributors. Meech seldom if ever showed his face at the Gate.

Two other houses also served as temporary shelter for the big shipments, and few distributors were allowed there. In fact, only the most trusted insiders could visit those locations. One was a brick home in a sterile Atlanta subdivision. It was dubbed "the Horse Ranch." The other, a classy town house, was called "the Elevator," because there was a small glass elevator in the home. Once the brothers fell out—and Terry assumed control of the White House—Meech and J-Bo took up permanent residence at the Elevator.

Unlike the White House, investigators were completely in the dark about the Elevator's whereabouts. But while Meech's living arrangement was shrouded in secrecy, his dominance in Atlanta was no mystery. Local cops and federal agents couldn't help but speculate about what Meech was thinking, but one thing was clear: He was advertising his presence in a way that got *everyone* talking. At several Atlanta intersections, including ones at I-75 and at Peachtree Road, Meech announced his intentions from the sky. The testament of his power was printed in white block letters on a black twenty-by-sixty-foot expanse. The words were a nod to *Scarface*—a frequent source of Meech's inspiration. In the film, Cuban-born drug lord Tony Montana looks to the Miami sky and sees a message ticking across the side of a blimp: THE WORLD IS YOURS. Likewise, the billboards that Meech placed around town declared, THE WORLD IS BMF'S.

Of all the rumors being tossed around about Meech and BMF, it was the news of the billboards that really got Fulton County Assistant District Attorney Rand Csehy worked up. By mid-2004, Csehy (pronounced SHAY-hee) was used to cops coming to him with increasingly outlandish stories about the Black Mafia Family. But a drug dealer advertising on a billboard?

Csehy had been with the DA's Office for two years, and he loved the work. As part of the office's narcotics division, he didn't have to deal with the heartache of violent crime (victims weren't his thing) or the monotony of theft investigations (not enough drama). Best of all, he got to work with a group of men he viewed as peers and equals. Csehy had close ties to the detectives who brought him their drug cases—some say too close. He knew that several of his coworkers frowned on his cozy relationship with the police, and as with all the other things about Csehy that caused a stir at the DA's office, he didn't care.

From the hoops in his ears to his tattooed triceps, his heavy silver rings to his tattered jeans, Csehy looked more like a narc than a prosecutor. He possessed an undeniable excitability, an intensity betrayed by wide eyes that flashed an almost too brilliant blue. Csehy was passionate, and if that sometimes got him in trouble, so be it. He often caught flak for speaking too much of his mind to his boss, District Attorney Paul Howard. Then there was his chumminess with the cops—an affinity that dated back to his days at a suburban DA's office. After moving from the small suburban office to the big city one, he found himself gravitating toward Atlanta's narcotics investigators. He rode with them when they executed search warrants. He participated in their stings. He carried a gun. And after wrapping up a day's work, he and some of the detectives would go out drinking—a ritualistic occurrence in the summer of 2004, when Csehy's second marriage in three years was falling apart.

Csehy made himself available to the police when they needed legal advice, and they, in turn, filled him in on the talk of the streets. At the time, there was a lot of talk about the Black Mafia Family, but not a whole lot of legal advice to hand out. That's because the DA's office had not landed a single indictment against the crew—in a town where hundreds of BMF associates were believed to be controlling the drug trade.

When one cop came to Csehy with the startling revelation that the crew was advertising on billboards around town, the prosecutor was incredulous. He went to Buckhead to check it out. And he realized that, as with so many other rumors, the billboard wasn't what people were making it out to be. The billboard was advertising a record label—in much the same way that Atlanta's iconic neon yellow So So Def billboard graced I-75 on the south side of town. "What are we gonna do?" Csehy mused to himself. "Take down So So Def while we're at it?" And so while the myth of the BMF crime syndicate was everywhere, the evidence to prove its existence was nil. In fact, there was only one person on the Atlanta police force with any institutional knowledge of BMF. He also happened to be Csehy's best friend.

Detective Burns had learned about the Black Mafia Family on a fluke. In 2001, after he was promoted from a patrol officer in the city's most dangerous police zone to an investigator in the department's elite organized crime unit, he was trying to squeeze information out of a suspect. The guy didn't have the insight Burns was looking for; instead, he wrote down a name on a piece of paper and slipped it to the detective. The name meant nothing to Burns at the time. A year later, however, the name came up when Burns went undercover in a white-collar crime ring. An Atlanta company called XQuisite Empire was using the identities of innocent men and women to buy cars and homes for drug dealers. One of XQuisite's employees was the same man whose name was printed on that slip of paper. And Burns soon began to suspect that XQuisite's president, William "Doc" Marshall, played a significant role in a drug crew that called itself BMF.

Burns's impeccable work in the XQuisite investigation helped qualify him for his next career move: inclusion in a multiagency federal task force that was committed to rooting out drug kingpins. DEA agent Harvey helped out with the task force as well. And Csehy, who like Harvey was not an official member, served as its liaison to the DA's office. Csehy would assist in obtaining search warrants and, hopefully, drafting affidavits seeking wiretaps on BMF associates' phones.

All three men—as well as a dozen others—were called together in the summer of 2004 to go over one of the task force's primary initiatives: Target the highly secretive, seemingly impenetrable Black Mafia Family. To some in the room, the letters *BMF* meant nothing, and the term *Black Mafia Family* seemed almost comical in what it implied. But to Harvey and Burns, who were well ahead of the curve, and Csehy, who was catching up, the difficulty of the mission was obvious.

The meeting made clear the need to nab a BMF associate on drug charges (most likely an associate on the organization's lowest rungs) and persuade him to talk. The information would have to be good enough to set up an undercover buy and, from there, build a case for a wiretap. For that to happen, someone inside BMF would have to get sloppy. Until then, the task force agents would watch the streets as closely as they could, hoping they might catch a break.

FOUR FALLEN PRINCE

For some reason, they took it to another level.
— WILLIAM "DOC" MARSHALL

Rashannibal "Prince" Drummond was a big kid who liked big parties. The aspiring musician with espresso-shaded skin and a wide smile had a knack for figuring out where the action was—and when he couldn't find it, he'd create it. His most recent bash, a celebration for his twenty-second birthday the year before, lasted two full days. Prince treated every party like it was his last. And while he didn't have the kind of money to do it up the way he hoped, he managed to pull off a lot with a little. That's something he learned from his mother.

Prince was the third of Debbie Morgan's four children, and over the years, she'd scraped by to make sure they wanted for nothing. Debbie's singsong lilt and sparkly black eyes, her close-cropped hair and petite frame, gave the impression of a woman eternally optimistic, perhaps bordering on naïve. But her pixieish looks masked a strong will. If she wanted something, she'd go after it with a fire that surprised those who mistook her peaceable nature for passivity.

Debbie had been through a lot. Her marriage had failed, leaving her to raise four kids on her own—until she later fell in love with a handsome Puerto Rican boxer. She'd weathered several years in one of Atlanta's sketchiest neighborhoods, a few blocks off Boulevard, only to see the area begin to turn around. She'd steered her three boys through several arrests on minor drug charges—charges that they beat. (Another, more serious aggravated assault charge against Prince proved baseless.) Debbie knew her boys would find trouble, as boys do, but she raised them well enough to know they'd somehow find a way past it.

Now that her children were grown, with their own aspirations, Debbie felt she could finally start tackling her own dreams. Before moving to the United States as a young woman, Debbie grew up in eastern Jamaica, and she was part of a culture that prized three things. The first is Rastafarianism, a religion that honors the African roots from which Debbie's ancestors were displaced, respects the value of all living things, and eschews the corruption of "Babylon," or modern society. Intertwined with Rastafarianism is another of Jamaica's most influential contributions: reggae, dub, and dancehall music. Those genres heavily influenced hip-hop, and Debbie's sons looked to their musical heritage for inspiration as they tried to make music of their own.

Not least of Jamaica's cultural offerings—not to Debbie, anyway—is the country's food. Debbie's longtime dream was to open her own restaurant. She wanted to serve Jamaica's staples, the spicy dishes adapted from African, Chinese, and East Indian dishes, but somehow uniquely Jamaican: curried goat, grilled plantains, barbecued tofu, and jerked chicken. She'd held down various office jobs over the years, but in the summer of 2004, Debbie felt ready to start something new. And with her children finding their independence, her goal seemed within her grasp.

Her daughter, who'd grown into a lovely likeness of Debbie, was the most responsible of the clan, despite being the baby. And her sons, whom Debbie treated like royalty, were working to carve out a spot in Atlanta's hip-hop scene. Her eldest, Rasheym (everyone called him "Sheym"), was learning to shoot video, and Prince and Raschaka (who went by "Tattoo") were writing and recording rap songs on a shoestring budget. The Drummond boys closely followed Atlanta's hip-hop players and the happenings in the city's clubs. And so it was to be expected that Prince and Tattoo, along with their cousin and three of their friends, headed to a Midtown club called the Velvet Room for what was hyped as the club's final night. If you were young, into the rap scene, and interested in rubbing shoulders with those who made the industry tick, there was no better place to be. On July 24, 2004, and well into the following morning, all the Velvet Room regulars would be on hand to offer the club a final salute.

Though small compared with other Midtown venues, the Velvet Room, up until the end, pulled in a steady crowd. And on its last night, the long rectangular space was as swanky as ever. The club's swooping drapes were no less dramatic, its red velvet ceiling still sultry, its crystal chandeliers just as sparkling. And the crowd of beautiful people, hip-hop flossers, and wannabe players was in full force. The neighborhood itself had its share of mega-clubs and celebrity sightings, but it was still a more organic place than its neighbor to the north, Buckhead. In Midtown, there were fewer of the tensions that arose between Buckhead's revelers and residents. There was a party atmosphere, for sure, but not quite an out-of-control one.

And yet as the Velvet Room's final night wore on, the vibe was getting more and more like Buckhead. Even after last call had long come and gone, the crowd was still spilling from the doors of the club, which faced Peachtree Street, and down into the sloped parking lot behind the building. The scene out back was not unlike the one inside. Music was blaring from the speakers of well-buffed cars. Groups of drunk and emboldened guys were trying to hook up with the departing cliques of girls. Some of the men in the crowd, a conspicuous group in a caravan of conspicuous cars including a silver Lamborghini, gray Ferrari, and black Porsche SUV, were even clutching bottles of Cristal that they had smuggled from the club.

In the middle of the lot were Prince's three friends: Marc, who at age twenty was the youngest of the three; Black, the quietest of the group; and Jameel, who at six-foot-five towered over the other two. Jameel had dipped into his car, a white Mitsubishi, to listen to music while Marc and Black chatted up some girls. They all were waiting on Prince, who'd been the last in their circle to leave the Velvet Room.

Prince's brother Tattoo and his cousin Jahmar had been the first to reach the parking lot. They stopped at Tattoo's car, and Tattoo was ready to roll. But Jahmar decided to stay. Just before Tattoo took off, Jahmar warned him, "Don't drive all crazy." Tattoo drove north on Peachtree and cut over toward Georgia Tech. Jahmar headed back toward the club. He didn't want to leave without Prince.

Back in the parking lot, Prince's friend Jameel was still sitting in his Mitsubishi, nodding to the music, when he glanced out the rear window and saw that Prince had finally left the club. He was shuffling down the hill toward the parking lot, Jahmar at his side. The cousins cut similar images as they made their way down. They both sported baggy jeans and Nikes. Jahmar wore a striped blue shirt, his dreadlocks tucked behind a blue Bullets cap, while Prince wore a gray T-shirt and let his shorter dreads hang loose. They were alike in stature, too. Both about five-eight, maybe five-nine, definitely under 150 pounds.

The security guards were still working crowd control in front of the club when Prince and Jahmar met up with Marc and Black. Those two were working the crowd out back—or at least trying to. They were vying for the attention of some girls when the motorcade of high-end cars that had been idling in the parking lot began to roll out. It was a slow process. The cars had to be lined up in the correct order by the crew's bodyguards and lower-rung members before gliding one-by-one to their next destination, which some of its members decided would be Club 112, one of Atlanta's few after-hours venues.

As the cars fell into their customary formation, the last one in line, the black Porsche SUV, nearly backed into Prince. Prince tapped the side of the Porsche. "Yo homeboy," he called out. "You hittin' me."

The driver, a chubby guy with a goatee, jumped out. At least four other members of his crew were close behind. Two of them were still clutching their Cristal bottles.

"What do you think you're doing?" the driver said, bowing up at Prince. "Y'all motherfuckers don't ever touch my car again."

One of the guys in Prince's camp, most likely Prince, turned to the driver and smarted off: "You aren't running nothing."

Marc, the youngest of Prince's friends, noticed that the crew began to form up, as if part of a single entity. He started backing away, explaining that they didn't want any trouble. His friends agreed, but there was little they could do. The crew jumped all four of them.

Marc and Black tried to defend themselves as best they could, but in the flurry of fists and feet and glass, they both had a hard time seeing what was going on. Jameel, still in his Mitsubishi, quickly realized there was trouble. He was parked about ten feet away from the fight and couldn't see his four friends—just bottles flying and fists swinging. But he was worried. He grabbed his .40-caliber Glock from the glove box and jumped out of the car.

The first thing he saw was Jahmar on the ground. Several men were stomping on his head. He didn't see Prince or the others, but he knew the odds were stacked way against them.

Jameel did the only thing he thought would help. He dared not fire into the crowd. Instead, he pointed his gun in the air and squeezed off two rounds.

Seconds later, two more shots rang out.

When Marc heard the gunshots, he hit the ground and rolled

toward the bumper of Jameel's car. Glancing up, he watched as the crew that had attacked him scattered. He chased after one of them, who ducked into a car and sped off. The entire motorcade was peeling out of the parking lot.

Tires were screeching. Jameel was screaming. Dozens of onlookers were running in every direction. And when Marc saw what Jameel had seen—their friend Jahmar on the ground, bleeding like crazy—he started running, too. He was desperate to make sure Jahmar hadn't been shot.

Crouching close to Jahmar's face, Marc realized that no, he hadn't been. But he'd been beaten, badly. Both his eyes were swollen shut. His left eyelid and cheek had been sliced open. Blood was pooling under his head. He was moving, but barely. He was totally incoherent.

Where were the rest of them? Marc looked up, scanning the parking lot. All he saw, a few feet off in the distance, was Prince.

He started running again, but before he got to Prince, someone grabbed him from behind—club security.

When the two security guards in front of the club had heard the initial shots, followed seconds later by a couple more, they rushed toward the parking lot. The first thing they noticed was a bunch of fancy cars speeding off. Then, they saw people running—scattering in so many directions that the guards couldn't tell where the trouble was. But when the crowd parted a little, the security guards found five men huddled on the ground: Prince and Jahmar, who were bad off but still breathing, and Marc, Jameel, and Black, who were pretty much fine. Except for Jameel's screams.

The three friends were whisked away so that the guards and the arriving Atlanta officers could secure the scene. Jameel, frantic to know what was going on, kept asking the security guard if Prince and Jahmar were going to be all right.

"Why do you want to know?" the security guard asked. "Were you involved?"

"Yeah, I was right here."

"What happened?"

Jameel explained to the guard that he'd been sitting in his car when he noticed a fight had broken out—and that his friends had been jumped. He told the officer that he grabbed his gun and fired in the air to get the fighting to stop. After that, he said, he heard more shots. He said he stashed the gun under the seat of the car before rushing to his friends' side.

The guard told Jameel to remain silent. He cuffed him and placed him in the back of one of the officers' patrol cars.

Marc, meanwhile, was yelling over and over for an ambulance. To quiet him, the other security guard placed him in a patrol car, too—but not before Marc reached for his cell phone and dialed a number he hated to call. When Tattoo answered, Marc told him what had happened to his brother:

"Prince got hit," he said.

Tattoo whipped his car around and headed back toward the club.

Still in the patrol car, Marc watched and waited. When the ambulance finally arrived, Jahmar awoke from his battered daze—and started swinging at the paramedics who were trying to help him. He wouldn't remember any of it, but he would fight them all the way to Grady Memorial Hospital, and once there, he'd turn combative toward the hospital's staff, too. After that, he would slip into a coma. He would stay there for twenty-eight days.

As Jahmar's ambulance pulled away, Marc continued to keep an eye on the scene from the back of the patrol car. He was still holding out hope. He believed Prince had a chance.

He didn't. One of the two bullets that hit Prince penetrated his right forearm, fragmenting beneath his skin. The other bullet struck him in the middle of his back. It traveled slightly upward, grazing his liver and causing a serious internal rupture. The force of the bullet also bruised his right lung before continuing on through the right ventricle of his heart. It exited just under his left nipple, leaving a small metal remnant behind.

The paramedics didn't even try to help Prince. They just laid a sheet over him.

Atlanta homicide detective Marc Cooper sped west on Eleventh Street toward the north end of the Velvet Room parking lot, responding to the call of shots fired. He arrived at 4:22 A.M., seventeen minutes after the security guards heard the gunfire. By the time Cooper rolled up, the men who attacked Prince and his friends were long gone. But they did leave behind a few clues—clues that were eerily similar to another scene Cooper had investigated eight months earlier and a few miles up Peachtree.

Like the men killed in the other incident, at Club Chaos, the two Velvet Room victims were attacked in the club's parking lot. (Fortunately, this time one of them would live.) Like before, a stream of high-end cars had fled the scene. And again, there was a strange silence blanketing the witnesses.

But this time the assailants were sloppier. A few yards from where Cooper discovered the two shell casings from Jameel's Glock—as well as the two other casings discharged from the 10 mm that shot Prince—he came across a pair of champagne bottles. He asked the crime scene technician to take swabs from the mouths of the bottles. One of the men involved in the attack might have left behind some DNA.

A second officer discovered another significant clue: two phones. One of them, a Nextel BlackBerry, bore the greeting, "Bleu, BMF Entertainment." The other was later traced to Deron "D-Shot" Hall, who was listed in DEA files as a known associate of the Black Mafia Family.

But what Cooper really needed were the same two things that had eluded him in the Chaos investigation: a murder weapon and a witness. None of Prince's friends wanted to give statements to the police. Jameel had to give one, because he'd fired a weapon. But the statement was brief, and it was consistent with other evidence. Jameel didn't see the fight break out, because he was sitting in his car. He did fire his gun, but only in an attempt to break up the fight. And though he heard gunshots shortly thereafter, he didn't see who shot Prince. "I can't describe anybody," he said.

Cooper let Jameel go. He was not charged with a crime.

For weeks after the incident, while Prince's cousin Jahmar was still in a coma, Cooper tried to convince Marc, Black, and Tattoo to provide written statements of what they saw that night. Though Tattoo wasn't in the parking lot during the fight, he returned to the scene shortly thereafter, and Cooper suspected he might have an idea about who shot his brother. But the young men refused. Marc finally agreed to meet the detective, then failed to show up for the interview. When Cooper called to find out why, Marc said he didn't trust the police and didn't want to meet with him after all. He hung up.

Finally, Cooper reached someone who could help. He got in touch with Prince's mother.

After she got the news about her son, Debbie lay in bed for weeks. Through the haze of grief, bits and pieces of what had happened seeped in. Then they cascaded. Debbie quickly became familiar with something called the Black Mafia Family. And she told the detective what she knew: The boys had little faith in the police—and a lot of fear of the suspects. She said BMF was a powerful organized crime family—so organized that they had sent word to her, via the street, that they didn't intend for her son to die. If she would handle this the street way, and bypass the police, she was told she'd be rewarded. She said the offer, which she refused, was extended more than once.

She then told Cooper that she'd do her best to convince the boys to talk. On the evening of September 15, 2004, more than six weeks after Prince was killed, Marc, Tattoo, and Jahmar arrived at the Atlanta homicide office to give their statements. (Black did not join them.) Each of the three spoke for less than thirty minutes. Marc went first. He said he didn't see who shot Prince, because he'd dropped to

the ground as soon as he heard the first shots ring out. "Can you further describe the driver that exited the vehicle?" Cooper asked. Marc
said he didn't want to talk anymore.

Jahmar, barely two weeks out of the hospital, was up next. Because
he was in a coma for so long, the news about Prince was still fresh in
his mind. "I didn't even know that my cousin was dead," he told the
detective. He talked about leaving the club with Tattoo, then going
back to grab Prince. He vaguely recalled one of the attackers drawing
a gun, but other than that, he remembered little about the fight.

"Would you be willing to testify in court?" Cooper asked.

"No," Jahmar said. "I've been through trauma. I have fear for myself and my family. I don't want to testify against this person."

Tattoo went last. Cooper quickly got to the point.

"Are you familiar with BMF Entertainment?" the detective asked.
"Yes."

"To your knowledge, were they involved in this incident?"
"Yes."

"How do you know they were involved?"

"That's what I've heard from people on the streets."

The information wasn't exactly going to hold up in court, and
Cooper knew it.

"Why have you been reluctant to provide a statement?" he asked.

"I've just been mourning."

None of the young men was the witness Cooper needed. But the
right witness did exist—a man who was close enough to the fight to
see what happened, yet far enough removed not to have committed a
major felony. Whether he would talk was another matter.

The day after the Velvet Room shooting, BMF chief financial officer
William "Doc" Marshall got an angry phone call from California.
Terry was on the line, and he wanted Doc to tell him what had hap-
pened the night before.

Doc told Terry that normally, when there's a fight like that, the whole crew will jump in, and it might drag on for a bit. But this time, it was a half dozen of their guys on four smaller ones. He said the smaller guys got banged up pretty quick.

That's what was so perplexing to Doc, and what he tried to explain to Terry. It just didn't make any sense. The guys on the ground were done for. Doc said there'd been warning shots from the other camp, but everyone knew they were just that: a warning. The shots were too far away for anyone to truly believe that a gun had been aimed at them. In fact, the crew already was back in their cars when one of them, for reasons unknown, grabbed his gun out of the Porsche. According to Doc, the gunman was a high-ranking member, a guy who didn't need to bother with shit like that, yet he decided to run back to the scene, to stand over the guy who was lying defenseless on the pavement, and to pump two rounds into him.

The guy on the ground shouldn't have been killed, Doc said. He wasn't sure why that trigger was pulled.

Terry was livid. He told Doc they were all out of control. And even though Doc said Meech wasn't involved (he'd been whisked away from the scene as soon as the fight broke out, Doc said), Terry still blamed him. "Man, my brother down there's still up to that stuff?" Terry vented. "Listen, I don't know what they *think* they got away with." But he said one thing was clear: Meech's guys hadn't learned their lesson. Their behavior in the clubs was endangering everyone.

Doc agreed.

"They could have pretty much said, 'Hey, man, get out of here,' and it could have been cool like that," Doc recalled. "But for some reason, they took it to another level."

FIVE STUPID AND THE GIRL

My heart goes out to all the families who face this type of crisis.
—ATLANTA MAYOR SHIRLEY FRANKLIN

It was 5 A.M. California time, dark and quiet in the Valley. Scott King, a business associate of Terry's, was asleep. At least he *had* been asleep. For some godforsaken reason, his phone was ringing.

The phone was a prepaid cell, the kind you buy when you don't want anyone listening in on your calls. Scott was on the run, and he had to be careful. The guy on the line, Scott's close friend and business partner down in Atlanta, had to be careful, too. Tremayne "Kiki" Graham was in nearly as much trouble as Scott was. For that reason, Kiki also was using a prepaid cell.

Scott should've seen this coming. He'd been given plenty of signs. Still, the phone call shook him. Things were bad for him and Kiki. But what Kiki was whispering to him—news that boiled down to six deflating words—would make their situation a whole lot worse.

Not that Kiki saw it that way. To him, this was his ticket to freedom. This would be his way out of the mess he'd stumbled into. At least that's what he was saying to those he trusted could keep their mouths shut.

Scott knew better. He sensed that their run soon would come to an end. Months earlier, he'd sought refuge in L.A. from the heat he was drawing down South. Back home, he was a wanted man. And considering what Kiki had just told him, now they'd want him even more.

Those six words that put an end to his slumber, cutting like a scythe through the L.A. predawn, were sure to come back and haunt him. They were haunting him already.

Scott and Kiki had been friends for a decade. In the late '80s, Scott attended North Carolina's Mars Hill College on a full basketball ride. Five years later, when Kiki was accepted to nearby Clemson University, he also fell in with the basketball crowd. Kiki roomed with two of Clemson's players, Devin Gray and Andre Bovain. Devin and Andre were friends with Scott, so Kiki became friends with him, too.

Though Kiki didn't play for Clemson, he looked the part. Like Scott, he stood six-foot-five, a born charmer with an elegant build and an easy smile. Scott and Kiki had a grace about them, one that earned them popularity not just on campus, but, later, among some of the country's most celebrated sports stars. The two men were personal acquaintances of NBA stars Charles Barkley and Michael Jordan. Scott and Kiki had something else in common, too. While in college, they both began running cocaine on the side. For Scott, it started as a summer thing. But after dropping out of Mars Hill in his fourth year, he turned to the drug business full-time. One of Scott's primary customers lived in Greenville, South Carolina, the biggest city between Clemson and Mars Hill. Kiki worked as a courier for that drug customer.

Four years after he ditched school, Scott's lifestyle caught up with him. He was busted in California in '95 after picking up twelve kilos from his supplier. As a result, he would serve three years in a state pen. He didn't turn on his crew, though. He kept his mouth shut about his customers back in South Carolina, a display of loyalty that won him points with Kiki.

Scott was released from prison in 1998 and moved to Atlanta, where Kiki happened to have relocated. They ran into each other one night while partying at the same club. Scott noticed that Kiki was doing pretty good for himself, and Kiki didn't hesitate to tell him why. He was still in the drug game, and it was treating him well.

Not long after, Kiki stopped by Scott's apartment, a parole-office-approved complex in Atlanta's historic West End. He pulled up in his new Range Rover, and he came bearing a generous gift. As a token of his appreciation for Scott's discretion following the drug bust, Kiki handed him ten thousand dollars—a little spending money for a man who recently reclaimed his freedom. It was only natural that the relationship progressed from there—especially after Kiki's cocaine supplier ripped him off. Scott offered to hook him up with some kilos through one of his old connects back in California, as well as some other cocaine contacts he'd made. Within months, the two old friends decided it made sense to go into business together. Scott and Kiki would split the cost of each drug package, and split the profits. Scott still had some hungry customers up in Greenville, after all, as well as a driver, a close college friend named Ulysses "Hack" Hackett, who was willing to make the two-hour delivery from Atlanta to the South Carolina city. Rounding out the arrangement, Kiki offered to turn a property he was still leasing, on Greenville's Singing Pines Drive, into a stash house for their South Carolina–bound shipments.

Their drug ring hummed along for a year or so until, in 1999, the two partners needed a bigger supplier. This time, it was Kiki who found him: a major cocaine trafficker named Jerry "J-Rock" Davis. (J-Rock's girlfriend, who lived in the same Atlanta apartment building as Kiki's girlfriend, had introduced them.) Though only a year older than Kiki, J-Rock was well ahead of him in the drug game.

He'd been born in Columbus, Georgia, and his family later moved to a seedy suburb, Phenix City, Alabama, just across the Chattahoochee River. The small town was infamous for its lawless past—so much so that it had been dubbed "Sin City" by the soldiers stationed at Fort Benning, on the other side of the Chattahoochee. In the 1940s and 1950s, Phenix City was in the tight grip of a crime syndicate run by good old boys turned bad. Under their reign, the town had morphed into a Western-styled outpost of freewheeling drug dealing, open-air prostitution, blatant gambling, and rampant violence. Among the syndicate's victims was Attorney General–elect Albert Patterson, who'd run in 1954 on the promise of rooting out the city's organized crime network, which included countless cops and politicians. One day not long before Patterson's inauguration, he was assassinated in front of his downtown law office.

By the '90s, the city had tried to overcome its unsavory history. But even among a population of a mere thirty thousand, Phenix City remained fertile ground for the region's drug trade. J-Rock, who birthed a crew called the Sin City Mafia, was resurrecting Phenix City's ignoble past. The feds estimated that the Sin City Mafia eventually would traffic as much cocaine as the Black Mafia Family, an organization with whom J-Rock built a lucrative alliance. The two crews each moved truckloads of cocaine, and authorities surmised that they relied on the same L.A. supplier.

After moving his organization's hub from Phenix City to Atlanta and L.A., J-Rock—like Meech and Terry—maintained stash houses that held hundreds of kilos at a time. As with BMF, Sin City's customers bought well upwards of ten kilos (or "keys") in a single transaction, and the packages were delivered in cars outfitted with secret compartments.

J-Rock, like Meech and Terry, was a formidable kingpin. Short, stocky, and boyishly handsome, his appearance did little to reveal his sinister reputation. On the one hand, J-Rock was a family man. He looked after his mother and grandmother, as well as his own growing clan. (He would father eight children by the time he was thirty-one.) He was good to his drug crew as well, offering similar compensation to what BMF doled out. And though he was generally more feared than the BMF bosses, defections did occur from their camp to his, and vice versa. Most notably, a high-ranking BMF distributor, Richard "Baa" Garrett, jumped to the "other side" to become J-Rock's right-hand man. Baa appeared to be a more benign manager than his boss was. Once, when a courier delivering drugs for Baa had his shipment intercepted by authorities, J-Rock stepped in and told the underling that, had the package belonged to him, the courier "would be dead."

Scott, for one, considered J-Rock's style a little too Mafia. Scott wasn't crazy about bowing down to the don, and the two never really saw eye to eye. Kiki was closer to J-Rock than Scott was. Overall, though, J-Rock's crew got along well, professionally and personally. Sometimes, they even took trips together purely for pleasure. Such was the case in February 2001, when Kiki, Scott, and five of J-Rock's associates (one of his partners, the partner's bodyguard, and three midlevel dealers) flew to Washington, D.C., for the NBA All-Star game. By then, Kiki and Scott had been doing business with J-Rock for over a year, and they were fully ingratiated. For the trip, J-Rock's crew was furnished with a limousine and driver from an Atlanta company to which the boss had ties. Unlike any limo they might hire in D.C., this one would let them smoke weed in the car, and carry guns.

The night before the game, the crew was out on the town. They hit up a downtown strip club before calling on the white stretch Mercedes to come pick them up and take them to a party. After the men piled in, the limo began crawling up Connecticut Avenue, near Dupont Circle. The streets were jammed with cars and people— including a group of men who'd just left a Connecticut Avenue strip club, Royal Palace. Two of the men darted across the street. To avoid hitting them, the limo slammed on its brakes, throwing the men in the back against their seats. The driver yelled out the window at the two pedestrians. They shouted something in response. The bodyguard who was traveling with J-Rock's crew, whom everyone called Dream, asked the driver if everything was cool. Yeah, the driver said. "I can handle it."

Dream wasn't convinced. He asked the driver if it was okay for him to try to defuse the situation with the pedestrians. The driver told him to go ahead.

Dream stepped out of the limo and walked toward the front of the car. But the sight of the oversized bodyguard did not deter the men in the street. The men, who were Hispanic, got into a racially charged shouting match with Dream and his entourage, who were piling out of the limousine. The men in the street started banging on the limo. One of them broke a bottle. As a retort, someone in Dream's entourage—accounts differ as to who—pulled a gun and began shooting wildly. A twenty-five-year-old Salvadoran carpenter named Raul Rosales was shot in the mouth. He was pronounced dead at Howard University Hospital. Two of Rosales's friends also were hit, but they survived. In the melee, Dream also took a bullet, to the back. He survived, too.

Three people in the crowd identified the shooter as Michael "Playboy" Harris, who was an associate of J-Rock. But Scott was sure that it wasn't Playboy who did the shooting. Rather, he claimed he clearly saw one of his fellow drug dealers, a man named Jamad "Soup" Ali, pull the trigger.

While Dream hobbled up Connecticut Avenue, the others hopped back in the limo. Not Scott, though. He'd had enough. He disappeared into the crowd.

The limo driver spotted Dream a few minutes later, and pulled over to pick him up. Dream climbed into the backseat, bleeding profusely from the bullet wound to his back. At that moment, Kiki realized Scott wasn't in the limo, and he was worried. He dialed Scott's number, to make sure he hadn't been hit. Scott picked up—and told Kiki he thought it would be smarter to ditch the car and come meet him. "Every police agency in the world is here," Scott warned. "They are going to stop that limo."

He was right. The limo was pulled over, and everyone inside was questioned. Before that happened, though, Kiki had followed Scott's advice. He bolted from the backseat and hit the sidewalk running. He and Scott stayed on the phone, weaving through the tangle of D.C. streets before meeting up on a busy corner. From there, they hailed a cab and headed to the party, later than expected but not deterred.

They were almost there when Scott noticed that Kiki's tie was spattered with blood. He pointed out the stains, and Kiki unknotted the thing and, after stepping out of the cab, tossed it in the trash. The two men then made their way inside. They weren't at the party long before their phones started lighting up. Word traveled fast, and friends and associates, including J-Rock, wanted to make sure they hadn't been hurt. Of course, J-Rock also expected a full account of what had gone down.

After the party, Scott and Kiki headed back to their hotel. They didn't meet up with the other occupants of the limo until the following day. When they finally reunited, the men told Scott and Kiki that they'd been questioned, that Playboy had been arrested on multiple charges, including murder, and that Dream was laid up in the hospital. At that point, Scott and Kiki decided to distance themselves as much as they could from the rest of the crew. They even switched hotels. They had to be careful, and not just because law enforcement was watching. Their girlfriends were flying in that day to meet them. They had to regain some semblance of normalcy.

Kiki was no longer dating the woman who'd introduced him to J-Rock. He had a new girlfriend, one he'd met through Scott. Scott, who was dating her younger sister, introduced them one night, when all four of them were hanging out at an Atlanta strip club. Kiki and the older sister hit it off. Kai Franklin was vivacious and attractive, curvy and petite—a full foot shorter than Kiki, even in heels. In that way, she took after her mother.

Despite her diminutive stature, Kai's mother, Shirley Franklin, was a powerful woman in Atlanta politics. Her ex-husband, David, was an influential political adviser, and she herself had served in two mayoral administrations. Franklin was the chief administrative officer and city manager under Mayor Andrew Young, and she went on to become the cultural affairs commissioner under Maynard Jackson, who, as Young's predecessor, had returned to the mayor's office for a third term after Young's two terms ended. (At one time, Jackson also was David Franklin's law partner.) Shirley Franklin wasn't so tightly bound to Mayor Bill Campbell, who would end up the target of a federal racketeering indictment—and was ultimately convicted only of tax evasion. But she was undoubtedly a crucial component of the Jackson–Young–Campbell machine that dominated the Atlanta political scene.

Which was why, when Campbell's two-term limit was nearing its conclusion, the machine was urging her to take aim at the mayor's seat. "To have Shirley Franklin running for mayor is just so delicious, because it's the first true draft I've ever seen," her ex-husband told the press shortly after she launched her campaign. (The two had remained close friends.)

Yet the rest of her family was surprised that her name was being batted around. She was a private person. She reveled in behind-the-scenes policy and strategy. She'd never been the type to seek the spotlight. Still, she was highly qualified and immensely likeable. Most important, she could win. And the machine was persuasive. Despite having never run for public office, and never before having seemed interested in such a thing, Shirley Franklin was game.

As Atlanta's 2001 mayoral campaign was heating up, it became clear to Kiki that he needed to legitimize his earnings. That's because he intended to make Shirley Franklin's eldest daughter his wife.

In his foray into legitimacy, as with his illegal endeavors, Kiki formed a partnership with Scott King. The two men decided to open a car dealership and customization shop on the outskirts of Buckhead, one that would offer $2,000 rims and $350,000 Bentleys. Kiki and Scott incorporated their business in September 2001, and they called it 404 Motorsports—so-named for Atlanta's intown area code. The dealership had a clublike setting, and it catered to the type of customers who might qualify for an AmEx black card. The walls of 404 Motorsports were graced with autographed jerseys of clients such as Atlanta Brave Andruw Jones and Cleveland Brown Corey Fuller. Graham's business would be a portal to celebrities, with whom he had an easy rapport. And his fiancée would be a liaison to Atlanta's political elite.

That year, both Scott and Kiki sat down for Christmas dinner with the Franklin family. There was much to celebrate: Shirley's recent victory and her upcoming inauguration (she'd taken the race by a seventeen-percentage-point lead), Scott and Kiki's new business, and, right around the corner, wedding bells. Kai and Kiki were married December 29, 2001. Kiki now had all the more reason to keep up appearances. Fortunately for him, he possessed an uncanny ability to come across as legit. There was a pleasantness about Kiki, an understated ambition that made people believe in him, to convince themselves he was someone he wasn't. He dressed in three-piece suits and smart ties. He hobnobbed with superstars. And his wife was the daughter of a wildly popular mayor—the first African-American woman to hold that post in any major Southern city. If he was careful enough, Kiki would be guaranteed a charmed life.

He and Scott ran into a snag, though. As 2002 wore into 2003, their business wasn't making money. Even with the two men continuing to move cocaine, they couldn't keep 404 Motorsports afloat without outside help. For that, they turned to Kiki's father-in-law, David Franklin. For over a decade, David had run a successful—and, some say, controversial—concessions business at Atlanta's Hartsfield International Airport. With his business partner Ed Wilson, Franklin

Kiki, and so he did a better job supporting his studio than they did their car dealership. J-Rock sank thirty thousand dollars a month into Platinum Recordings between the studio's equipment, bills, and salaried employees, one of whom was paid to make sure members of Dep Wudz made it to their shows and stayed out of trouble. Another Platinum employee, hired to do accounting work, began to suspect that the studio was a front, but continued to work there for fear that J-Rock wouldn't accept a resignation without retribution.

Looking to expand his roster, J-Rock assumed the role of manager in 2002 to an aspiring teenage rapper out of North Carolina. Born Walter Tucker, Oowee was a promising addition to J-Rock's label, which he renamed Bogard Records in early 2003. Oowee also was tight with BMF. Meech had made a habit of befriending young rappers, even those who had other representation and pending record deals, and he was particularly fond of the tough-but-pretty lyricist (fond enough to feature him prominently in Bleu's video, "Still Here"). As for Meech and J-Rock, they were cool, both in matters lawful and otherwise. J-Rock had one crew and Meech had another, but the two bosses looked out for each other.

In fact, in many ways, Meech and BMF Entertainment took after J-Rock and Bogard. Both bosses had a genuine passion for the industry, and the industry, in turn, valued their street smarts. Meech and J-Rock also possessed the bravado, if not the acumen, of more traditional music moguls. But there were some notable differences between the two bosses. For starters, J-Rock was a silent partner in his label and recording studio, presenting himself as a freelance artist's rep rather than the money and leadership behind the venture. (He went so far in his charade as to meet Bogard's accountant in random parking lots, usually behind the wheel of a Ferrari or Lamborghini, to clandestinely hand off any cash the studio might need.) Meech, on the other hand, put himself out there. He was the very public face of BMF Entertainment, which, even as record labels go, was a highly noticeable organization. The fact that BMF, like Bogard, was financed with drug money appeared not to dissuade Meech from flooding the market with excessive displays of exorbitant wealth—money that had no verifiable, legal origin. J-Rock was more understated.

Yet no matter how careful he was in separating himself from Bogard, J-Rock remained inextricable from the Sin City Mafia. J-Rock *was* Sin City Mafia. And once investigators started sniffing around J-Rock's crew, the boss had reason to worry—but only to a point. That's because J-Rock, like Meech, considered himself fairly impenetrable. He was near the top of his game, after all. Only further down the food chain, or so the logic goes, does one become vulnerable.

Barron Johnson existed somewhere along the middle of that food chain. The Greenville coke dealer had a few street-level guys working for him, and he was buying about ten kilos at a time from his supplier. Vice detectives at the local police department stumbled onto him in 2002, after orchestrating a few undercover, street-corner buys from West Greenville dealers, whom Barron was supplying. From there, the detectives landed a wiretap on one of Barron's phones. Based on what they heard, it appeared he was getting his drug shipments from Atlanta. One of his Atlanta suppliers, they learned, was a man named Scott King. And one of Scott's associates, Ulysses "Hack" Hackett, was driving the coke up to Barron on a regular basis.

After nailing down Scott as Barron's supplier, the local investigators went to the Greenville office of the U.S. Drug Enforcement Administration in the summer of 2003 to see if the federal agents might be interested in the case. The DEA *was* interested, as was the criminal division of the IRS. The two agencies immediately launched a full-scale investigation into Scott King's drug ring and assets.

In December 2003, Barron Johnson, Scott King, and Ulysses Hackett were indicted under seal in federal court in Greenville. The indictment charged them with conspiracy to distribute cocaine and to launder drug money. Barron was quickly apprehended, and it didn't take long for investigators to convince him to talk. He went so far as to arrange a four-kilo shipment from Scott, who knew nothing of Barron's arrest or his own pending charges. And so Scott sent Hack to Greenville with the package, as he'd done countless times before. Hack planned to meet Barron at the stash house on Singing Pines Drive, the one Kiki had leased.

But he didn't make it that far. On the afternoon of January 21, 2004, a highway patrol trooper acting on DEA orders pulled over Hack's SUV on I-85, a few miles shy of his destination. In the backseat, investigators found four neatly wrapped and barely disguised kilos of cocaine. That same day, a federal judge signed off on a search warrant for the house on Singing Pines Drive. During the search, investigators found another ten keys inside the stash house. The drugs, along with eighty thousand dollars, were tucked away in five underground safes.

Later that afternoon, Scott was hanging out at his town house when Hack's girlfriend, Misty Carter, knocked on his door. She'd heard about Hack's arrest, and she wanted to help. Misty was twenty-four years old, a graduate of Atlanta's historically black, all-female Spelman College, and a salesgirl at an upscale Atlanta boutique. Not that she needed to work. As the daughter of a well-to-do physician in the idyllic town of Fayetteville, North Carolina, Misty was still pampered by her parents. She had little experience with the ins and outs of the drug game, or the workings of the legal system. But she did have access to cash. She broke a savings bond in order to free Hack from jail, and Scott promised to pay her back.

Immediately after she left, he called Kiki. The two made arrangements to pay for Hack's lawyer, a move they mistakenly believed would give them access to the sealed evidence filed in the case—which in turn would allow them to see how close the government might be to nabbing them, too. Scott, however, didn't have to wait long to find out what the feds had in store for him. Days after Hack's arrest, the full indictment was unsealed—and Scott learned that he (though not Kiki) had been charged. Scott wasn't going to wait around for authorities to find him. Using a fake ID, he caught a flight to California, where he intended to start over.

The move across country was an easy one. J-Rock had just relocated to L.A., too, along with his new wife. The couple had taken up residence in one of three houses where J-Rock stored his fresh-to-the-U.S. drug shipments. The $2 million home was still in the L.A. hills, technically, but close to the belly of the Valley—and even closer to Terry Flenory's primary stash house, the Jump. You could walk from one home to the other in less than five minutes. Like Terry, J-Rock had little choice but to maintain several L.A. properties to keep up with the drugs he purchased—allegedly from their supplier-in-common, the one with a direct Mexican connection.

J-Rock's crew called the house where he lived First Base. It was located in a neighborhood called Sherman Oaks, at the crest of a long, climbing driveway. The three-story stucco-and-terra-cotta structure was exposed to the road—but so far away from it that, as with Terry's Jump, any outside surveillance was all but impossible. J-Rock's Second Base was a nearby pad where his crew usually stayed, in the same L.A. neighborhood. And Third Base was way out on Ventura Boulevard, in a part of L.A. so far west that even the locals, who had a looser definition of sprawl than most of the rest of world, considered it the distant reaches. That house, on a cheerful, tidy street called Oso Avenue, was home to the largest of J-Rock's drug shipments—several hundred kilos at a time.

With all that property, there was plenty of room for Scott King. And also plenty of work. While living as a fugitive, Scott stayed deep in the game, and he maintained regular contact with Kiki, who seemed to be better situated in this whole mess. Barron Johnson didn't know Tremayne "Kiki" Graham. He'd never seen him, never spoken to him. And so while Barron could (and did) contribute to Scott's undoing, Kiki would prove a harder catch.

The one thing that concerned Kiki was the possibility that Hack might turn government's witness. Hack did, in fact, meet with federal investigators. In the early spring of 2004, he agreed to provide a statement. In that statement, he talked, a lot, about the fugitive Scott King. That's what the feds were expecting to hear. What surprised them, though, was how little Hack was willing to say about Kiki. Even at that point, investigators had enough on Kiki to know that Hack was hiding something. Hack, they believed, was lying to protect him. And so one of Hack's interrogators, DEA agent Jay Rajaee, let him know that he saw right through the act. "This is over," Rajaee told him. "I'm not talking to you anymore."

Hack told Kiki about the meeting—an admission that had the unintended consequence of further fueling Kiki's paranoia. Kiki was sure that Hack would cooperate against him—if he hadn't already—and he confided this to Scott. By then, the two friends had begun to refer to Hack as "Stupid," because of the little white lies Hack was always telling. To Kiki, those white lies were beginning to assume a darker hue. Kiki was convinced: Hack was out to get him, and the only way he could possibly be indicted would be if Stupid were to fold.

Yet despite his growing belief that he was, in fact, fallible, Kiki continued to traffic cocaine. He was more careful about it than ever. He came up with what he thought was a foolproof plan, and to put that plan into motion, he decided to join Scott and J-Rock in California for a while. He was a free man, after all, one who could travel anywhere he pleased. And if he were added to the federal indictment while he was out in L.A.? Well, maybe he'd make the move permanent.

Before Kiki came up with his plan, J-Rock's primary method for transporting his drugs from California to Georgia (and his drug money in the opposite direction) was by private jet. Of course, you couldn't send just anyone on a thirty-thousand-dollar flight across the country with luggage that contained three hundred kilos of un-cut cocaine, or $4 million in bundled bills. Such a job called for a professional. In early 2004, J-Rock had learned that a man named Eric "Mookie" Rivera was up to the task, and he quickly brought Mookie on board. As with past couriers, Mookie lived where J-Rock lived, which meant Atlanta at times, alternating with L.A.

J-Rock typically would have his couriers make at least one "clean" cross-country trip. During that flight, neither drugs nor drug pro-ceeds, the latter of which were typically packed in boxes and topped with rap flyers, would be brought on board. The idea was to get a feel for things. But in 2004, Kiki arrived in California to meet with both J-Rock and Mookie—and based on what he proposed, the practice flight would not be necessary. With Kiki's help, J-Rock was about to change things up.

Kiki's cocaine-trafficking plan was so impressive that the boss of-fered to pay him sixty thousand dollars for every load of drugs he shipped. "The Graham Method," as one associated called it, relied on a friend of Kiki's, Ernest "E" Watkins. It utilized the well-oiled de-livery system of the United Parcel Service. And it was designed in such a way to protect everyone involved. That's because the only people who could possibly get caught transporting the drugs across the country could claim complete ignorance if they happened to be busted.

The first time they tried out the plan, Kiki met J-Rock at First Base, where they snugly packed bricks of cocaine into large card-board boxes. Once full, the boxes weighed in at about seventy pounds each. They were addressed to a fictitious address in Atlanta, from a fictitious sender in L.A. One of J-Rock's associates then met them at the house, having been forewarned by Kiki to dress conservatively. The associate loaded the boxes into a van and drove them to a UPS store just up the street, off Ventura. Once the shipment left the asso-ciate's hands, the rest of the trip was cake. The boxes were uncere-moniously pushed, hoisted, and shoved, passing from van to plane and back to van again, along with countless other large brown boxes. They plodded across the country, indistinguishable from other packages—the difference being that the contents of these particular boxes couldn't be insured to their actual value. Even wholesale, the cocaine inside was worth well over $500,000. If street value was taken into account, each box would be worth millions.

Once the boxes landed in Atlanta, Kiki's friend Ernest, who had an inside source at UPS, orchestrated the interception. The insider watched for the boxes bearing the fictitious Atlanta address. Sure enough, he found them. After setting the boxes aside, he then hand-delivered the precious cargo to Ernest.

After seeing the boxes off in L.A., Kiki and Mookie flew to Atlanta a few days later to catch up with the shipment. Ernest met them at the airport with the good news. The plan had gone off without a hitch. And so Kiki and Mookie returned to L.A., to do it all over again—and again. The two went back and forth several times in early 2004.

During one of those trips, however, Kiki received news from back home. The news brought his involvement in the scheme to a screeching halt. His wife Kai called him. The feds were at their house in East Cobb. They had a warrant. And they were digging through everything.

DEA agent Rajaee, the one who'd interviewed Hack a few months earlier, had traveled to Atlanta from Greenville to participate in the search. Fellow DEA agent Jack Harvey, out of the Atlanta office, had drafted the warrant for Kiki's house, which was located on Hallmark Drive. Harvey was deep in the throes of his investigation into BMF, and several of his subjects had trickled over into Rajaee's investigation. So the two agents joined forces.

When they first arrived at the house, a handsome, two-story brick traditional with a circular drive, it appeared that no one was home. The agents knocked on the door, sat back, and waited. Finally, Kai Franklin Graham, the mayor's daughter, answered. The agents gathered several items as they combed through the house, including a receipt for a storage shed issued to someone named Ernest Watkins. The name meant nothing to them at the time. That would change.

As Kiki soon would learn, the search warrant coincided with his name being tacked onto Scott and Hack's indictment. Out in California, Kiki and Scott discussed what he should do and, more important, how they were going to climb out of their deepening hole. The next day, Kiki and Scott headed over to First Base to continue the conversation. They needed guidance from J-Rock. As the three men sat and talked, Scott decided he would remain a fugitive. He might as well ride this one out, make the feds sweat him a little more. Kiki, on the other hand, was leaning toward surrendering. After all, he bragged, his mother-in-law was the mayor. He seemed to think she'd pull some strings, and he'd be out of jail in no time.

Two weeks after his indictment, Kiki showed up at the U.S. Attorney's Office in Atlanta to turn himself in. A few days later, a federal magistrate set a $300,000 bond for Kiki—with the condition that he wear an ankle monitor and remain under house arrest. The bond had nothing to do with the fact that he was the mayor's son-in-law, though, and everything to do with his clean criminal history. Federal prosecutors didn't even push to keep Kiki locked up. His wife, Kai, with the help of her younger sister, found a bonding company willing to spring her husband. In the application for the bond, she noted that she earned an $80,000 salary through her father's airport concessions company—her father being the well-connected ex-husband of the mayor. The woman behind the desk at Free at Last Bail Bonds was impressed with Kai, and the fact that she was driving a Porsche convertible. The bondswoman didn't require Kai to secure the bond with any asset, such as her and Kiki's home. It was an unusual move, but it also was an unusual case: the defendant was the son-in-law of the mayor.

Instead of putting up her house, Kai paid thirty thousand dollars out of pocket, and Free at Last assumed the rest of the debt—with the understanding that in the unlikely event her husband was to flee, she'd be responsible for the $300,000 (though her house wouldn't be on the line). While Kiki's bond had plenty to do with the standing of his wife, it had little to do with Mayor Shirley Franklin. The mayor pulled no strings for Kiki. All that talk back in California, about how easy it would be for him to get out of jail, amounted to a bunch of boasting in the company of friends.

Despite having no direct connection to the mayor, Kiki's arrest pained her on a personal level. "I am saddened to hear of the indictment," Shirley Franklin told the Associated Press, stressing that she was speaking not as the mayor but as a mother. "I am hopeful that he will be found innocent, but we must let the legal system run its course.

"My heart goes out to all the families who face this type of crisis."

Those words would be of little consolation to another family that was about to be dragged into the crisis, in a far harsher way.

Rather than use his time under confinement to step back from his situation and take pause, Kiki dived right back into the game. On the outside, he was quiet, repentant even. But beneath that doleful facade, Kiki was plotting. Amazingly, he continued to oversee the UPS scheme, this time from his home on Hallmark Drive—and presumably because he was hurting for money. He stayed in close contact with Ernest "E" Watkins, who handled the shipments on the Atlanta end through his UPS insider, and with Eric "Mookie" Rivera, who'd flown back and forth from L.A. with him. Mookie had grown fond of Kiki. He had sympathy for his situation. The two talked often on the phone (Kiki using a prepaid cell, of course), more like friends than drug associates.

Kiki complained to Mookie that J-Rock wasn't helping out with his legal expenses as much as Kiki had hoped, and Mookie thought that was highly unfair. Kiki and Mookie had helped J-Rock make tens of millions of dollars. Yet those directly under J-Rock saw nowhere near that kind of money. Paying some attorney fees was the least J-Rock could do. Fueled by the injustice of it, Kiki hatched another scheme—this time behind J-Rock's back. Mookie wanted to help, so Kiki asked him to arrange a flight on a private jet from Atlanta to L.A., and to get to Atlanta as soon as possible. It would be hard, Mookie said, because he was still under J-Rock's command in California, and J-Rock watches everyone and everything so closely. But somehow, he said, he'd swing it.

One night in the summer of 2004, Mookie made good on his promise. He arrived at the house on Hallmark Drive and stayed the night with Kiki. Ernest, the guy with the UPS connection, joined them the following afternoon. The three men sat in the house, counting and packing stacks upon stacks of cash. With that task out of the way, the operation was solely in Mookie's and Ernest's hands.

Mookie had arranged for a jet to meet them at a small private airport in Atlanta, and Ernest had called for a car to take them there—along with the suitcases filled with money. They flew the cash to L.A., where Mookie's work was done. Ernest then took the money, bought a decent-sized cocaine package, and shipped it to Atlanta using the UPS method. He'd done it plenty of times before, but this occasion would be different. This time, the drugs belonged to Kiki, not J-Rock. Kiki would see the bulk of the profit. J-Rock wouldn't even know about it.

But Kiki did confide in J-Rock about other matters. Chief among them was Kiki's mounting distrust of Hack. Kiki couldn't shake the notion that Hack was a threat. And Kiki was beginning to suspect that Hack was a threat to J-Rock, too. Over the years, Hack's dealings with J-Rock had been minimal. He wasn't high up enough in the organization to interact with the boss. But once, when Scott and Kiki were out of town, they'd asked Hack to bring J-Rock some drug money they owed him. Hack handed over the cash to J-Rock himself. That was the extent of the connection between J-Rock and Hack, but it was enough to directly implicate J-Rock in the drug trade. And Kiki kept harping on it. He said that if J-Rock didn't want his name tacked onto the indictment, something had to give.

To Katie Carter, Hack came across as a very nice young man. She first met him during a trip to Atlanta in 2003. He was clean-cut and clearly crazy about her daughter, Misty. It was easy to see why. Misty was a pretty girl. She had wide, sparkling eyes. A shiny black bob framed her oval-shaped face. And according to her daddy, Misty had a million-dollar smile. She was a little naïve but deeply kind—and, when it came to her boyfriend, deeply in love.

She was spoiled, too, and Katie Carter is quick to admit it. As an only child, Misty consumed all her parents' attention. When she graduated from Spelman, the Carters bought her a townhome on Atlanta's trendy Highland Avenue. They paid for her car, her clothes, and whatever else Misty could possibly need. To the Carters, it was worth it. She was a good daughter.

When Katie first met her daughter's boyfriend, he picked them up at Misty's place and took them to breakfast, then to his place of work. Katie could tell he was proud of the business. And she herself was impressed. 404 Motorsports was a high-end operation. Even with a mechanic working on a car in the back of the showroom, the entire place was spotless, Katie recalled, just like a freshly mopped kitchen floor.

At first, Katie thought Hack was one of the dealership's owners. But she soon realized he only worked for them. Misty mentioned one of the owners, Scott, to her mother in passing. She boasted that he hob-nobbed with the city's elite and played golf with genuine sports stars.

Hack and his friends seemed to be good people. But a couple things about him bothered Katie. One, Hack was so much older than Misty—a full ten years. Katie Carter also began to notice how often

Hack went out of town. "Misty, where's Hack going?" Katie asked her daughter over the phone one day. "Why is he always going to South Carolina? Did you ask him?'"

"Yes," Misty answered, exasperated. "I asked him."

"What did he say?"

"He said some things are better that you not know."

Misty didn't tell her parents that her boyfriend had been arrested. But Katie would soon suspect her daughter was keeping something from them. Misty wouldn't have wanted her parents to know, of course, because they'd have insisted she come home, to Fayetteville. Misty wanted to stay in Atlanta, to support Hack.

Weeks later, in the summer of 2004, the Carter family went to San Diego. Paul Carter, a vascular surgeon, had a medical conference to attend, and his wife and daughter wanted to tag along. Katie took the opportunity to press her daughter for more info on her boyfriend's frequent trips.

"He doesn't say anything about it," Misty insisted.

"Well, you need to know," her mother said. "He's probably going to see another woman. He could have a wife somewhere. You don't know. You just don't know."

The questions didn't seem to bother Misty. Throughout the trip, in fact, she remained upbeat. And as always, she was disappointed when she and her parents had to part ways. On their way home, Paul and Katie were on a separate flight from their daughter, though they did have a short layover in Atlanta before heading on to Raleigh. Misty's flight arrived in Atlanta not long before her parents', and she ran to their terminal to give them yet another good-bye.

Over the next few weeks, Misty spent a lot of time on the phone, chatting with her mother. That was the norm. A few years earlier, Misty had insisted that Katie buy a cell phone. Misty had grown frustrated when, time after time, she would call her mother at her father's medical practice, where Katie worked, too, only to find her out on an errand. Misty was the type who wanted to check in with her mother about everything: the fact that she was going across the street for ice cream, the property she was interested in renting to open a men's spa (the Carters wanted to help their daughter start her own business), the furniture she was considering for her town house, and whatever else happened to cross her mind.

One day in September 2004, Katie spoke with her daughter no fewer than four times. During the last call, Misty mentioned that she and Hack were staying in that evening. And so, unlike those nights when Misty went out with her girlfriends, Katie didn't worry. She didn't go through the ritual that mothers often endure, waking in the middle of the night to wonder if her only child was okay. She didn't sit up in bed and glance at the clock. She didn't stare at the ceiling and ask herself whether she knew for sure that her daughter was safe. On that night, Misty was home.

Though Kiki kept Scott apprised of just about everything going on with him, he didn't say much about the gun. Only that it came in such a nice case. Ernest, a gun collector and enthusiast, had gotten it for him—Ernest who'd been so integral to Kiki's UPS scheme. Anyway, Kiki didn't keep the gun for long. He told Scott he passed it along to J-Rock. He said J-Rock was going to take care of this.

At first, Kiki had the audacity to ask Scott to handle it. Scott balked. Hack was like a brother to him, he'd known him for that long. No way, Scott told him. He didn't want any part of it. Eventually, Kiki backed off. And Scott was able to put it out of his mind—until September 4, 2004.

Police would speculate that at least three people were involved in the incident that occurred in those early morning hours, at an upscale town house off Highland Avenue. One of the men, investigators believed, waited in the car. It appeared that two others hopped the iron fence that separated the sidewalk from the buildings' manicured grounds. They hurried noiselessly across the damp grass, unseen in the hushed predawn. They kicked in the door of one of the units and bounded up the stairs, toward the master bedroom. They left nothing to chance. Hack and Misty both were shot in the head.

As the killers rushed back to the getaway car, they most likely believed that they'd left behind a pristine crime scene. The gun wasn't theirs, and it would soon disappear. There were no fingerprints left behind, no shoe imprints, no fibers—no forensic evidence that could link them to the murder of Ulysses Hackett and Misty Carter.

What they didn't take into account was that someone in the complex saw them run. The person got a good enough glimpse—at one of the men, at least—to remember his face. The witness later would point to a picture in a photographic lineup and unequivocally state that the man in the photo was the one who sprinted from the town house after the shots rang out.

The sun already had risen in Atlanta when Scott King was shaken from sleep and forced to face the California darkness. Kiki knew the hour was crazy, but he had to call right away. His explanation was succinct. He would get back to Scott later with the details, another of those what-to-do-next conversations that he and Scott often had. But in the meantime, he thought Scott ought to know: "Stupid and the girl are dead."

SIX SPACE MOUNTAIN

If they want O, they comin' to get O.

—OMARI "O-DOG" MCCREE

n the evening of October 22, 2004, BMF's lieutenants were scrambling. Regardless of whether they were disturbed by—or even clued into—what had gone down a few weeks earlier at the town house off Highland Avenue, they were faced at the moment with a more pressing matter. Meech needed a ride. The problem was, he needed a ride from the DeKalb County jail. No one wanted to show up at the lockdown in a sparkling new Porsche or late-model Benz. That would send the wrong message. But one of them needed to get the boss out, fast. And they definitely needed to figure out what had landed him there in the first place.

Meech's go-to girl, Yogi—the woman through whom most of his administrative orders passed—was hoping to take control of the situation.

"I need a low-ass-key car," Yogi mused, her husky voice taking on a softer tone. "Like a Honda."

Omari "O-Dog" McCree, clearly one of Meech's favorite soldiers, was quick to offer his services to Yogi. "What time you have to pick him up? 'Cause I might could, um, get a—"

She didn't let him finish. "See, I just talked to the court officer, so the paperwork is goin' in as we speak." Yogi was always bailing people out, taking care of business, looking out for the Family. That was her job. In fact, she'd warned Omari earlier that day that he needed to take his new car home and park it. He couldn't be doing any extra driving, not in a $100,000 Porsche. According to Yogi, Vince Dimmock, an attorney working several of the Family's cases, advised that all those new cars doubled as big, fat targets on wheels. "Vince said anything we're drivin' without a license tag on it, they're pullin' it," she'd told Omari earlier that day. Then Yogi personalized it—in a way that must have made Omari cringe. "They know who you are," she'd told him. "You got pendin' shit. You know, it ain't even worth it, ridin' around or whatever-whatever."

"All right," Omari had conceded.

"So take it in, sit it down."

"All right."

Now, however, several hours later, it was Yogi who was at a loss for a vehicle. She couldn't drive her new Benz to the jail to get Meech, but what else could she do? Nobody seemed to have a modest ride these days. "What I need is a fuckin' rental," she told Omari.

But compared with everything else going on, her car frustrations were a minor inconvenience. More disturbing was the fact that someone seemed to be keeping too close an eye on the Family. The rumor was that Omari was to blame. He and his friend Jeffery Leahr—the two were so close, most people thought they were brothers—were the prime suspects in a quadruple shooting at a nightclub the week before. Nobody had been killed, and the incident quickly blew over in the local press. But the gun battle at the Atrium, one of the city's veteran hip-hop clubs, was arousing suspicion in BMF circles. Were the cops tailing Omari and Jeffery with the hope of charging them with the shootings—or were they biding their time in an attempt to gain wider insight into the organization? Was the Atrium incident somehow responsible for Meech getting nabbed on bunk charges—or was that just a fluke? Never mind that Meech seemed to have a soft spot for O-Dog, perhaps seeing something of himself in the rebellious young tough who rose up from the corners of Boulevard to bona fide baller status. Getting your boss, even a sympathetic one, in trouble because of your own heat? Not good.

The barrage of phone calls Omari was fielding wasn't exactly encouraging, either. The streets were talking, and the talk was not casting him in a positive light. About an hour after Omari hung up with Yogi, his phone rang again.

"Oh, I just callin' to check on you, make sure you was all right," a sweet-voiced girl gushed. "I had heard some stuff. I said, 'Let me call him.'"

"Yeah, I been hearin' shit, too. What you heard?"

"Huh? Uh, somethin' 'bout some shootin' shit at Atrium. And, um, I guess it's like, they got him at the club or something."

"They what?"

"They was sayin' they had got Meechie at the club," the girl said.

Two days earlier, in the predawn hours of October 20, 2004, DeKalb County police had set up a roadblock outside a strip club called Pin Ups on Ponce de Leon Avenue, a few miles east of Atlanta's city limits. The department claimed that the incident at the Atrium, as well as another recent shoot-out at a strip club called Jazzy T's, warranted a "safety checkpoint" at the Pin Ups intersection—though it wasn't particularly close to the site of either shooting.

Shortly before 5 A.M., the roadblock snared a Dodge Magnum that was leaving the club. Officers claimed the car smelled suspiciously of weed. They arrested the driver, Hamza Hewitt, who was once Jay-Z's bodyguard and was now believed to be Meech's, and both passengers. (Charges against Hewitt were later dismissed.) One of the passengers gave the name Ricardo Santos. At the station, Santos was placed in an empty interview room. Shortly after 9 A.M., a detective passed by, glanced through the small observation window embedded in the door, and caught sight of something that stopped him in his tracks: The man, who'd been strolling back and forth across the interrogation room's floor, suddenly paused—and with an air of nonchalance hanging over him, he pissed on the wall.

After a while, the man finally agreed to speak to investigators. Almost immediately, he let slip his real name; an officer asked if his last name might be Flenory, and he corrected the pronunciation. Regardless, one of the cops already had recognized him as Big Meech. After all, his pictures had been all over the papers the year before, when he'd been arrested for the Buckhead double-homicide.

By the time of the Pin Ups roadblock, the Buckhead case had gone stale, and most of the conditions of Meech's bond had been lifted. And so DeKalb County didn't have much to pin on Meech following his arrest. They couldn't get him for bond violation, because there was nothing left to violate. After charging him with carrying false identification and interference with government property ("interfering" with the wall of the interrogation room), the county granted him a thirty-thousand-dollar bond. Two days later, the Family was readying to spring him—and to get to the bottom of what was going on.

Meech had been locked up for nearly three days when, shortly after midnight on October 23, 2004, Yogi called Omari with marching orders: "Your boss said, have your ass at the Elevator."

"He act like I did something wrong," Omari laughed, a trace of uneasiness in his voice. "But all right."

Omari had reason to be nervous about the meeting. As the girl on the phone suggested, there appeared to be some sort of connection between Meech's arrest and the Atrium incident. Had he known the real reason why trouble seemed to be following him, however, he'd have been infinitely more stressed. That's because by the time those four people were shot at the Atrium, investigators were well on their way to cornering Omari "O-Dog" McCree. And they were inching ever closer to their ultimate prize: Omari's boss.

For months, a special drug task force had been climbing the food chain of local drug dealers, using confidential informants and undercover cocaine purchases as points of entry—and eventually graduating to a hard-earned wiretap investigation. It wasn't the Atrium shootings that had piqued investigators' interest in Omari McCree and the crew to which he belonged (though for the purposes of the investigation, the shootings couldn't have happened at a more opportune time). Rather, it was a seemingly unrelated drug deal in a down-and-out Atlanta neighborhood that eventually would lead a team of undercover agents to the curb outside Omari's swanky Buckhead town house.

Across the country, local cops and federal agents had been teaming up for what were called High Intensity Drug Trafficking Area, or HIDTA, task forces. HIDTA was the brainchild of the Office of National Drug Control Policy, an effort to stymie the flow of cocaine, crack, and heroin into the country's most blighted urban neighborhoods. The Atlanta HIDTA office comprised two units, manned by the best and brightest of the DEA, Atlanta Police Department, and Georgia Bureau of Investigation—including the APD's detective Bryant Burns, who was working with the DEA's Jack Harvey and Fulton prosecutor Rand Csehy to break the Black Mafia Family's code of silence.

HIDTA's responsibility was to dismantle drug trafficking organizations—the kind that, due to a lack of resources, typically evade most big-city police departments—and cut short the reign of violent career criminals. To that end, task force agents were given luxuries that cash-strapped police departments coveted: high-tech wiretapping equipment, fleets of undercover vehicles, and most important, unimpeded time. Agents had the benefit of months, or even years, to develop confidential sources, track the finances of kingpins and sit, wait, and watch as the tide of drugs ebbed and flowed into such downtrodden Atlanta neighborhoods as Boulevard, the Bluff, and Bankhead.

The idea was to track the large shipments by starting with the smaller sales that trickled down to the street, working backwards from the corner dealers who delivered the product to the consumer, and blazing a trail toward the three-car garages of upper-level suppliers who had direct connections to overseas sources. As with most cities, Atlanta in the early 2000s was serviced by a handful of major drug distributors from whom all the city's cocaine—bound over from Colombia or, more likely, Mexico—originated. And in Atlanta, all those distributors got their coke from BMF.

And so while HIDTA's work could be tedious, the reward in Atlanta was clear: Follow any street-level drug purchase back to its source, and you're bound to find yourself at Meech and Terry's doorstep. Of course, it wasn't so easy as strolling up to the door of the White House with an arrest warrant. For years, cops and prosecutors had fielded countless tips and rumors implicating BMF in the drug trade, but hard and fast evidence was more elusive. The dealers—even those several steps removed from BMF—usually suspected they were being watched, and so they spoke in code, relied on near-untraceable prepaid cell phones or phones in friends' names, and made a habit of ditching numbers they thought were hot. Once word spread that a dealer had been nabbed with dope, he was immediately excommunicated, and so the dealer often was useless, even in the off chance he agreed to cooperate with authorities. Getting to those upper-level guys at the heart of BMF was like running up a down escalator; falter even for a moment, and you're right back at the bottom.

Rafael "Smurf" Allison wasn't exactly at the bottom rung, but he wasn't high up, either. He was a modest crack-cocaine trafficker, a big fish in a small pond known as Pittsburgh. The Atlanta neighborhood, just across I-75 from Turner Field, was less congested than

Boulevard or the Bluffs. But street-level drug deals there were just as rampant.

Twenty-two years old and dealing in multiple ounces at a time, Smurf took in between one thousand and three thousand dollar per deal, and he sometimes did several deals a day. He'd been a HIDTA target for three years, since 2001, and he was considered by agents to be sloppy enough to maybe, possibly serve as a line to a bigger catch. In July 2004, HIDTA agents had been lucky enough to secure a confidential informant who'd ingratiated himself to Smurf—and was able to buy multiple ounces of crack from him three times in a month. Smurf even gave the informant his cell phone number, so that the informant could buy dope any time.

The agents also had an idea of who Smurf's supplier might be. One day, a surveillance team followed Smurf to a suspected "re-up" (a replenishment of one's drug supply). At a BP gas station on the corner of Ponce de Leon and Monroe Drive, it appeared that a man sitting in a brown Pontiac Grand Prix stepped out of the car to hand a package to Smurf. The Grand Prix, the surveillance agents learned, was titled to a woman named Charmela Hoskins.

Armed with proof of the drug deals and with Smurf's digits, Fulton County prosecutor Rand Csehy put together a thirty-page application seeking a wiretap on Smurf's phone. Csehy had been collaborating with the task force agents for months—ostensibly to advise on legal matters such as those pertaining to the Smurf wiretap, and perhaps more to the point, because he felt a certain kinship with cops who went after major drug dealers. Csehy felt at home with the task force. Through it, he was connected to Harvey at the DEA, whom he admired, and the APD's Bryant, who was his best friend. It took an excruciating month and a half for the wiretap application to pass District Attorney Paul Howard's muster, but finally, in early September 2004, the wiretap was approved. And the agents, holed up in a series of cubbyholes flanking a long hallway at HIDTA headquarters, began to pore over Smurf's calls.

Working the wire was difficult at times. The voyeuristic novelty wore off fast. In the meantime, the higher-ups wanted results. And so the agents listening to the calls had to try to deliver that which only fate could provide. Unlike some of the other task force agents with whom they worked in tandem, the guys assigned to the wire didn't get to experience the rush of surveillance or the satisfaction of laying their eyes on their target. They would pore over the "line sheets," the call-by-call synopses of what came over the wire, and try to find a pattern. And it was through their work that the case finally started coming together.

The idea was to get the informant to make another crack purchase from Smurf, then listen in as Smurf rang his supplier to replenish his cache—thereby nailing down the supplier's number. Sure enough, when the informant met with Smurf on September 3, 2004, asking if he could pick up four ounces, Smurf promptly dialed up the food chain. He asked for a "four hundred tray." The supplier let Smurf know he had only "a deuce hard and a deuce soft"—two ounces each of crack and powder.

The task force now had Smurf's supplier's number. What's more, the phone was listed under the name Charmela Hoskins, the same name that appeared on the title of the Grand Prix that the agents had eyeballed in the BP parking lot. But to succeed with another wiretap application, for the supplier's phone, the agents would need more than the name Charmela Hoskins.

Over the next two weeks, the wiretap agents kept a close listen on Smurf's calls, hoping he would carry them closer to the supplier whose voice materialized on the other end of the line. One day in mid-September, the wiretap team listened as Smurf told his supplier he was on his way to meet him. One of the agents contacted the surveillance team that was camped out at Smurf's house and told them to follow the target. Keeping a safe distance, the surveillance agents split up into several cars and followed Smurf to a posh apartment complex on the city's industrial West Side. Now they had a suspected address for Smurf's supplier.

Two days later, a county judge authorized a wiretap on the supplier, whom investigators later identified as Decarlo Hoskins, Charmela's husband. Right away, as soon as the wiretap was up, Decarlo called *his* supplier. Agents perked up at the all-too-obvious drug talk. Decarlo had a complaint about a recent delivery. It sounded as if his supplier had floated him some bad dope.

"I had, like, one more that was fucked up real bad, homey," Decarlo said.

"There wasn't anything wrong with that, Lo," the voice replied.

"I ain't doin' nothin' out of it," Decarlo practically spat. "But you could tell it was real fucked up. It got a logo on it, but the whole shit just like, brown. You know what I mean?"

"You sure?"

"If you'd seen it, you'd know it wasn't right."

Two days later, investigators caught another break. Decarlo was plotting what sounded like a major drug sale to three men from out of town. Decarlo told the potential buyers to meet him at "his spot." HIDTA agents took that to mean his West Side apartment. They positioned themselves at the complex, one car in the lot and another in the parking deck, and they waited.

Based on what was discussed during the call, the investigators were expecting a gray Nissan Altima to pull into the apartment complex between noon and 1 P.M. After picking up the drugs, Decarlo's three customers were supposed to head down Northside Drive to the Georgia Dome, to watch the Falcons game.

Sure enough, agents watched as a gray Altima pulled into one of the visitor spaces at around 12:30 P.M. Two minutes later, a black Infiniti, which agents believed was driven by Decarlo, pulled into the space in front of it. One of the guys in the Altima hopped into the Infiniti, and it took off across the parking lot to a place the surveillance team couldn't quite see. A few minutes later, the Infiniti returned, and the man climbed back into the Altima. Both cars bolted.

The Altima headed south on Howell Mill Road, past the neighborhood's loft buildings and warehouses, with the surveillance agents in slow pursuit. Merging onto Northside Drive—maneuvering through the game-day traffic that snaked toward the Dome—a HIDTA agent radioed Atlanta Police. It was time to request a traffic stop.

As soon as the patrol car flashed its lights, the guy in the Altima's passenger seat called Decarlo. He said they were about to be pulled over. And he said that if the police asked them to get out of the car, they'd gun it instead.

Keep it in drive, Decarlo warned.

An Atlanta police officer approached the Altima and asked the driver for his license. A moment later, one of the HIDTA agents approached the car on the other side. He told the passenger to quit talking on his cell phone and step out of the vehicle. That's when the agent saw a Smith & Wesson .357 on the Altima's floorboard.

The men didn't act on their promise to Decarlo; they didn't hit the gas. They didn't put up a fight, either. And in the trunk of the car, agents found a Louis Vuitton tote bag packed with seven individually wrapped kilos of coke, and another shopping bag stuffed with two more. The coke was wrapped tightly and professionally, as if it had been cut only once or twice since landing in the States. To Csehy, that was a good sign. That meant they were closer to the Black Mafia Family than he first imagined.

Down at HIDTA headquarters on Juniper Street, the men refused to talk. But the agents didn't need them to. Investigators now had enough evidence to take down Decarlo, the suspected source of the dope—and hopefully, by extension, Decarlo's supplier.

Yet finding Decarlo proved trickier than expected. He was cautious. After his three customers were busted on the way to the Falcons game, he decided to ditch his phone. It would have been a smart move—had he not used his old phone to call and establish a new account. The wiretap agents were listening as Decarlo's cell phone provider recited his new number.

During another call, Decarlo and a drug associate tossed around the idea of throwing their phones away. The agents braced themselves for the likelihood that the wire would fall silent. But it never did. Decarlo kept on talking.

After dialing someone else, Decarlo mentioned he wasn't sure whether state or federal officers had busted his three customers. Either way, he said, he was getting his shit together in case the police were coming for him, too. The man on the line said one of his associates was worried about Decarlo and wanted to make sure that if he were arrested, he'd hold his tongue. Decarlo said he would—and that if authorities caught up with him, he wouldn't call anyone for a week, which would serve as a heads-up. Decarlo then called another of his suppliers, Keith "Big Homey" Patterson, to ask for a "handshake"—a term that the surveillance agents knew to mean five kilos.

Nine days later, the task force had obtained a wiretap on Big Homey's phone. One day in October 2004, nearly a month after the West Side bust, agents listened as Big Homey set up a four-kilo cocaine deal, and they sent a surveillance team to the location where the deal was about to go down. At the same time, another set of agents tracked Decarlo to the same location, a building just off Boulevard, in the neighborhood known as Old Fourth Ward.

Csehy, eager to be part of the action, typically was on hand to listen to calls moments after they had been captured. (The law forbids anyone but the task force agents from listening to the calls in real time.) That day, he was at the HIDTA office, and he immediately started readying a stack of search warrants. If the surveillance agents were to catch Decarlo, they'd need to act fast and hit any address that could be linked to him or to Big Homey.

Decarlo knew something wasn't right. Talking on the phone to someone inside the house, Decarlo mentioned "the white guy with the binoculars" stationed outside. Yet he wasn't so spooked that he turned around and left. Instead, Decarlo walked inside. Shortly thereafter, Big Homey's customer walked out of the front door and toward his car. Moments after he pulled away, the HIDTA agents asked the Atlanta Police Department to stop the car—and the officers conducting the stop discovered the four-kilo package. The agents then moved in on the building where the deal had gone down. Inside, they found six more kilos, as well as fifteen pounds of marijuana. They also found Decarlo and Big Homey, both of whom were arrested.

That evening and into the next morning, a team of agents hit up Decarlo's suburban home, where they found $55,000; the apartment on the West Side, where they found another $10,000; and Decarlo's mother's house just south of the city, where they turned up $100,000. Decarlo was looking at a steep sentence on cocaine trafficking charges. The threat of prison, however, appeared not to be so deflating as another likelihood raised by investigators. Csehy told Decarlo's lawyer that the government might try to build a case against Decarlo's wife, Charmela. Decarlo was devastated by the news.

Of course, there was a way for Decarlo to keep her out of this—and even a way for her to keep their home, which would have been subject to forfeiture had the government been able to show it was purchased with drug proceeds. The thing was, Decarlo would have to talk—both now and, if necessary, in court. He'd have to give up the names of the people supplying him with his dope. If he did that, the judge would be made aware of Decarlo's assistance during his sentencing, and he might end up serving a lighter sentence, too.

Decarlo folded. Two days after his arrest, he and his lawyer sat down with Csehy and a couple of HIDTA agents. Decarlo told them he got his packages from two dealers he'd known since the three were kids growing up on Boulevard. Usually, the coke was given to him as a front, meaning he didn't have to pay them for it until he sold it. In fact, those two dealers were the ones who fronted him with the dope that he in turn sold to the three men busted near the Dome. He said they belonged to a drug crew, BMF, that didn't deal out of one particular location, per se. Instead, BMF delivered—and only to people they knew and trusted.

Decarlo said he'd be willing to let agents listen as he called and tried to arrange a deal. He knew the suppliers only by their first names: Jeffery and Omari.

Agents immediately told Decarlo to make the call. Sitting in the HIDTA office, Decarlo dialed Omari. But it was a dead end. Omari's phone had been turned off. Decarlo then called Jeff to ask him for Omari's new number. (Omari likely had ditched the old one after suspecting it was hot.) The agents watched as Decarlo jotted down the digits. He then tried Omari again. This time, Omari answered.

Decarlo asked Omari if he was "on deck"—meaning holding cocaine. "If you have anything," Decarlo continued, "I want to get two blocks." Omari's reply was succinct: He wasn't talking on the phone anymore.

But that wasn't exactly true. In the weeks to come, Omari would continue to talk on the phone—just not to Decarlo. Because he had suspected, correctly, that Decarlo had been busted.

The weekend after Decarlo's call, Omari wasn't doing the best job of avoiding trouble. He and his friend Jeffery Leahr were hanging out at the Atrium when somebody opened fire on the club-goers. Police suspected Omari and Jeff were behind the shootings, but after the two men were questioned, police let them go.

A week later, the judge granted the agents yet another wiretap, this time for the phones of Jeffery Leahr and Omari McCree. And on that first day up on the wire, just after 4 P.M. on October 22, 2004, agents knew they'd hit it big. They heard Omari talking on Jeff's phone to a security guard from the Atrium. The two were discussing, in terms as vague as possible, the shooting that had gone down at the club.

On Omari's phone, the chatter was even better. The agents heard several conversations referring to the Family's efforts to bond Big Meech out of jail.

First, agents heard the warnings about the cars: Watch your flash. Then, there were hints that Omari and Jeff would be called to a meeting later that night. "You and Jeff stay available," Yogi told Omari—and with that, four agents set out for Omari's town house on the outskirts of Buckhead. From a safe distance and from several vantage points, they would watch the comings and goings from Omari's half-million-dollar residence, and hopefully be ready to lay chase when the call came from Yogi to mobilize BMF's ranks.

Finally, seven hours later and shortly after midnight, Meech was out of jail. And BMF was on the move. Omari got the call at 12:45 A.M. In a voice weary but still upbeat, Yogi gave as many details as she could. "He fillin' out paperwork right now," she said. "He ain't talkin' on no phones. He said he want to *see* everybody at the Elevator spot."

"All right, well, just call me when y'all almost there so I can come on," Omari said. "We ain't but down the street."

Five minutes later, an unidentified man walked out of Omari's front door and drove off in a black Land Rover. One of the agents told another agent, camped out up the street, to note which way the Land Rover headed. That agent watched as the Land Rover turned right out of Omari's subdivision onto North Druid Hills Road, and he radioed a third agent, who was even farther up the street, with the instructions to follow the vehicle. That agent tailed the Range Rover from North Druid Hills to Roxboro Road to Wieuca Road and, finally, onto Peachtree, in the heart of Buckhead Village. By then, however, Omari was walking out his front door, and the agent pulled off in order to help the others keep up with their primary target.

After disappearing into his garage, Omari sped off in a silver Porsche SUV. One of the surveillance cars took off after him, onto North Druid Hills Road, then onto Roxboro and from there to

Wieuca. The other agents didn't even have a chance to join the pursuit. Omari was driving so fast and taking so many sudden turns that nobody could keep up. They lost him.

The following evening, Yogi called Omari to chat. It quickly became obvious to the agents that she and Omari were close confidants—and that she was a confidante to Big Meech as well. Yogi spoke at length with Omari. She said that Meech tells her "more and more" every day. She said she has the "inside scoop" on what the boss is thinking and doing. She described J-Bo—Meech's hawk eyed second-in-command—as her boss as well (though not nearly so likeable a boss as Meech). Those two, she told Omari, "are the biggest tricks out there." She also mentioned that Meech, Baby Bleu, and Ill currently were out of town on business.

An hour later, Omari got a call from Jeffery. The news wasn't good. Jeffery said the security guard, the one from the Atrium, had been fired—presumably because someone found out the guard had been covering for them.

The day after, the agents again staked out Omari at his house. This time, though, they had a bigger team—eleven guys to the four who took part in the prior effort. They didn't want Omari to get away again, but they also needed to be sure they followed him to a destination that mattered. They were hoping he'd lead them to the mysterious Elevator, which the chatter over the wire revealed to be a headquarters for BMF's crew. Of course, they'd settle for a traffic stop—as long as he was in possession of enough dope to maybe, somehow, convince him to talk.

When Omari called Jeff late that afternoon, moments before he pulled into the driveway, his language suggested he might be arriving with a drug shipment.

"When you hear the doorbell thing, come help me get the stuff."

"Say what?" Jeff asked.

"I'm fixin' to pull in. Just come help me get this shit out the car."

An hour after Omari's Porsche pulled into the garage, he took off again. Agents followed him as he made several stops. He picked up Yogi at a house in the posh Atlanta neighborhood of Brookhaven. From there, Omari and Yogi stopped by a CompUSA and a Sprint cell phone store, then drove to a gated subdivision in north Atlanta. Agents waited just beyond the iron gate, and the Porsche reemerged minutes later. The next stop was a gas station, where agents watched as Omari, Yogi, and a young woman (whom they must have just picked up) dipped inside the store. Finally, after the Porsche made a ten-minute pit stop at Omari's home, the occupants started on a longer trip—and the agents took that to be a sign that there might be something valuable in the car. The surveillance team followed the Porsche along several surface roads before finally hitting the highway. When the Porsche topped out at 85 mph, the agents radioed local deputies to request a traffic stop.

Obliging the flashing lights, the Porsche pulled to shoulder on the ramp between I-285 south and I-20 east, about twenty miles from Omari's home. The young woman who'd been spotted at the gas station was now driving, and Omari was a passenger. Pointing at Omari, the woman told the officer, "Everything in it belong to him." When officers asked if they could search the car, the woman consented. But the search was in vain. They found zilch.

Thirty minutes later, Jeff called Omari.

"We just got pulled over by the police," Omari told him.

"For real?"

"Yeah."

"They searched it?"

Omari didn't want to get into all that. "Um, I'll call you back, man."

The next day, agents listening to the wire perked up at what sounded like not-so-well-guarded drug talk. Yogi had called Omari for help in figuring out how to tally different piles of bills.

"Hey, um, listen," she said. "One rubber band of, uh, twenties is what?"

"Um, a stack."

There is a difference, however, between a stack, which totals $2,500, and a double stack, which is worth twice as much. Omari sensed that Yogi wasn't too sure about how to differentiate between them. "It's not double is it?" he asked.

"One stack," she said, "but it's got two rubber bands."

"Both tied?"

"Yeah.

"That's five."

"Ooh, well, I was about to fuck up. That's why I asked. Thank you very much."

In another call, Yogi used an unusual euphemism for what the agents believed to be a dope shipment. And the term she used later would come in handy for the investigators.

"Look," Yogi said to Omari, "if Ralphie got somethin' on the back of the truck, would he leave it there all night?"

"If he got somethin' on the back of the truck?"

"He, um, put all his 'dry cleaning' on the back of the truck. You don't think he should leave them clothes on the back of the truck like that, should he?"

"I don't know. Where he takin' 'em to?"

"He was takin' them from the, uh, from the Elevator."

"Uh, I don't know. Whatever man, just tell him it's whether he want to or he don't."

"I mean, it's just a call," she said. "What would you do?"

"Umm, I wouldn't go back, I tell you that."

"Oh, leave it where it is?"

"Yeah."

Two days later, Yogi had some interesting gossip to share. She brought Omari up to speed on matters involving the rapper Young Jeezy. She claimed that Jeezy was behind on some payments for his Lamborghini, which he'd gotten from a dealership in Orlando that regularly secured cars—Lambos, Ferraris, and the like—for BMF.

The owner of the shop was Eric "Swift" Whaley, a 350-pound man with a heart condition that rendered him a far cry from the image his nickname conjured.

Yogi was clearly getting a kick out of the situation. "Jeezy called me talkin' 'bout, 'Let me tell you what that punk-ass Swift did.' I said, 'I know—took your car.'"

"He took it?" Omari asked, incredulous.

"Yep. He runnin' round here tellin' everybody his paperwork wasn't straight," Yogi said. The car, she claimed, had been impounded. "Jeezy just ain't made a motherfuckin' payment on the car in five months," Yogi continued. "Swift told me if I get Jeezy to pay a car payment, he'll pay *my* car payment."

"What the hell is wrong with that boy?"

"Swift told him the only way he can get it back is if he pay it all the way off. He said that's fucked up. He said, 'No, I'm gonna get the Medina.' I said, 'Okay, Hollywood.'"

"I ain't never heard no shit like that."

"Isn't that crazy? Niggas be frontin' one way and shit. Mmm, mmm, mmm . . . rappers."

As for Yogi and Omari, both were having some self-restraint problems with their new rides—she with her Benz and he with his Porsche. Meech, whom she and Omari often referred to as "Dude," had noticed their dilemma. "Dude said, 'Yogi don't drive the motherfuckin' car,'" she told Omari a few minutes after the Jeezy story. "I need to just stop bein' hardheaded, but when you know you ain't got no transportation, sometimes you just gotta do what you gotta do. I know it's especially hard on you, 'cause you hate bein' in the house."

From that, and from what Omari said next, it appeared to the agents that Meech's crew was under a sort of self-imposed house arrest.

"Not really," Omari said. "I ain't got no problem with it. It's just, I wanna get out like one time. But I see that's not possible."

"That's for sure. You know these motherfuckers are actually for real laying in wait for a nigga to leave the motherfuckin' club."

Omari was getting a little stir crazy. Yogi, too. And the fact that they fell back on talking on the phone as opposed to going out—that they let their guards down on their cells and that, likely out of boredom, their lips got looser and looser—well, that turned out to be better for investigators than had the two of them been hanging out all over town. Their chatter was the foundation of the HIDTA case.

Three hours later, Yogi and Omari were on the phone again. During this call, Omari's mood had taken a turn for the worse. Yogi, who was constantly trying to lift his spirits, did her best to combat his fatalistic mumblings. She reminded him of his rather fortunate standing with her—and with Meech.

"Half the shit that I tell you, I break confidence in my boss to tell you," she admitted. "I know I shouldn't be tellin you. But it's because I just see you in a totally different light. I think sometimes I see more than you see yourself. And I have conversations with Dude, and I know certain things that he think of you."

Omari wasn't having it. As Yogi's tone shifted from admonishing to nurturing and back again, he remained morose. He was worried about the Atrium shootings—and Decarlo's bust, too. He also mentioned that he thought he was being watched.

Take heart in one thing, Yogi reiterated: You are in Meech's good graces.

"Dude just asked me how's everybody," she said. "I'm tellin' him everybody cool, but motherfuckin' everybody gettin' an attitude. He's like, 'Shit, everybody just got to sit in then.' I don't want you to sit around your house mopin' about everything bad that's goin' on with you. You gotta take all of that energy that you spendin' mopin' around and get on with your fuckin' life, O. You still in a good position right now, a real good position."

"I'm not mopin'," Omari skulked. "I'm not doin' shit, man. I'm rollin' with everything that comin' my way. But I'm not fixin' to be sittin' round here all happy-go-lucky, smiling at everybody."

"Like I was sayin', everybody ain't against you, O."

"I never did say anybody was against me. Ain't nobody with me or against me."

"I ain't tellin' you how to run your life," Yogi said, laughing a little, trying to lighten the mood.

"Shit, well, maybe I just don't feel like talkin' sometimes. Maybe I'm just sittin' here thinkin'. Maybe that's what I'm doin'."

"You just my friend," Yogi explained. "I care about you, and I don't like seein' you like this, that's all. If it's wrong to be carin' about you, then I'll deal with that on my own but—"

Omari cut her off. "I appreciate all the care," he said. "I appreciate everything, for real, from everybody and whatever. But when it's all said and done, or when it all comes to an end, if they want O, they comin' to get O. I'm still the one that got to deal with it at the end of the day. I do. Maybe I'm preparin' myself for the worst."

The following day, the worst seemed to be on its way. The security guard from the Atrium called again. He reminded Omari that he had been fired. As compensation, he said, he wanted a car. He told Omari, "I've done my part."

An hour later, the security guard talked to Jeffery. "I need my little bit right now," he said.

"Tomorrow," Jeffery replied.

The guard had been partly responsible for Omari and Jeffrey becoming suspects, and now he was helping undo the damage. For that, he'd already been paid $2,500 up front, and he was guaranteed another $2,500 when the case was dismissed. Somewhere along the way, though, the guard decided he wanted more.

After hanging up with him, Jeffery called his twenty-two-year-old girlfriend, Courtney Williams, to vent. The guard had been fired, Jeffery complained to Courtney, because he said too much about what had happened—though not enough to get Jeffery and Omari arrested. Now, the guard wanted Omari and Jeff to compensate him

for his loss of income. Such demands were unwise, Jeffery hinted to Courtney. "People need to realize how much clout we got in this motherfuckin' city," he told her.

The Atrium situation was clearly stressing out Omari and Jeffery. Yogi wanted to ease their worrying. So she stayed on top of the situation, claiming to be in contact with the attorney, Vince Dimmock, who was handling the case. So far, neither of them had been charged—and they might not be, thanks to the security guard's willingness to hold back on what he'd witnessed. That's what Yogi wanted to discuss with Omari on November 2, 2004.

"Vince said they really don't have all that they want," she said. "So you just really gotta take what he said, and stay ahead of the game."

With that bit of business out of the way, Yogi and Omari wound up talking for nearly an hour—or, to be more precise, *Yogi* talked for the better part of an hour. Omari, as usual, mostly listened. She chattered on about the progress over at the club Meech was opening. It was going to be called Babylon, the same name as Tony Montana's club in *Scarface*. She complained about J-Bo, who, compared to Meech, didn't seem to appreciate her. J-Bo didn't hold a candle to Meech, not in her book.

Noticing that Omari was zoning out, she switched topics.

"What are you doin'?" she asked sweetly.

"Just thinkin'," Omari said in a far-off voice.

"About what?"

"I don't know, everything."

"Tell me one thing you're wonderin' about."

"Um, why I keep gettin' calls from somebody sayin' I'm fixin' to go to jail and shit."

"You don't think that's just the talk in the streets?"

"Yeah, it might be."

"Who's discussin' you?"

"I don't know. Just different people."

"You talkin' 'bout people from Boulevard, right?"

"Nah, no. Somebody called and was like, 'So-and-so said this.'"

Yogi believed she had an explanation for all that talk: envy. "I can name thirty niggas on Boulevard that wanna see you go to jail right now and hope that they could take your place," she said. "Nigga, don't give them that."

Then, she got deep.

"I see the character traits in you that are in Dude," she said. "I see you bein' a leader. I see a lot of you in him, and I see a lot of him in you. I know what Meech used to be like in his younger days. The conceit that you have, he had—but he's a little more humble now, because he's a little bit older. I just see you and him bein' the same kind of people, and I think people in the Family see that also."

These were treacherous times, she continued. People felt the heat, because the heat was real. Take St. Louis. Thirteen BMF guys had just been indicted there, including a high-level manager named Deron "Wonnie" Gatling—who'd gone on the run. "I'm talkin' about St. Louis so hot right now, I'm sure everybody think the world is on fire," Yogi said. "We all a little warm around this motherfucker. But I just don't see why they keep singlin' you out. I just think that it would have been done by now, you know what I'm sayin'? That's just my opinion. I just feel like you sittin' there stressin' yourself out and it's not time for you to stress yourself out, you know? Everybody got their time. I don't think it's yours, though."

The most Omari could offer in response was a long "Hmmmm."

To which Yogi responded, "Let it go, baby."

Of course, Omari couldn't.

November 4, 2004, was a day of bad omens—some of them obvious, others not. Two days had passed since Yogi's extended pep talk, and Omari was as paranoid as ever.

His first order of business that afternoon was to help bond one of his associates out of jail. Decarlo Hoskins had been locked up for nearly three weeks and had just that day been granted a $100,000 bond. Omari felt obligated to help. You had to look after those who could incriminate you, after all. Little did Omari know that it was too late.

A couple of hours later, Omari got an ominous phone call. The man on the line identified himself as Omari's brother. Investigators knew that wasn't the case, though they didn't know who the caller was.

"I need to talk to you real urgent," the man said. "Real, real important, my nigga."

"It's bad?" Omari asked.

"Hell yeah. I think it is."

"About me?"

"Yeah, nigga, you heard me?"

"Man . . ."

"Your shit is all right? Your, um, your jack?"

Omari wasn't all that sure anymore. Despite the fact that he and Yogi had been talking freely on his cell, he began to doubt it was safe.

"Um, I'm gonna call you from another," Omari said.

"Hurry up, son."

Omari's paranoia was mounting. One of his next calls showed just how freaked out he'd become—and how close he was to figuring out what, exactly, was going on. Omari called to request a favor from a woman, who in turn called a friend of hers on another line. Her friend worked at the Atlanta Police Department.

Omari was worried that a black truck he kept noticing, a truck parked on the curb just up the street from his house, might be part of a surveillance team. Earlier, he'd jotted down the truck's tag number. Now he was reading it to the woman, who repeated it to her police source. The agents listening in could tell that the person who betrayed them was inside the APD, because they were able to trace the number back to the department. The actual perpetrator, however, was never identified.

The woman told Omari that she'd get back to him soon with some info.

A half hour later, Jeffery called Omari with an idea that he thought might help ease some of their pressure. Jeffery's girlfriend, Courtney, was out of town, so Jeffery offered to bring the "clothes" to her apartment on Highland Avenue. She just so happened to live in the same complex where, exactly two months before, Misty Carter and Ulysses Hackett were shot to death in Misty's bed.

"Yeah," Omari said. "That's cool."

The surveillance agents weren't able to maintain a tail on Jeffery as he drove the "clothes" over to Courtney's. Thus the agents were left thinking that they'd missed out on a golden opportunity, a convergence of events that surely wouldn't happen again—until they realized, listening to the wire the next day, that all was not lost.

Just before 5:30 P.M. on November 5, 2004, a taxi pulled up to Omari's house, and the surveillance agents watched as Courtney stepped out. She'd just come from the airport, according to the wire, and was about to leave town again. Ten minutes later, agents saw her pull out of the garage in a white Cadillac SUV, followed moments later by Jeffery, driving the Porsche. The agents, who were joined by the DEA this time around, split into two teams. Three guys took off after Courtney, the other three after Jeff.

The Porsche was driving wildly. Jeffery gunned it through a red light at Spring Street and North Avenue, entering the thick of downtown Atlanta. The agents lost him.

It was at around that moment, while Jeffery and Courtney were both driving, that Jeffery decided to call Courtney to let her know the "clothes" were at her apartment. Courtney said she wanted the clothes out of there—and she wanted to be rid of Jeffery, too. So the clothes had to be moved, and quick.

Back at HIDTA headquarters, the agents were scrambling to let the surveillance team know what was going on. The team *had* to get to Courtney, and quick.

"I'm sick of this dirty business," they heard Courtney say. "So I'm just tryin' to figure out if you're gonna be there within the next thirty minutes, because I'm about to go out of town."

"You're fixin' to go outta town? Where you goin'?"

"Outta town," she said dryly.

"Damn, well, can I keep your key while you're outta town?" Jeffery pleaded.

"Can you keep my key while I'm outta town? You missed the point. I just changed my number—"

"Courtney, I need to keep those clothes over there for real, 'cause . . . you don't even understand right now."

"You're right," she said. "I don't understand."

"Can I just keep those clothes over there, please? Can I just keep the keys until you get back?"

"I'm sorry. You can't keep my key."

"Courtney, can I please keep the key. Please."

"I already said no."

"All right, if you're going to be selfish like that—"

"I'm not being selfish."

"All right, well, I'm on my way."

Courtney, fortunately, was easier for the surveillance team to keep up with. The agents followed her all the way to her Highland Avenue apartment complex. A few minutes later, Jeffery pulled up in the Porsche. Both of them went inside her apartment. Shortly thereafter, the couple emerged with a duffel bag. They climbed into the Porsche and headed toward the highway.

The agents pursuing them called in Atlanta Police. It was time for another traffic stop.

The cops caught up with the Porsche on I-75 at Pine Street, near the heart of downtown. Jeffery pulled to the shoulder of the exit ramp. Investigators, who were met on the scene by Fulton prosecutor Csehy, approached the SUV, guns drawn. They ordered Jeffery and Court-ney out of the vehicle, then cuffed them and put them in separate cars. In the backseat of the Porsche, in plain view, the agents found an open duffel bag stuffed with ten kilos.

Csehy and the agents drove the couple to Courtney's apartment, where she consented to a search. While some agents were digging through her stuff, others tried to pressure her to talk. They said she should've been well aware that Jeffery and Omari were up to no good. "These guys don't work and they live in a half-a-million-dollar home and they drive an eighty-thousand-dollar truck," one of them told her. "Where do you think they get their money from?"

But Courtney wouldn't budge. She just sat there staring at them.

In the course of the search, the agents didn't turn up anything, though the ten kilos in the back of the Porsche were more than enough to arrest the couple and put them away for a while. Instead, Csehy decided to let them go. It was a ballsy move, but he figured Jeff and Courtney would keep talking on the phone, and that might yield even better information over the wire.

When Omari called Jeffery a few hours later, Omari knew some-thing was up. Yet he pressed Jeffery to talk, despite Jeffery's insistence that it was a bad idea.

"Don't wanna talk right now," Jeffery said as soon as he answered. "Bye."

"What?" Omari asked.

"Bye."

The line went dead. Thirty seconds later, Omari called again. Jeffery greeted him with a terse, "Don't wanna talk."

"Hey, what the fuck you talking 'bout?"

"Don't wanna talk, man. Listen to me, please. Just listen to me for real."

"You in trouble?"

"Don't wanna talk. Come on, for real. Please come on."

Jeffery hung up. A minute later, he called Omari with instructions.

"Yogi Bear's house," Jeff said.

"Huh?" Omari asked.

"Yogi Bear's house."

"Who?"

"Yogi Bear's house."

"Yogi *what*?"

"Yogi Bear's house! Go to Yogi Bear's house."

"Go?"

"Go to Yogi Bear's house, all right?"

"Are you all right, though? That's what I'm askin' you."

"Can you just go there? I'm all right right now, but can you . . ."

"All right."

Omari tried Jeffery's girlfriend next. She could barely form the words around the tears.

"Hello?" Courtney mumbled.

"What you cryin' for?" Omari asked.

"He didn't let you know?"

"What?"

"Everything just went wrong, O," Courtney sobbed. "Just leave the house, all right? Are you at your house?"

"No."

"Okay, well, as long as you left there, you should be straight."

"Would you stop? Look, just tell me what happened."

"I don't wanna talk on the phone, you know what I'm saying? The fuckin' feds, whoever they was, just dropped out on us."

Three days later, Yogi called Meech to discuss business. By then, there was a wire up on her, too.

Of course, Meech wasn't into talking on the phone. He said they could talk about whatever they needed to discuss once she arrived in L.A. That day, Yogi boarded a commercial jet bound for California. So did two task force agents. They followed her to California, hoping to shadow her all the way to her meeting with Meech. But Yogi proved difficult to keep up with. While driving through L.A., she made abrupt turns, turning back on her tracks and traveling in broad circles. Eventually, she shook them.

Two days later, Yogi was back in Atlanta. Over the phone, Meech told her he'd be back the day after next.

Even then, Jeff and Omari were still talking on their cell phones, but their conversations were waning. They needed to come up with a plan—and some cash. The package they'd lost was a front, meaning they owed a bunch of money to the boss. But they had no product to sell.

They weren't exactly making themselves scarce, though. Both men were at their house when Csehy stopped by on November 19, 2004, to talk to Jeffery about the bust. Omari, who wasn't sure whether he, too, had been tied to the cocaine in the backseat of the Porsche, jumped off the balcony in back of the house, gun in hand, and ran. A surveillance team stationed outside watched his retreat.

Jeffery's girlfriend was smarter. Within days of the bust, Courtney ditched her Highland Avenue digs. She moved, she would later say, out of fear.

That evening, Meech called Yogi for an update.

"What happened?" he asked.

Yogi mentioned that the police had shown up at Jeff and Omari's, and that Omari had skirted them.

"I thought he moved," Meech said.

Yogi said he hadn't.

"He's being very stupid," Meech told her. "And that's why I'm not fucking with the man right now."

Out of an abundance of caution, Meech had switched things up. He no longer felt safe distributing cocaine out of the same location Jeffery and Omari had visited. The house, in a residential, wooded part of Buckhead, would have to be shuttered. It was time to close the Gate.

Meech didn't move the operation too far. About a mile away, in a similar upscale neighborhood, Meech set up shop at an even more impressive abode. The ultramodern house was so grandiose that some BMF associates referred to it as "the Bugsy Siegel," because it was the type of place that only the flashiest gangster would inhabit. Meech had another name for it. He called it Space Mountain. During the first few weeks that BMF operated out of Space Mountain, the limos from California came and went, delivering a hundred kilos at a time, and driving off with millions in cash. The house held as much as $6 million at a time, which BMF associates, including a convicted murderer named Ralph "Ralphie" Simms, counted by hand.

Meech tried to make his presence scarce around Space Mountain. As always, he had J-Bo oversee the drug shipments. The customers would call first, to let J-Bo know how many kilos to set aside. J-Bo would tell the lower-tier workers, including Ralphie, to be ready and waiting for the customers to arrive. The transaction would take mere minutes. Even so, years later Ralphie would remember two of the customers vividly. One was Doc Marshall, who did BMF's books. The other customer to whom Ralphie allegedly handed kilos of dope was hard to forget. After all, he was a soon-to-be famous rapper: Young Jeezy.

Ralphie also was on hand the day a frantic order came down from Meech. It was two days before Thanksgiving 2004. Everybody was getting ready to go to Miami for the holiday. That afternoon, Ralphie left Space Mountain, but just for a minute. He was only going to stop at the store for cigars. But shortly after he pulled out of the driveway, he was stopped by police. It appeared they'd been watching the house. Ralphie handed over a license with a fake name. Had he not adopted the alias, he'd have found himself in serious trouble. He currently was in violation of his probation, which he'd received the prior year after serving time on a Missouri murder charge.

The cops ran the license, and it came back clean. Like most of the rest of Meech's crew, Ralphie had gotten a "legitimate" license through a crooked source inside the Tennessee DMV. The cops let him go.

At around the same time, Meech was driving over to 404 Motorsports to check on one of his cars, which was being worked on at the dealership's shop. He noticed that someone—apparently an undercover agent—appeared to be following him. Once he heard about Ralphie getting pulled over, he knew that Space Mountain had been compromised. He called J-Bo and told him what to do: "Clean up the house." There were a hundred kilos inside, and they had to be moved, fast.

That same afternoon, a contractor was at Space Mountain, doing repairs to the roof. He knew most of the crew that hung out at the house by sight, because he'd done numerous repairs at both that house and the Gate. In fact, he'd installed the gate at the Gate. The contractor believed that the men whom he'd met—both J-Bo and Ralphie, as well as a short, charming, likeable guy called Ill—were in the music business. That's what they told him, anyway. Their claim was supported by the fact that there often were the limos, Lambos, Ferraris, and Hummers parked in Space Mountain's driveway.

As the contractor was finishing up the job on the roof, he noticed people running from the house, scrambling for their cars. He recognized one of them as J-Bo. Soon thereafter, he packed up and left— only to return a few hours later. He was supposed to fix a leak inside the house. By then, it was dark. And he was startled to find that the house was crawling with local police and federal agents. They were executing a search warrant. But they were a few hours too late.

In his affidavit for the search warrant, HIDTA task force agent Walt Britt had cited the search a year earlier of the Flenory brothers' White House. He described the Porsche, driven by Jeffery Leahr, that had been pulled over two weeks earlier, loaded with ten kilos. He laid out Meech's connection to Yogi, his assistant, and her relationship with both Jeffery and Omari. He also wrote that a confidential source had claimed Meech was supposed to be paying off debts that very day—including money he owed to attorney Vince Dimmock, for his representation of Jeffery, Omari, and a handful of other BMF members. That meeting was supposed to take place at a room inside the Ritz-Carlton Buckhead. Britt even went so far as to claim that a recent article in hip-hop magazine *The Source* hinted at Meech's role as a drug boss.

In the article, Meech was quoted as saying, "We all are hard-working hustlers. But none of us rob, steal, or kill for our money. . . . We always just hustling in whatever way we can, whether it's selling CDs or whatever we have to do out here." In his affidavit for the search warrant, Britt wrote: "Missing amongst the crime denials is selling drugs."

That evening, November 23, 2004, the judge signed off on the warrant, and Britt, Csehy, Harvey, Burns, and several other law enforcement agents showed up at Space Mountain. Nobody was inside the boxy structure, which sat off the road behind an iron gate and featured a wall of windows facing the woods. But the elegant interior, which featured a spiral staircase ascending to an open-air loft, did turn up some items of interest. Inside, the agents found guns, several BMF jerseys, and a Tennessee driver's license with J-Bo's picture and a fake name: Derrek Williams. In the garage, they found cloth wrappings that tested positive for cocaine residue. But they didn't find any drugs.

When the contractor showed up, DEA agent Harvey broke away from the others to talk to him. The contractor said that he had a phone number for one of the men who hung around the house. His name was Ill. Harvey told the contractor he'd follow up with him.

Upon leaving, the contractor went directly to Ill's house in the suburbs. He knew where Ill lived, because he'd done renovations for him, too. He knocked on the front door. No answer. So he went around back to the deck, to peek through the glass doors. He knocked on the glass. A very nervous Fleming "Ill" Daniels opened. He was hanging out with Ralphie. Both men were dressed down—in their boxer shorts. In the background, *Scarface* was on the TV. They seemed to be spooked by something. The contractor told Ill what he'd seen at Space Mountain. But Ill, as well as the rest of the crew, already knew.

The next day, Meech decided he was done with Atlanta for a while. He was already planning on heading down to Miami to get away from things for a bit, and he figured he might as well extend the vacation. In Miami, he'd find a warmer reception—and a more grandiose home. The week before Christmas 2004, he leased (through an associate, of course) a deco-styled mansion in South Beach. The rent was thirty thousand dollars a month.

By that time, it seemed, Omari McCree had finally disappeared.

We've not yet pinpointed a motive.
—ATLANTA POLICE DEPARTMENT SPOKESMAN

By the time the sun came up in California, leaving Scott King face-to-face with the news about Misty and Hack, Tremayne "Kiki" Graham was calling him for the second time that morning. And, in true Kiki fashion, he had a plan.

Kiki told Scott that he'd come up with an idea that would immediately throw investigators off his trail. (Never mind, Scott thought, that it was he, Scott King, who'd now look like the prime suspect, seeing as how he was on the run—and how Hack had been his codefendant, too.) Kiki would create the illusion that, as a result of the double shooting on Highland Avenue, he was in grave danger. He would prompt law enforcement to believe he needed protection. He would let everyone know that he now had to fear for his life.

It was widely known that Kiki was under house arrest at his and his wife Kai's East Cobb home. That meant that if someone wanted to target him (or if he wanted people to *think* someone wanted to target him), he'd be easy to find. So to demonstrate just how serious the situation was, Kiki made a temporary move—to a place where any would-be attacker would be loath to tread. He sought refuge at the home of his mother-in-law, Atlanta mayor Shirley Franklin. No one, including the mayor herself, would believe for a second that Kiki had the gall to move into her house if he'd been tied in any way to the murders.

Surprisingly, the double-homicide didn't make much of a public splash. Two days after the early-morning shooting, the deaths warranted a mere hundred words in the *Atlanta Journal-Constitution*, buried deep inside the newspaper's metro section. The paper quoted an Atlanta Police Department spokesman, who described the killings as baffling, but not quite out of the ordinary: "We have no suspect, no motive and no arrest at this time. It was a home invasion, but we've not yet pinpointed a motive." The story did not mention that one of the victims had been the codefendant of the mayor's son-in-law.

Apparently satisfied with the public reaction to the killings, Kiki later moved back to East Cobb. And for a time, all resumed to normal—or at least some semblance of it. With Kiki still under house arrest, his friend Eric "Mookie" Rivera continued to meet with him at his house—and to plan more trips from L.A. during which he could traffic cocaine on Kiki's behalf. During one of Mookie's visits, in the fall of 2004, he asked Kiki how his case was going.

"It's looking good right now," Kiki told him.

"What's goin' on?" Mookie asked.

"The one guy that could say anything about me got murdered," Kiki said casually, as if citing some obscure case law that worked to his advantage. "The guy is gone."

At that point, Mookie didn't want to hear any more. And for a while, he didn't.

He'd be seeing a lot more of Kiki, though. On October 29, 2004—four days before jury selection was scheduled to begin in Kiki's federal drug trial—his attorney requested that Kiki be allowed

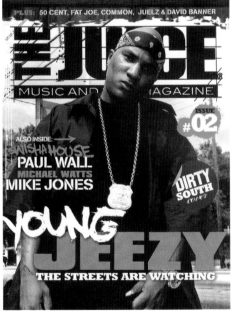

The first issue of hip-hop magazine *The Juice*
featured Meech on one cover and the rapper
Young Jeezy on the flip side.

Meech (seated), Bleu DaVinci (standing behind him), and Meech's second-in-command, J-Bo (far right) on an Atlanta street corner. *(David Stuart)*

At his thirty-sixth birthday party in June 2004, Meech toasts the massive crowd at Atlanta mega-club Compound. *(Ben Rose/benrosephotography.com)*

8-30-06

'WHAT'S "CRACKIN" WORLD

AS YOU CAN SEE THEY CAN LOCK UP MY BODY', BUT NOT MY MIND!
SO I JUST WANT EVERYONE TO KNOW THAT THIS IS THE "REAL BIG MEECH"
MY SPACE WEB SITE. AND I APRIECIATE EVERYONE for Logging ON SENDING
YOUR PICTURES, MUSIC, And COMMENTS EVERYTHING GETS FORWARDED TO ME
IN ST CLAIR COUNTY JAIL WHERE I'm TEMPORARELY being HELD UNTIL MY BOND
HEARING ON NOVEMBER 8TH, SO I will bE RESPONDING "PERSONALLY" TO
YOUR QUESTIONS AND COMMENTS, THE WORLD IS STILL B.M.F's WE
STILL HERE AND WE'RE NOT GOING ANYWHERE! SO AII YOU LADIES WHO
THINK YOU HAVE WHAT IT TAKES TO bE A JUICE OR JUICY GIRL PLEASE
SEND ME YOUR BEST PHOTO'S SO I CAN PUT YOU IN OUR FUTURE
ISSUE AND HELP JUMP START YOUR CAREER. EVEN THOUGH I'm LOCKED UP
I'm STILL FOCUSED ON MY "VISION" mAKING MY CHALLENGES TEMPORARY
but MY "VISION" PERMANENT, SO UNDERSTAND THAT NOTHING DISTURBS
THE TRIALS of THE PRESENT LIKE THE EXPECTATIONS OF THE
FUTURE!!! I will bE BACK N BLACK SOON SO UNTIL MY PENCIL
MEETS MY PAPER AGAIN REMEBER LOYALTY IS NOT JUST A WORD ITS A

LifeSTYle

LET NO MAN SEPARATE WHAT WE CREATE
FROM EVERY HOOD TO HOLLYWOOD comING
TO A GHETTO NEAR YOU DEATH B4
DISHONOR THE GREATEST SHOW
ON EARTH AFTER US THERE WIII
BE "NO OTHER"

LOVE

THE REAL
BIG MEECH

Above: The letter Meech posted on his MySpace page in 2006, months after he was arrested outside Dallas.

Left: The home on southwest Detroit's Edsel Street where the Flenory brothers came of age. *(Sandra Svoboda)*

BLACK MAFIA FAMILY & ASSOCIATES

JAY "YOUNG JEEZY" JENKINS, platinum-selling, chart-topping Atlanta rapper whose career Big Meech claimed to have given an early boost.

RADRIC "GUCCI MANE" DAVIS, fellow Atlanta rapper and onetime nemesis to Jeezy.

JERRY "J-ROCK" DAVIS, leader of the Sin City Mafia ("the Family"), a sister crew to BMF that shared a common cocaine source.

OMARI "O-DOG" MCCREE, a midlevel cocaine distributor under Big Meech who received a shout-out from Young Jeezy in one of the rap superstar's tracks.

BARIMA "BLEU DAVINCI" MCKNIGHT, sole rapper signed to BMF Entertainment, whom Meech treated as a little brother.

DEMETRIUS "BIG MEECH" FLENORY, charismatic co-leader of national cocaine syndicate the Black Mafia Family, CEO of Atlanta-based hip-hop label BMF Entertainment, and older brother to Terry.

CHAD "J-BO" ("JUNIOR BOSS") BROWN, right-hand man and second-in-command to Big Meech.

FLEMING "ILL" DANIELS, a BMF cocaine distributor who became Meech's third-in-command.

WILLIAM "DOC" MARSHALL, Meech and Terry's CFO and one of the few BMF associates who continued working for both brothers after their split.

JACOB "THE JEWELER" ARABO, New York jeweler to the stars and self-described "king of bling" who outfitted the Flenory brothers with millions of dollars in diamonds.

INVESTIGATORS

JACK HARVEY, highly regarded agent with the U.S. Drug Enforcement Agency in Atlanta who spent close to a decade on the BMF case.

MARC COOPER, Atlanta homicide detective who investigated three high-profile crimes tied to BMF.

 **SCOTT KING**, one of J-Rock's top cocaine associates and Kiki's close friend and business partner, both in the luxury car business and in the cocaine trade.

 **TREMAYNE "KIKI" GRAHAM**, another of J-Rock's top drug lieutenants, who later married the mayor of Atlanta's daughter.

 **ULYSSES "HACK" HACKETT**, cocaine courier to King and Kiki who came under Kiki's suspicion after a drug bust.

 **ERIC "MOOKIE" RIVERA**, courier to J-Rock who was skilled at smuggling cocaine across the country in private jets; later went to work directly for Kiki.

 **ERNEST "E" WATKINS**, another of J-Rock's couriers, who assisted Kiki in a different cocaine-smuggling scheme.

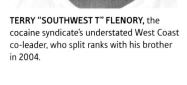 **TERRY "SOUTHWEST T" FLENORY**, the cocaine syndicate's understated West Coast co-leader, who split ranks with his brother in 2004.

 **ERIC "SLIM" BIVENS**, trusted underboss to Terry, making him lateral to J-Bo.

 **CHARLES "POPS" FLENORY**, father of Terry and Meech, longtime carpenter and gospel musician.

 **BENJAMIN "BLANK" JOHNSON**, childhood friend of the Flenory brothers and high-ranking member of Terry's cocaine crew, later to be replaced by his half brother A.R.

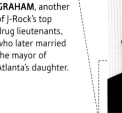

 **ARNOLD "A.R." BOYD**, Terry's Detroit manager, who took over his brother's position after Blank was busted.

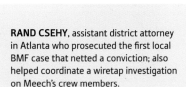

BRYANT "BUBBA" BURNS, Atlanta police investigator assigned to the department's organized crime unit, who would become the APD's most knowledgeable source on BMF.

RAND CSEHY, assistant district attorney in Atlanta who prosecuted the first local BMF case that netted a conviction; also helped coordinate a wiretap investigation on Meech's crew members.

ROLANDO BETANCOURT, acclaimed bounty hunter hired to track down federal fugitive Tremayne "Kiki" Graham.

Top: The sprawling "Space Mountain" in Atlanta's upscale Buckhead neighborhood doubled as a party pad and cocaine stash house for Meech's crew. *(Joeff Davis)*

Center: The house on L.A.'s Mulholland Drive where authorities believed Terry Flenory lived with his longtime girlfriend. *(Mara Shalhoup)*

Bottom: Jerry "J-Rock" Davis's San Fernando Valley home, known as "First Base," was the suspected hub of BMF's sister crew, Sin City Mafia. *(Mara Shalhoup)*

Meech (center, right) and his close friend rapper Barima "Bleu DaVinci" McKnight (center, left) soak up the attention of camera crews at Meech's birthday party. *(Ben Rose/benrosephotography.com)*

The rapper Nelly (left) admires Meech's eye-catching fur at a holiday party held at Atlanta mega-club Vision. *(Ben Rose/benrosephotography.com)*

to leave his home to attend a meeting. The meeting would take place at the attorney's downtown law office, a thirty-minute drive from East Cobb. The attorney and client had much to discuss in preparation of the trial. The attorney thought an exception to Kiki's house arrest was warranted. As such, the request to the U.S. Probation Office was granted.

But the meeting never happened. After Kiki left his house that day, he made a run for it. He cut off his electric ankle monitor and hit the road. Ernest Watkins, his associate with the inside man at UPS, rented him a car. From the highway, driving west from Georgia toward Texas, Kiki called Scott. He told him he was going to catch a plane from Dallas to Burbank, and that he'd need a ride once he landed in California. Scott said he'd be waiting.

Sure enough, Kiki took a cab from Burbank to Van Nuys, at which point Scott picked him up and brought him to his place. The following day, they met with their boss, J-Rock, who offered to put Kiki up at the stash house way out in the burbs, the one on Oso Avenue called Third Base. As long as Kiki didn't mind keeping the company of several hundred kilos of cocaine and a veritable arsenal of guns, the arrangement would work out just fine.

More than a week passed before the bonding company that had sprung Kiki found out that he was now a fugitive. Free at Last didn't get a call from the U.S. Marshals Service, or from any government agency, for that matter. Instead, one of its employees happened to be watching the local news. (Had the employee been reading the newspaper instead, Free at Last would still be in the dark; the story of Kiki's flight didn't even make the paper.) The newscaster was saying that the mayor of Atlanta's son-in-law had skipped bond on major drug trafficking charges and was on the lam. That meant the bonding company, because it hadn't secured any real collateral on the bond, such as Kai and Kiki's home, stood a good chance of losing $300,000—should Kiki remain a fugitive.

Back when the bond was posted, Kai Franklin Graham entered a contract with Free at Last stating she'd pay the full $300,000 in the event that her husband was to flee. But wrenching that kind of money from someone was sure to initiate a lengthy—and costly—legal battle. And despite the fact that Kai had provided the bonding company with a financial statement outlining her ability to repay the bond in the event of a situation like this, that didn't mean she actually had the money. In fact, her father's airport concessions business, where she'd been employed for ten years, had tanked. She didn't even have a job.

Free at Last didn't want to count on Kai to come up with the money she owed. Nor did the company want to leave the task of finding Kiki up to law enforcement alone. So Free at Last's owners decided to take matters into their own hands. They hired an Atlanta bounty hunter, Jean Gai, to track down any possible leads that could result in the apprehension and arrest of Tremayne "Kiki" Graham.

Kiki was willing to turn his back on many things: his trial on federal cocaine charges, his home and his business, his third-of-a-million-dollar bond, and his reputation as a repentant former drug dealer who feared for his life. But there were other things Kiki couldn't give up. He refused to abandon his young son, born four years earlier of a previous relationship. And he could not cut all ties to his wife.

Whether or not Kiki maintained contact with Kai would be a subject of dispute. Scott would later claim that Kiki and Kai spoke regularly on a prepaid cell that was dubbed "the Kai phone"—an allegation Kai vigorously denied. Scott said he spent enough time with Kiki over at the Oso Avenue stash house to conclude that Kiki had certain obligations to his wife that he intended to uphold, including helping her pay the five-thousand-dollar monthly mortgage on their home. According to Scott, Kiki figured out a way to funnel the cash to Kai, after which she would have to be careful how she handled it; the wife of a federal fugitive couldn't just deposit tens of thousands of dollars, origin undocumented, into her bank account—not without attracting attention.

Scott also claimed that Kiki needed to send money to Kai for the two Porsche SUVs that were in her name, the ones that Kiki had given to Terry Flenory as a return on his 404 Motorsports investment. It wouldn't be wise to default on those loans. That could put Terry at risk, and Kiki had enough trouble as it was.

According to Scott, Terry might even have spoken with J-Rock about the murders of Misty and Hack. The way Scott described it—a version of events allegedly relayed to him by Kiki, who Scott claimed had witnessed the meeting—J-Rock stopped by the White House some time after the killings. During the visit, J-Rock allegedly boasted to Terry that there was nothing to worry about with Hack anymore. J-Rock told Terry that he "had took care of it," Scott claimed.

Now that Kiki was out in California, with debts mounting back home, he needed to rake in some cash. The obvious way to accomplish that was to do what he'd always done best. Unfortunately, Ernest Watkins, who was integral to Kiki's UPS scheme, had called it quits. Ernest was beginning to think that Kiki was the only one who was ever going to get rich off that plan. It just wasn't worth it to him anymore. (Ernest's complaint was nearly identical to Kiki's grievance, a few months earlier, that J-Rock was seeing the windfall of everyone else's hard work.)

Kiki and Scott's fallback plan was to transport the drugs out East, and the drug proceeds back West, using private jets. For that, Scott and Kiki needed Mookie, who'd already proved himself highly capable of the task. And Mookie was more than game. In fact, he needed Kiki as much as Kiki needed him.

A few days after Kiki cut his ankle bracelet and fled, Mookie suffered a falling out with J-Rock. It started when Mookie helped arrange a deal by which J-Rock gave one of Mookie's acquaintances thirty thousand dollars for a couple of cars. But the cars never materialized, and J-Rock held Mookie responsible. Mookie got the feeling that J-Rock wanted the guy killed and that Mookie should be the one to off him. Mookie wasn't interested in that, though. He knew that killing the guy would come back to him one way or another. So he kept avoiding the situation until, finally, J-Rock told Mookie that he'd waited too long. Mookie was forced out of J-Rock's crew—and he now owed J-Rock the thirty grand.

Kiki witnessed J-Rock's excommunication of Mookie. And since Mookie already had been running drug money for Kiki on the sly, they figured they might as well make it official. Mookie would work for Kiki, and Kiki would pay him well enough that he'd eventually be able to pay J-Rock back.

Over the next several months, Mookie flew on private jets back and forth from L.A. to Atlanta no less than half a dozen times. He ran multiple kilos of cocaine on the outgoing flight, and tens of thousands of dollars on the return. But that wasn't all. Mookie also would drive some of the drugs up to Greenville from Atlanta and collect payment for them. And while he was in Atlanta, Mookie would deliver some of the cocaine proceeds to Kiki's wife.

During his first trip after Kiki became a fugitive, Mookie flew to Atlanta, then drove to Greenville to pick up fifty thousand dollars that was owed Kiki for a past drug deal. Mookie would later claim that he counted the cash, divided it in half, and dropped off twenty-five thousand dollars for Kai. According to Mookie, Kai wasn't home at the time that he showed up. So, using the garage door code that Kiki had given him, he went inside the house and left the cash on the stairs. Mookie then taped the other twenty-five thousand dollars to his leg, wrapped an Ace bandage around it, and flew back to California on a commercial jet.

The second time Mookie allegedly delivered cash to Kai, Kiki had him give it to her directly, Mookie would later claim. He would describe how he flew to Atlanta, checked into a hotel, and packed a bag with twenty thousand dollars in neatly bundled bills. Kiki then called him and said Kai was on her way to the hotel. Mookie, still on the phone with Kiki, walked down to the lobby and stepped out onto the hotel's circular driveway. Mookie would allege that Kai promptly pulled up in her Lincoln Navigator. He claimed that he dropped the money-stuffed bag onto the passenger seat of Kai's car, and she drove off.

Back in L.A., Mookie and Kiki were arranging yet another drug flight when, in the course of the conversation, Kiki mentioned that he missed his little boy. He asked if, this time around, Mookie would be willing to transport the child as well. Mookie said sure.

Mookie would later claim that on that trip, after dropping off the cocaine he'd hauled from L.A. and collecting the payment, he met Kai in the parking lot of the Cheesecake Factory restaurant, where she handed over Kiki's son. Mookie took the boy with him to a private airport in Atlanta. He loaded the child and the cash onto the plane, and accompanied them to L.A. On the flight, he played a Disney DVD for the boy, to occupy him.

During the child's visit, Scott stopped by the house on Oso Avenue to see Kiki. He was concerned to find Kiki's son there. He told Kiki that he needed to "tighten up."

"You can't let the authorities track you through your son," Scott warned him.

But Kiki was careful. When it came time for the boy to return home, he allegedly had Mookie escort the child again. This time, however, Mookie and the little boy weren't in the presence of any drug money. In fact, they took a commercial flight, occupying two first-class seats on the red-eye. Mookie even flew under an alias, Gary Rich. After landing in Atlanta, Mookie would later claim, he and the boy took a car service directly to Kai's house, where he handed the child over to her. He then got back in the car, returned to the airport, and flew straight back to L.A.

If Kiki was drawing attention to himself this way, so be it. There's no point being free if it means cutting all ties to the people you love.

And anyway, he'd gotten this far without getting caught. Who knew if he ever would?

For J-Rock, keeping up with his family was far easier. Inside First Base, the three-story house that sat atop a steep L.A. hill, J-Rock lived with his new wife, Tiffany Gloster, their newborn son, another two sons (one from each of their previous relationships), and J-Rock's niece and nephew. To help care for all the children, J-Rock employed a live-in nanny who drove them to and from school (the Communion Christian Academy of Arts & Sciences). The nanny also helped them with their homework and tutored them on the weekends.

Things were looking good for J-Rock. His family was happy. His drug business was humming. Even his record label, Bogard Music, was making strides. Bogard recently had signed a manufacturing and distribution deal with WEA Urban, a subsidiary of Warner Music Group. That meant J-Rock's artists, Oowee chief among them, would be better equipped to sell their albums to a wide national audience. What's more, J-Rock—at least in connection to the fugitives Scott and Kiki—wasn't really on the feds' radar.

But DEA agents were poking around—not more than three blocks away.

Over at Terry's stash house, the one called the Jump, Terry's crew had assembled one night with a plan: celebrate the boss's thirty-fifth birthday. It was early January 2005, and Terry's entourage—which included his trusted Detroit manager, Arnold "A.R." Boyd, and his second-in-command, Eric "Slim" Bivens—was getting ready to head to a club where a big party was planned. As they were leaving, though, A.R. noticed something unusual. The home's security cameras, which were tucked away in the bushes surrounding the house, were registering a bunch of activity. It looked as if a team of law enforcement officers was scurrying about. He couldn't be sure, but there was no point in hanging around to find out. The crew booked it out of there and headed to the club.

The party was well under way when, all of a sudden, people started scattering. A.R. thought someone might have been shot. But it wasn't that. It was the feds. They swarmed the party, and they brought Terry's festivities to an abrupt end. The crew, including Terry, made it out to their cars and took off—rattled but at least not arrested.

That night, Terry's crew lay low and, for the most part, steered clear of the Jump. One of them, though, headed back to the house, just around the corner from J-Rock's, to see if it was safe. He quickly realized that the home had been raided, probably during the party. DEA agents had left the signed warrant inside, listing all the items that had been confiscated: a few drug ledgers from the exercise room, a money counter from the master bedroom and, from the bedroom's closet, a black duffel bag stuffed with roughly $600,000.

It was the ultimate fuck-you to Terry, a raid, perfectly timed, to what would have been a day of celebration. The feds didn't have enough to haul him in, not yet. But with each wiretapped call (of which Terry was still clueless), with each confiscated notebook (there had been others before these, pulled from the White House), and each haul of cash (the latest, at $600,000, wasn't exactly chump change), the case the feds were assembling grew stronger.

On January 24, 2005, one month after Kai and Kiki's third wedding anniversary, Kai Franklin Graham filed for divorce. The divorce papers stated that her husband's "whereabouts have been unknown" to her since he went on the run in November 2004 and that she "has no manner of contacting" him. The grounds for the divorce, the papers claimed, was "abandonment."

A week later, the owners of Free at Last, the bonding company, were growing frantic. If Kiki truly was that far gone, they were in trouble. In Free at Last's experience, 95 percent of clients show up at court as expected. The remaining 5 percent almost always are caught within 120 days. Kiki was pushing ninety. And at over $300,000, his bond far exceeded the norm.

The bounty hunter the company had hired, Jean Gai, had turned up a couple of leads, including information that suggested Kiki had rented a Ferrari through an accomplice. But Gai wasn't exactly close to tracking down Kiki—or, for that matter, the Ferrari. Three days before a February 9, 2005, court hearing during which Free at Last stood a fair chance of being ordered to pay the $300,000 bond in full, the company offered a ten-thousand-dollar reward for information leading to Kiki's capture. (Earlier that week, incidentally, an anonymous donor offered the same reward for information leading to a conviction in the murders of Misty and Hack.) Free at Last also began to publicly pressure the mayor to take action. The company wanted her to hold her daughter accountable for the debt. "She's the matriarch of the family," Jennifer Greene, the company's co-owner, told the *AJC*. "I would want [the mayor] to be a mother and encourage her daughter to do what's right."

After the February 9 hearing, Free at Last's situation was looking even more grim. The company was ordered to pay the court fifty thousand dollars by the end of the month and thirty thousand per month every month thereafter until Graham was captured—or the $300,000 was paid in full. The company, however, still had a binding contract by which they might recover that money from Kai. And Free at Last had every intention of wresting the money from her.

Yet that would prove even more difficult than previously imagined. A week after Free at Last made its first fifty-thousand-dollar payment, Kai filed for bankruptcy, citing the looming burden of having to pay for the bond her husband skipped out on, as well as the expense of the two Porsches that were in her name. In court papers, she admitted that she'd been a "straw purchaser" for the Porsches. She stated that she signed the paperwork on the vehicles to help her husband, and that she neither saw the pair of $100,000 cars nor had any idea where they might be.

The bankruptcy filing also described how Kai's "estranged husband" took all the couple's portable assets with him, including most of Kai's diamond jewelry. "His whereabouts," the filing said, "are still unknown." The suggestion was that Kai was destitute.

As for Kai's belongings, she claimed to have $250 on hand, $200 in checking, $1,000 in savings, $1,000 worth of clothes, and $10,000 in jewelry. She stated that she was subsisting on a $2,000 monthly handout from her parents—an amount that wouldn't even cover half her mortgage.

Now, Free at Last faced more pressure than ever to capture Kiki. If Kai's bankruptcy was approved, and if Kiki wasn't caught, the small family-run company would have a hard time recovering from the $300,000 hit.

The day after Kai initiated bankruptcy proceedings, Free at Last took what it believed was the next logical step—and perhaps its last gasp. Jean Gai was a fine investigator, but considering what was at stake, Free at Last needed to up the ante. The company hired Rolando Betancourt, who was considered one of the best bounty hunters in the country. His fee was forty-five thousand dollars, plus expenses. And Free at Last was willing to make that investment.

As soon as Free at Last handed over the Kiki file to Rolando, on March 8, 2005, he went to work. The most promising lead was the 2004 Ferrari Spider that Kiki supposedly was driving. Chase Manhattan was the lien holder on the vehicle, which had been leased in California. The last payment had been made on January 25, 2005.

Rolando's first stop was Kiki's last known address—the East Cobb home that he had shared with Kai. At the very least, Rolando wanted to check out the vehicles that were coming and going. But all he saw was Kai's Lincoln Navigator. Rolando talked to the neighbors. No one had seen anything like a Ferrari.

Three days later, Rolando got a call from Free at Last's attorney.

She told him that the Ferrari was registered to an address in Sylmar, California. Running a check on the address, Rolando found that the income levels in the neighborhood weren't exactly consistent with $150,000 Italian sports cars.

Rolando's next stop was Greenville, South Carolina. He met with deputy U.S. marshal John Bridge, who gave him a full briefing of the government's attempts to track down both Kiki and Scott King. John Bridge's investigation thus far had revealed that Kiki and Scott might be in Las Vegas or L.A. Both men had traveled there frequently in the past, booking trips through an agency called Outbound Travel, out of San Leandro, California. He also mentioned that Scott and Kiki had ties to several NBA players and were acquainted with Charles Barkley and Michael Jordan, the latter of whom already had been interviewed by the U.S. Marshals Service.

During a second meeting with John Bridge, Rolando was told that the phone number listed in connection to the Ferrari, like Outbound Travel, also had a San Leandro address. The number no longer was in service, but that didn't matter. Rolando had heard enough to convince him that a trip to California was in order. He boarded a flight to L.A. the following morning.

Once he landed, Rolando immediately headed to the address listed on the Ferrari's registration, a down-and-out apartment complex in the thick of the San Fernando Valley. The property manager said the woman who lived in the apartment drove a Ford pickup, not a Ferrari. He also told Rolando that her rent was subsidized, meaning she had to provide him with bank statements. And it just so happened that the apartment manager recalled some strange activity on one of those statements, from back in November 2004. During that month— and mere days after Kiki went on the run—the woman's bank statement included several airline tickets, a bunch of prepaid cell phones, and the deposit of a six-thousand-dollar check.

Later that day, Rolando watched as the woman and a young child walked out of her apartment and took off in the Ford truck. Rolando tried to keep up with her, but lost the tail somewhere in Pacoima.

Before the day was over, Rolando stopped by a post office in the Valley where a money order had been issued back in December, to make a payment on the Ferrari. He chatted up the clerk who had issued the money order, and she said she remembered the man who purchased it. Rolando showed her a picture of Kiki. Yep, she said, that's him. Another clerk piped up that she had seen Kiki in the post office even more recently, definitely within the past month. Rolando then stopped by another post office that had issued a money order used to make a Ferrari payment. The clerk there said that both Scott and Kiki were frequent customers. She remembered them well—after all, two men standing six-foot-five and dressed to the nines are hard to forget.

Ten days passed before Rolando caught his next big break. He went back to the apartment complex in Sylmar, to try his luck again with the woman who drove the pickup. This time, she emerged from her apartment, climbed into the Ford, and took off. Rolando followed her as she wound through several side streets, toward Ventura Boulevard. He lost her in a neighborhood just south of Ventura, and then caught up with her again. Rolando glimpsed her pickup pulling out of a long winding driveway on Libbit Avenue. The driveway led to a three-story house with a three-car garage and a pool. There was a silver Infiniti SUV and a pair of black and white Land Rovers parked outside. Little did Rolando know that he had just stumbled upon J-Rock's First Base.

Two days later, Rolando went to talk to the manager of the dealership where the Ferrari had been leased. (He would have gone sooner, but the manager had been out of town.) Rolando asked who had put the money down for the Ferrari, because surely it couldn't have been the woman whose name was on the lease. The manager said no, it wasn't her. Rather, a man named Eric Rivera had written the $92,000 down payment check. Rolando passed Mookie's info on to deputy U.S. marshal John Bridge, back in Greenville.

The following day, Rolando hit up Outbound Travel. The owner, who explained that his company was the exclusive travel agency of the NBA, said he knew Scott and Kiki and had booked tickets for them in the past. But it had been a year since their last trip. He also said that he'd heard from Charles Barkley that the two men were now fugitives.

Over the next month, Rolando pursued whatever seemingly small lead had been left dangling. He subpoenaed bank records that would show who'd written the six-thousand-dollar check that the woman from the Sylmar apartment complex had deposited back in November. He learned that the woman's cell phone records showed she'd been traveling on a regular basis between California and Atlanta. He discovered that the silver Infiniti parked in the driveway of the house on Libbit Avenue house a few days back was registered to Eric "Mookie" Rivera's sister. He obtained a picture of Mookie, a mug shot from a past arrest out of Miami. Mookie's bond file listed a Beverly Hills address. Rolando checked out the address, which was a mail drop. An employee there recognized the photo of Mookie, but the P.O. box itself was registered to a woman who lived in an apartment on Riverton Avenue, in Studio City. Rolando went there, too, and talked to the apartment manager. The manager didn't recognize Mookie's photo. But Rolando, just to be safe, handed him his card and said that if Mookie happened to come by, please give him a call.

What Rolando really needed, though, was to figure out how to keep a closer watch on the Libbit Avenue house. It belonged, on paper, to a Massachusetts man who had purchased it the year before for $1.8 million. But something wasn't adding up.

Rolando called deputy marshal John Bridge on May 13, 2005, and told him that he wanted to put together a high-tech system of surveillance cameras that could keep an eye on Libbit in real time. That way, Rolando could watch the house from any location, at any hour—and from several angles simultaneously. The equipment, he said, would take three weeks to assemble. But he felt it would be worth it. Every clue was pointing toward the three men—Kiki, Scott, and Mookie—hovering around the same part of L.A. And the multimillion-dollar home on Libbit seemed to be the hub. The house also appeared to be consistent with a drug kingpin's pad. There were fancy cars out front—and not-so-fancy cars, including the Sylmar woman's pickup, were regularly stopping by. There was, on paper, an out-of-state owner, and that owner didn't live there. There also was the physical layout of the property itself. The house, like so many other drug-lord domiciles, was very, very hard to surveil.

John Bridge told Rolando he'd do whatever he could to help. Unbeknownst to him, however, the answer to the Libbit Avenue mystery was practically right in front of him. The man who actually lived in the Libbit house was, at that very moment, in Atlanta on business—and had been questioned two days before by Bridge's fellow marshals. In fact, J-Rock and some of his associates had landed themselves in a rather treacherous confrontation with both the U.S. Marshals Service and the local police.

For the past eight months, a federal manhunt had been under way for a St. Louis fugitive named Deron "Wonnie" Gatling. Wonnie (or "Magic," as he also was known) was the leader of a midsized BMF hub in Missouri, and thanks to an aggressive investigation in that city, several midlevel BMF members, Wonnie included, had been indicted in federal court back in September. (The indictment had brought much grief to Yogi, who had complained about it to Omari during one of their many wiretapped conversations.)

Finally, on May 11, 2005, U.S. marshals got a tip that Wonnie was hiding out at his girlfriend's house in a northeast Atlanta suburb called Chamblee. Shortly after 2 P.M. that afternoon, a team of marshals pulled up to the house, on Anastasia Lane, and knocked on the door. The man who answered wouldn't let the marshals inside. Instead, he said he'd speak with the homeowner, and he turned around and headed upstairs. He didn't return, despite the marshals' repeated knocking.

The team then split up. A few of them walked around back, to see what they might find. Behind the house, they peeked through a window and saw four men in the basement. The marshals called for the men to come outside. They did, and as they opened the door, a strong scent of marijuana followed them. The men then insisted to the marshals that they were the only people in the house.

At that point, the team out front decided to head inside the home. At the top of the stairs, the man who'd answered the door reappeared—and contradicted the men who'd just emerged from the basement. From the landing, he told the marshals that the homeowner (Wonnie's girlfriend) was the only other person inside. Investigators called for her, and she, too, appeared at the top of the stairway.

"There's no one else here," she claimed.

The marshals decided to check it out for themselves. As they headed up the stairs and down the hallway, they noticed a .45 lying in the master bedroom. From there, they climbed into the attic—where they noticed footprints in the insulation, and noises coming from the far corner.

Behind the wall paneling, hidden beneath a layer of insulation, the marshals found their fugitive. Wonnie was finally in custody. But the sting didn't end there. After discovering Wonnie, the marshals called DeKalb County police for backup. Several units pulled up to Anastasia Lane—and as the DeKalb officers walked around back, to meet the other team of marshals that was still gathered there, bullets starting whizzing by.

At least seven rounds were fired, from somewhere beyond the fence at the edge of the property. The bullets struck the house within feet of where the officers and the marshals were standing.

After pulling Wonnie from behind the insulation—and then

hearing the shots outside—the marshals grabbed his phone. They saw that he had dialed a number while he was hidden back there, not long before the shooting started. The marshals asked him whom he called.

"An uncle in St. Louis," Wonnie said.

"What's your uncle's name?" they asked.

He wouldn't answer.

Investigators quickly pulled Wonnie's phone records and saw that he'd dialed a local cell phone. And the phone, according to cell-tower-mapping technology, was located not in St. Louis but in a neighboring Atlanta suburb, Dunwoody. The agents were able to determine that the number Wonnie called immediately called a third number—a cell phone that, the technology revealed, had been drifting around downtown Atlanta. And as soon as that third number got the call, both phones—that one and the one Wonnie himself had called—started moving toward the house on Anastasia Lane, the cell towers giving their locations away. In fact, both cell phones were in the immediate vicinity of the house on Anastasia Lane at the exact moment when the agents were fired upon.

Not long after, both cell phones returned to the Dunwoody location. The mapping technology was able to pinpoint the exact address. It was a house on Spalding Drive. Atlanta DEA agent Jack Harvey, who had immediately joined the investigation into who might have fired on the marshals, was familiar with the house. From his extensive research of the Black Mafia Family, he knew the house was a BMF hangout.

Shortly after midnight, investigators obtained a search warrant for the house. Before charging inside, however, they set up a surveillance operation to see who might be leaving the house. Less than an hour later, a gray Chrysler 300 fell into the trap. The Chrysler was pulled over. The driver, Michael "Playboy" Harris, had been arrested four years earlier for the murder of Raul Rosales during the NBA All-Stars game in D.C. (The charges, however, were later dropped.) Jerry "J-Rock" Davis was in the Chrysler's passenger seat.

The investigators confiscated both men's cell phones. They wanted to compare their numbers to the two numbers believed to be involved in the attack that afternoon. It turned out that the number Wonnie had called while hiding behind the insulation was J-Rock's.

J-Rock told the investigators that he and Playboy were temporarily staying at the Dunwoody house. He also admitted that he received Wonnie's distress call earlier that day. But he denied making any other call to assist his friend. After that, he shut his mouth.

Once it became clear that they'd be coaxing no additional info from J-Rock or Playboy, investigators cuffed both men. By then, they had moved forward with the search warrant.

The investigators forced their way through the front door of the house on Spalding Drive, only to find that there was no one inside. It seemed, however, that the occupants had just recently left, and that they left in a hurry. There were six cars in the driveway, an impossibly strong scent of weed in the living area, and guns and cash lying all over the place. One of those guns, ballistics tests would later prove, was the one used to fire on the marshals. And in one of the bedrooms, investigators found the cell phone that J-Rock had called after Wonnie called him, presumably to request the hit.

While the search warrant was being carried out, investigators read J-Rock his rights. But there wasn't enough to hold him for good. They detained him for a total of nine hours, after which he was not charged with any crime. The following morning, J-Rock was released.

EIGHT STAY STRAPPED

All of a sudden I feel a pop, and fall to the ground.

—HENRY "POOKIE LOC" CLARK

ig Meech was done with Atlanta. Back in October of 2005, after he'd given a fake name at a roadblock outside the strip club Pin Ups, he was warned by the local cops to stay out of DeKalb County. A month later and one county over, authorities raided the Buckhead house where they believed Meech lived, on Paran Place. Meech was in Miami by the time the search warrant was executed on Space Mountain—a search that, to him, seemed way out of line. At that point, he decided he'd had enough.

There were certain rules to the game, even on the other side of the law. And the Space Mountain raid seemed to him to be a signal that authorities in Georgia weren't playing fair. No investigator ever saw him at that house. There was nothing on paper that tied him to it. Basically, he told himself, they were just operating on the *assumption* that he lived there. Meech believed the Space Mountain search warrant was filled with such assumptions. To him, the investigator who drafted the warrant crossed the line when he quoted an article from hip-hop magazine the *Source*. In the article, Meech stated that his crew didn't rob, steal, or kill for their money. The investigator took that to be an admission of sorts. "Although Flenory denied killing people *for money*," the investigator wrote in the warrant, "he did not claim that they do not commit murder."

If they wanted him so bad, Meech wondered, why didn't they just keep him in jail after the roadblock arrest at Pin Ups? Why not save themselves the trouble of trying to shadow his every move? *Oh, yeah,* he told himself. *They don't have shit.*

In Atlanta, Meech felt he'd never be able to live down the hype. The Chaos killings had seen to that. It was as if once he stepped into the club parking lot that night in 2003, he'd crossed into an inverted reality. The deaths of Wolf and Riz followed him everywhere. He'd never be the guy he was just five minutes before. He'd been branded a murderer, and the scar was permanent. Never mind that he'd been shot that night, too—shot from behind (literally *in* the behind). Never mind that no indictment was ever filed. From that point on, everywhere he went in the city, Meech was the guy who killed Wolf, despite the fact that he swears he wasn't.

Even the billboards, which were an attempt, however indiscreet, to restore his reputation, had been misconstrued. He put them up to make a point: *I'm a businessman, with a legitimate product to promote— and I'm not going to back down.* They were intended as damage control. After all, what killer would put his face on a billboard? For that matter, what drug dealer would advertise his merchandise in such a place? BMF Entertainment was a record label, pure and simple, and that's what the billboards were trying to say.

Never mind, though. He'd say it in Miami.

Miami was a friendlier place, a place where the authorities didn't seem so interested in him, and that's where he intended to stay. He'd still have to go back and forth between the cities, for business. But for pleasure, Miami would be home. Sheltered in his South Beach mansion and encouraged by the locals to come out and party, Miami was easy. Miami was perfect weather and glitzier clubs and more beautiful women than you could stand around and count. Atlanta, on the other hand, was aggressive roadblocks and after-dark search warrants and his name in the paper for all the wrong reasons.

In Miami, Meech would deliver his message not through the use of billboards but with another documentary-style video, a follow-up to the 2004 DVD chronicling the making of Bleu DaVinci. Meech invited DVD magazine *Smack* to come down to Miami and check out BMF Entertainment in action. He hoped that what the film crew captured would resonate throughout the industry, all the way to the big-time record execs who Meech believed could validate him. Meech made the video exclusively for them, to get their attention and, ideally, some of the money they're known to invest in smaller, up-and-coming labels.

The docu-video was split into four chapters, each named for one of BMF Entertainment's top players: "Meech," "J-Bo," "Ill," and "Bleu." Miami couldn't have been a more perfect setting. The "Ill" chapter showed all four men milling around a reception in an all-white, lofty space in South Beach. Dressed identically in black cargo shirts over black tees, with black bandannas tied around their heads (with the exception of J-Bo, whose bald head gleamed unobstructed) and huge sparkling chains hanging from their necks, the four of them hobnobbed with some official-looking types. A white-haired man in a dark suit, his skin so flushed that it had assumed a hue not far from that of his ruby-red tie, appeared to be hosting the soiree. The mood in the room was celebratory, if a bit awkward. Ill, who is short, tough, and more boyish than the other BMF attendees, motioned to the corner and said in a measured and breathless voice, "That's the mayor over there." Miami Mayor Manny Diaz, dressed in jeans and a white linen shirt unbuttoned at the neck, waved in recognition.

"We appreciate Miami," Ill said, turning back to the camera. "We appreciate the hospitality. . . ."

Meech, standing just to Ill's right, smacked the gum he was chewing and grinned.

Before Ill could continue what he was saying, the guy in the suit ambled up from behind him and placed both hands on Ill's shoulders. He hovered over him for a second, then leaned in.

"Miami appreciates you," the man said, a trace of Kennedy-era Massachusetts in his ambassador's voice, though he stumbled slightly over his words. "Thirty years ago, it was rhythm and blues, soul, all of that. It was what it was." Motioning to Meech, Ill, J-Bo and Bleu, he continued, "This is what it is. The dichotomy, the community, the people, the culture, the variation—it's a big event, with this group here. Unparalleled as far as peace."

Meech turned to face the man, stretching his grin even wider until he beamed. The glee of the smile rivaled the sparkle of his trademark diamond cross. He shook the man's hand. "That's what's up," he said, a low, friendly grumble.

In the next scene, the "J-Bo" chapter, a large crew of BMF members arrived at South Beach strip club Teasers to celebrate J-Bo's birthday. By then, the crew had switched outfits. This time, the four main players, as well as their followers, wore matching white jerseys printed with BMF.

"This is one of the greatest men alive right here," Meech said to the camera, arm slung around J-Bo's shoulder as they walked inside the club. "It don't get no better than this."

"It *can't* get no better than this," J-Bo responded.

Meech had just set up a six-month deal with one of South Beach's wildest nightclubs, Crobar. BMF Entertainment would host a party there every Sunday, and depending on the size of the crowd Meech pulled in, he'd get a decent cut of the money earned at the door. Crobar boasted three VIP areas, including a three-story, glassed-in, club-within-a-club, and it could accommodate 1,600 people who often paid upward of fifty dollars each. It was legitimate money earned on street cred, and Meech was ecstatic.

On the night of J-Bo's birthday, as with most nights that BMF was out partying in South Beach, the VIP area of Teasers was BMF's exclusive stomping ground. For much of the night, Meech and J-Bo sat on the highest ledge within the all-red room, and rappers and BMF members pushed through the mass of bodies to pay their respects.

"J-Bo!" a voice called out from the crowd. It belonged to the pint-sized, tomboyish rapper Da Brat. "Happy birthday, brother!" Seeing who it was, J-Bo extended an arm to pull her up, as if reaching down from a throne.

Moments later, Meech descended from his seat alongside J-Bo to join Bleu, who was rapping in synch with one of his songs. It was playing over the club's sound system. The VIP crowd bounced and swayed to the track, a sweaty mass to which Meech had arrived fully prepared. In one hand, he gripped a bottle of Cristal, dancing gingerly enough so as not to spill the precious champagne. In the other, he clutched a bottle of water and a hand towel, rehydration tools for his intense level of partying.

In the DVD's next-to-last scene, Bleu offered the camera crew a tour of the cars parked on the grounds of the South Beach house where the crew was staying. There, in matching silver, were the Lamborghini Gallardo, Rolls-Royce Phantom, and Bentley GT coupe. Opening the door of the Phantom, Bleu spoke in mock British refinement and acted out a drug transaction during which the passenger of the Rolls seeks some high-grade marijuana.

"Do you have any Grey 'Chronic' Poupon blunts?" he giggled.

"As a matter of fact, Bleu," he said, answering his own question in the same ridiculous voice, "we have some kush."

"It'll be a pleasant day, sir."

The DVD concluded with a soliloquy from Meech. The sun was setting, and in the breezy Miami dusk Meech stood, illuminated by a dim spotlight, in the courtyard of the lemon-tinted, Spanish-tiled home. Walled in by eight-foot hedges and a stucco privacy wall, dressed in a crisp oversized white T-shirt and staring dead-on into the camera, Meech spoke with the calm authority of a seasoned prophet, his diamond cross flickering in the cool, bluish light. He spoke plainly, offering an in-depth description of his crew's rare camaraderie. Yet his intended audience wasn't immediately clear. His words didn't have the luster or substance of a business pitch. Rather, he seemed to be delivering an anti-pitch, an assertion of his independence and a testament to his prowess—not as a CEO, but as a mob boss. If Meech hoped to win over a music mogul—one who was willing to boost BMF Entertainment's legitimacy with a distribution deal establishing the company as a major-label subsidiary—the mogul would have had to be sold on Meech's street cred alone.

"You don't get nothing like this nowhere," Meech told the camera, motioning to the group of men who, one by one, whether by stepping into the frame or by the camera zooming out, begin to fill the shadows behind him. "Everybody move like brothers, and everybody is from different places: St. Louis, Detroit, Texas, Atlanta, Cali, Florida. We got people from everywhere in our mob. Everybody move as one. Everybody is prospering in some kind of way, in their own way. Every man plays his own role. And everything starts with the leader."

The men in the background nodded.

"I'm a good leader," Meech continued, his voice rising and falling in a gravelly cadence, "so I got good people that follow. It's simple. You can only be like the nigga that's running your crew. If you've got a robbin'-ass boss, then you're gonna be a robbin'-ass crew. If you got a real boss, who knows how to sacrifice and take the bad along with the good and show his crew how to be men, then that's what you get. Everybody's shinin' like new money."

As he continued to speak, his movements became more hypnotic. He stepped forward and back, forward and back, giving a gentle, steady sway to his broad shoulders. He moved in time to a deep instrumental hip-hop beat, and the motion mimicked a charmer trying to tame a snake. But considering it was a camera, not a cobra, into whose eye Meech stared, there was a hint of self-consciousness to his words, a trace of him trying to convince the outside world that the hardships that have plagued other crews won't spread to his:

> There ain't no other crew like this in the world, and there never will be another one—not black. If niggas like this are shinin' all together, doing shit every day, then they're going to fall out over some money, or somebody's going to rob, steal, or kill. I have yet to see that. All of us get along, with money. We've had money. Money ain't nothing without us being together.
>
> And we can't be stopped. I don't see nobody stopping us. I don't see no one to come after us, either. None. Nobody will ever do this again, because this many niggas and this much money can't get along and stay together. They gonna fall out over girls or something.

From there, he crossed into offensive territory, straying from the style of an old-fashioned sexist preacher into that of a stereotyped hip-hop player. "We don't fall out over no girls," Meech told the camera. "We hit 'em all. They hit my hos, I hit they hos. The ones that don't want to be shared, then that's your own personal one. Other than that, we ain't fallin' out over no hos."

In summation, Meech assigned a purpose to the partying and excess that filled the preceding thirty minutes of video. He might have stretched the numbers a tad, for effect, but the point was clear. Meech was answering a calling. He felt he had a responsibility to spend as much cash as possible, and he had to do it fast. Because you never know when someone might burst in and put an end to all that overkill.

> A lot of niggas don't like to spend their money. We love to spend money. We can't take none of this shit with us. None. Ain't no armored trucks pulling up at no funerals. So you better enjoy this

shit. Just a fool and his money won't part. When we go out at night, whatever we spend, $50,000, $100,000 in the muthafuckin' club, we can afford to do it, because we can't bring it all with us. Simple.

At about the time that the *Smack* DVD dropped, so did Jeezy's street video, "Trap or Die." It was packaged along with his album-length mixtape of the same name, which had been for sale, in various incarnations, for months. Jeezy's DVD, which eclipsed *Smack* in sales, did far more to boost his career than Meech's would. And though similar to the *Smack* video, down to a fatalistic mini-soliloquy from Jeezy toward the conclusion of his disc, *Trap or Die* felt more authentic, more like a genuine documentary compared with BMF Entertainment's stagier antics—which revolved around the label's sole artist, Bleu. By the spring of 2005, *Trap or Die* sold a reported 250,000 copies. And the buzz surrounding Jeezy was bubbling up from the streets and into the mainstream.

Daily newspapers and national magazines were building huge momentum for Jeezy's first major-label album, *Let's Get It: Thug Motivation 101*, which was scheduled for release later that year. In the months leading up to the album, *Vibe* called Jeezy "Atlanta's next big thing." He was described by the *Montgomery Advertiser* as "arguably the hottest rapper in the South right now." And the *New York Times* christened Jeezy's new DVD as "charming" and lauded his delivery of "tightly packed lyrics in an appealing rasp."

Jeezy also piggybacked off BMF's Miami blitzkrieg. He and Bleu hosted a party at club SoBe Live with then–Philadelphia 76er Allen Iverson, and he performed at several of Meech's Sunday night events at Crobar, along with the equal parts raunchy and sultry rapper Trina, known as "the Diamond Princess." Even as early as March of 2005, Jeezy was a pretty big draw. His performances were attracting crowds one-thousand-people strong, all of them willing to pay twenty dollars a pop.

Jeezy also was as skillful a self-promoter as he was a rapper. In interviews, he answered questions with the same eloquence that characterized his lyrics. And his promises, though big, were genuine.

"When my album comes out, all the dots will connect," Jeezy told *Billboard* in March 2005, four months before the album was released.

> You're going to feel sad with me, you're going to go through the struggle with me, you're going to hang out with me, you're going to hit the trap with me. You're going to see the 'hood through a young man's eyes who has really seen it, really felt it, really touched it, really tasted it.

Basically, Jeezy was guaranteeing that he was the real thing.

At the end of his *Trap or Die* DVD, he described, with similar authenticity, what life had been like for him thus far, a twenty-seven-year-old native of the streets who'd seen "fifty or sixty" friends fall to the game. "I ain't had a good night sleep in ten years, because I don't know if my motherfuckin' door's gonna fly open, you know what I'm saying? I *still* don't know. I'm just here, my nigga. At the end of the day, I just wanna be heard, dog. However it go, if it go for good or it go for bad, I was here, and I made it this far."

Soon, his words became more chilling than even he could have imagined.

A few months earlier, in the fall of 2004, Jeezy had brushed shoulders with a younger, lesser-known rapper at the downtown Atlanta shoe store Walter's. Against the backdrop of Walter's rainbow of Adidas and Nikes, Radric Davis, aka "Gucci Mane," was passing out promo CDs. He offered one to Jeezy, who was "iced out" with diamonds and buying what looked to Gucci like ten or fifteen pairs of shoes. Jeezy took the CD and complimented Gucci on his skills; he'd already heard some of the up-and-comer's tracks.

Though they came from different territories—Gucci from Atlanta's East Side and Jeezy, by way of Macon, from Boulevard's Old Fourth Ward—the two rappers claimed similar backgrounds. They both professed to have lived the ghetto life. And they both had been effective in channeling their street experiences into more professional ones.

The two rappers hit it off, and they agreed that they ought to get together in the studio. Jeezy thought a collaboration track between the two of them might work, and Gucci was game. Gucci, who had recently signed with Atlanta-based Big Cat records, was in the midst of cutting an album, and he hoped that Jeezy would contribute a few verses to one of his singles. Gucci wanted to attach some of Jeezy's star power to one song in particular, a lighthearted track (at least compared with Jeezy's fare) called "Icy," which touched on rappers' and groupies' fascination with bling.

When Gucci and Jeezy met in the studio, Gucci explained what he was going for with "Icy." But Jeezy didn't seem all that interested. That kind of stuff wasn't really his style. The concept was too sing-songy, almost cheerful held up against Jeezy's darker repertoire. Jeezy tried to steer Gucci toward other material, but Gucci kept bringing them back to "Icy." At the very least, Gucci wanted to pay the better-known rapper to lay down a couple of rhymes. It would be a coup for the more underexposed artist to have a guy like Jeezy on the track. Then they could move on to something else, something more Jeezy's speed.

Jeezy complied, rattling off his distinctive brand of poetry: "In my hood they call me Jeezy da Snowman . . . I'm iced out, plus I got snow, man."

To everyone's surprise, including Gucci's, "Icy" became an underground hit. In December 2004, it got heavy play on Atlanta's influential urban radio station, V-103. Its video later earned a regular-rotation spot on BET. And when Gucci or Jeezy—or, on occasion, the two of them together—would perform the song live, the crowd would go wild, screaming the chorus.

In the winter of 2004, Gucci and Jeezy took the stage together at Macon's career-making hip-hop club, Money's. Club owner George "G. Money" Willis, the fatherly benefactor of Macon's rap scene, remembered Jeezy from years earlier, in the late '90s. Back then, he was still Lil J and hadn't yet left Macon for Atlanta. Even so, the young man, not yet a rapper, had big aspirations. He and his close friend, Demetrius "Kinky B" Ellerbee, were pushing a mixtape label they'd launched, called Young Gunz Entertainment. Jeezy and Kinky B were so close, they considered themselves brothers. They'd met as teenagers, at a boot camp for wayward boys, and as soon as they were out, they hit the streets with a singular purpose: succeed in the hip-hop biz. The goal was a common one in Macon's down-and-out neighborhoods, but Jeezy and Kinky B's combination of street smarts and business sense was not.

G. Money had appreciated the young man's hustle. He noticed something in Jeezy, a quality that distinguished him from other young men with similar dreams. To G. Money, Jeezy was a born star. And now, with Jeezy filling his club with hundreds of adoring fans, he watched as his early premonition came true.

After Young Gunz had dissolved, Kinky B convinced Jeezy that he had the skills to be a great rapper, and Kinky B's hunch paid off in a huge way. He and Jeezy formed Corporate Thugz Entertainment to promote and package Jeezy's talent. And while the label started as an underground mixtape venture, by 2005 it had grown as much in stature as Jeezy's rap career.

Like Jeezy himself, his and Kinky B's label forged a deal with Def Jam. A seven-figure infusion of Def Jam funds would allow Corporate Thugz Entertainment (or CTE, as everyone called it) to cultivate new talent—perhaps so that Jeezy could do for another rapper what

Def Jam had done for him. CTE built a stable of artists, including the rapper Slick Pulla and the group Blood Raw, with the hope of turning them into eventual stars. Jeezy and Kinky B also were on the hunt for new talent. And in the spring of 2005, they'd set their sights on another act, a rap trio from Macon called Loccish Lifestyle.

No doubt about it, Jeezy and Kinky B had hit it big. Jeezy's stardom as a rapper was all but guaranteed. And CTE possessed both street sensibilities and major-label backing. Those two things were a sure recipe for record sales—and, some claimed, bullying rights.

In what came to be construed as a case of big label versus little one, Jeezy's camp had approached Gucci's label in the spring of 2005 with an unwelcome proposition. "Icy" had gotten so hot—*Jeezy* hot—that Def Jam wanted to acquire the track from Big Cat Records. The problem was, neither Big Cat nor Gucci was interested in selling it. "Icy" was Gucci's biggest hit to date. He birthed the song. And so he and Big Cat felt it belonged on Gucci's soon-to-drop album, not Jeezy's. In fact, Gucci and Big Cat already were battling the perception that the song belonged to Jeezy. In one newspaper article about Jeezy's rise, "Icy" was described as, "His song (along with Gucci Mane)." Gucci had been reduced to a parenthetical.

And yet even after negotiations over the rights to "Icy" broke down, Gucci tried to get Jeezy to appear in the video for the track. Despite a few near-concessions, that didn't work out, either. By the time it came time to shoot the video, in April 2005, two things were indisputable. The first was that, on the set, Gucci was just as "icy" as Jeezy had been the day they met at Walter's. The young rapper was decked out in a fifty-thousand-dollar yellow-diamond-studded watch designed by New York's Jacob "the Jeweler" Arabo, and a 37-carat pendant that spelled SO ICY in forty thousand dollars' worth of diamonds. The other certainty was that by the time the cameras were rolling, the term *icy* also applied to the relationship between the once-friendly rappers. The tug-of-war over the track had gotten personal. And the personal was about to get public.

To make his feelings on the matter abundantly clear, Jeezy released a "dis" song aimed at Gucci. The practice was common in hip-hop. For reasons ranging from disrespect to attempted murder, feuding rappers would dishonor the other party in rhyme, and would record the ensuing put-down for all the world to consider. The Biggie–Tupac imbroglio in the mid-'90s was the most significant of all such battles, ending in both rappers' deaths and the loss of two of rap's most talented artists. Back then, dis songs mostly were released on traditional albums, ones that took months, at least, to drop—elongating the pace of the feud to a frustrating trickle and dampening its ferocity. By the time Jeezy and Gucci found reason to loathe each other, though, the art of dissing had grown more sophisticated. Thanks to the mixtape phenomenon, dis songs could be released to the street within the week.

As a result, neither Jeezy's verbal assault of Gucci nor Gucci's razor-tongued response was served cold. Jeezy's track took several well-aimed swipes at Gucci. And it placed a steep bounty on his forty-thousand-dollar necklace:

"[If] you just happen to snatch that muthafucka off his neck . . ."

"I'm gonna shoot you the ten-stack, man."

As if the ten-thousand-dollar bounty wasn't obvious enough, the title of the track, "Stay Strapped," doubled as a threat. If Gucci wasn't already carrying a gun, he ought to start.

Gucci was quick to fire back. And his track, "Round 1," showed he was eager to play this game. In "Round 1," Gucci insulted Jeezy's skill: "Jeezy can't make a hit with a Louisville Slugger." And, in a verse that took balls, if not a disregard for self-preservation, to record, Gucci elevated the feud to the next level: "Put a dress on, nigga, you Meech's bitch."

In May 2005, two members of the rap trio Loccish Lifestyle hopped in the car to make the hour-and-a-half drive from Macon to Atlanta.

They'd been to the city countless times before, to perform in rap tournaments and hit the clubs to catch up with friends. But this trip was different. This time, Henry "Pookie Loc" Clark III and Shannon "Luke" Lundy were hoping to meet with representatives of Corporate Thugz Entertainment—and maybe sign a record deal.

The anticipation leading up to this trip was not unlike the thrill of another visit to Atlanta five years earlier, back in Loccish Lifestyle's infancy. On that occasion, Luke, Pookie Loc, and Loccish's third member, Carlos "Low Down" Rhodes, came to town for a freestyle rap competition at hip-hop club the Atrium. The three of them didn't even have a song ready, just a beat from somewhere, an undeniable chemistry, and a name for their three-man crew.

Loccish refers to a way of life on the streets, *loc* having its origin in Crips gang lingo. (The term *loc* is used to refer to a friend, supposedly standing for "love of Crips.") In Macon, a lot of people claimed the lifestyle. But few actually lived it. For a while, Pookie, Luke, and Low Down did. They shared a callused, survival-at-all-costs mentality. And so when the three of them started writing songs together, their material blended seamlessly. In life and in art, they were part of the same song. Back in 2000, when the Macon trio drove to Atlanta to perform in the rap tournament at the Atrium, they were mostly unrehearsed and had no real repertoire from which to draw. And still, they managed to take home the prize.

Loccish Lifestyle spent the next five years putting out two albums and building their name in the street, without the assistance of a label. Without so much as a push from its three members, Loccish Lifestyle's songs reached up from the ghetto to grab airplay on the radio. The three rappers were surprised to hear their songs there. The men never really had a plan for their music. There was no trajectory that they knew to follow. There was just their reputation, followed by a succession of shows that drew a decent crowd, mostly to Macon's hip-hop ground zero, club Money's. For a long time, their attitude was to just have fun with it.

Not that their music was "fun." Over the years, Loccish Lifestyle went from glorifying ghetto life to waxing moody and introspective about it. Their delivery was stoical, and their lyrics unapologetic. Loccish Lifestyle's biggest single, "Ridin' High," described a young man trying to navigate, and rationalize, the pull of the streets: "You know I ride since I was five," followed by, "Don't blame me, nigga, blame the game."

The group had been hustling for five years when they heard that Young Jeezy, whom they remembered from his Macon days, might be considering making them an offer. Pookie and Luke were thrilled at the prospect. The two of them drove to Atlanta in May 2005 and checked into the Marriott Courtyard downtown. They were ready to sign. Low Down, however, was holding out. He wasn't exactly opposed to a deal with CTE; he just wasn't yet convinced it was the right move. All three of them were getting older, at least by street standards. They were nearing thirty. Even Pookie, the wildest of the three (he'd been arrested twenty times in less than a decade, on charges ranging from participating in gang activity to possessing a weapon), was slowing down. But Low Down was by far the most cautious. They'd been so alike at one time, but Low Down was starting to drift. He'd gone through the jungle, so to speak, hoping he might make it out—and come to appreciate what was on the other side. His path diverged from the others. He wasn't sure they wanted the same thing anymore. And so Luke and Pookie had gone to Atlanta without him.

On a dead-end Decatur street called Springside Run, five men dressed in black piled out of a van and began trudging up one of the driveways. One of them carried brass knuckles. Another had duct tape. A third had a gun. A neighbor glanced up from trimming his hedges and thought it odd, a sight so menacing in broad daylight. He watched as the door swung open and men disappeared behind it. There was no knock, nothing.

Inside the house, Gucci Mane was hanging out with a woman he'd met earlier that afternoon at Blazin' Saddles, a strip club on the southernmost stretch of Atlanta's busy Moreland Avenue—the part where the $300,000 condos and colorful boutiques fade away, replaced by trucker bars, wearied strip malls, and industrial yards. Gucci had gone to the club to shop a few songs around. He hoped the strippers would like one of his tracks enough to want to dance to it on stage, a move that would help generate some buzz. One of dancers, in fact, seemed particularly interested. She even invited Gucci and his friend back to her place, where the listening party could continue.

They weren't at her house long before company arrived.

One of the men dressed in black, the one with the brass knuckles, punched Gucci in the head. Another pistol-whipped his friend. They said something about killing him. Someone drew a gun. Gucci drew faster. "Stay strapped," he'd been warned.

He aimed and fired.

The five men piled out the front door. As they made their way to the van, one became separated from the others. He ran along Springside Run, away from the dead-end and toward the busier Columbia Drive. A middle school was up ahead. So was a cop car. He veered into the woods, stumbling, stumbling, falling.

When the neighbor heard the shot and saw the five men come rushing out of the house, he dialed 911. While driving to the scene, the responding officer saw the man running. But he proceeded to the house. There wasn't much to find there. Gucci Mane and his friend had already bolted.

Three days later, DeKalb County Police got a call. Four men had shown up at Columbia Middle School to search for something in the woods. Based on what they discovered, the school's security guard called the cops.

One of the four men was Loccish Lifestyle's Shannon "Luke" Lundy. Another was Demetrius "Kinky B" Ellerbee, co-owner, along with Young Jeezy, of Corporate Thugz Entertainment. Luke gave the police their story. He said they'd been at a video shoot across town, in Atlanta's West End, when he overheard someone talking about a shooting on Springside Run. Luke told the officer that his bandmate, who'd gone missing, happened to know a woman who lived on that street. So he and his buddies came to check out the area. What they discovered was an eerie reflection of lyrics from one of the band's tracks:

All of a sudden I feel a pop and fall to the ground . . .
Realizing that I'm shot, and real slowly I'm dying.

Luke had found Pookie Loc there in the woods. He was dressed in all black, a white Braves cap lying at his side. There was a sound coming from him—a buzzing. It was the flies. They had descended, like a funeral shroud, over his body.

A week later, Gucci Mane was in New York, promoting his album *Trap House*, which was due out in days. BET had asked him to appear on its hip-hop talk show *Rap City,* and he was on the set in New York when he heard the news. A warrant had been issued for his arrest. Gucci was wanted in the murder of Henry "Pookie Loc" Clark.

Gucci flew back to Atlanta and, in the presence of his attorney, turned himself in to authorities. On May 24, 2005, exactly two weeks after his visit to the stripper's house, he was released from jail on a $100,000 bond—the same day that *Trap House* hit the streets. Judging from the response at local record stores, his arrest was generating greater-than-expected interest in his record. His single "Icy" debuted at a solid (though not outstanding) number twenty-four on Billboard's rap-singles chart. But Gucci was not celebrating. He was on a mission to clear his name.

"As a god-fearing person, I never wanted to see anyone die,"

Gucci told hip-hop Web zine SOHH.com the day he got out of jail. "I found myself in a predicament, and even though there was an attack on my life, I truly never intended to hurt anyone. I was just trying to protect myself."

His lawyers raised the defense that the assault at the stripper's house was the culmination of a business dispute. One of Gucci's attorneys, Dennis Scheib, told the press shortly after Gucci's arrest that his client had refused to relinquish control of his music to "some people." He didn't name names.

Jeezy and his camp denied any link to the events. During an interview with AllHipHop.com, Jeezy said he'd never even been interested in the rights to "Icy." "It was our song, but it was always understood that it was for him to blow up," Jeezy told AllHipHop. "And that's how it was supposed to be, and I was cool with that."

Jeezy's attorney, Janice Singer, fired back more fiercely: "It is offensive and outrageous that Jeezy's name is being used by Gucci Mane's defense team and his CD producer as a strategy to sell CDs and defend against the charges leveled against Gucci Mane," she told the *Atlanta Journal-Constitution*.

Gucci's label, Big Cat Records, then announced that it was seeking evidence to prove that Gucci was the real victim on Springside Run. The label offered a ten-thousand-dollar reward for information leading to the arrests of the four men who accompanied Pookie Loc during the attack on Gucci.

But none of those men was arrested or identified. Neither Jeezy nor anyone else was named a suspect in the incident, even after DeKalb County authorities turned the case over to the FBI—and even after the charges against Gucci were dropped.

After conducting their own investigations, Gucci's two attorneys (he fired one to hire the other) continued to claim that a business dispute was to blame—and that, in some way, so was the Black Mafia Family. "Here's the situation," Scheib would later say. "Five guys came in. They were BMF." Gucci's other attorney, Ash Joshi, made a similar claim: "Law enforcement was always interested in BMF, throughout all this." Law enforcement officials, however, would not confirm those allegations.

Looking back at the situation more than a year later, Low Down didn't want to speculate too much. As the third member of Loccish Lifestyle, the one who decided not to go to Atlanta with Pookie and Luke, he wasn't sure what to think about what happened on Springside Run. But he wasn't angry—or even surprised—about Pookie's death. He did have his doubts about BMF's supposed involvement, though. Like anyone close to the streets, Low Down knew that in the weeks and months following the shooting, BMF was getting so hot, the crew would be easy to blame for just about anything. In the spring and summer of 2005, BMF was about to be on fire.

The soaring dining room at Justin's on Peachtree Street, hung with floor-to-ceiling ivory drapes and a massive chandelier, was set on May 22, 2005, for a birthday party. And the guest of honor was the father of the former-R&B-icon-turned-Atlanta-bad-boy, Bobby Brown. The past year had been hard on the fallen star. He'd been jailed several times, first for probation violation that stemmed from a DUI conviction, then for failure to pay child support to an ex-lover, and, finally, for accusations that he assaulted his wife of twelve years, super-diva Whitney Houston. By the time of his father's birthday party at Justin's, however, Bobby Brown was making a comeback—of sorts. It would be a uniquely American resurrection. Brown's sagas, including his tumultuous relationship with his famous wife, had been deemed surreal enough for reality TV. A month after the party, the voyeuristic cable show *Being Bobby Brown* was set to air on Bravo.

Had there been cameras capturing the festivities at Justin's that night, *Being Bobby Brown* would have been all the more disturbing. On that night, the film crew would have captured footage of a crime scene.

Sundays at Justin's drew a celebrity-heavy crowd, thanks in large part to the restaurant's owner, Sean "P. Diddy" Combs. Performers would pop in and take the stage unannounced, or just soak up the scene. Brooklyn rapper Fabolous, who had appeared in the BMF Entertainment video for Bleu DaVinci's "Still Here," showed up the night of Brown's event. So did several BMF members, who paid regular visits to the restaurant. In fact, three years earlier, Meech had hosted his own birthday celebration there.

The party was packed. And it was about to get interesting.

The Brown family sat down for dinner, after which the pop star took the stage at the far end of the dining room. A few hours after his performance, at around 1:45 A.M., Bobby Brown, his sister, his niece, and two nephews pushed through the crowd to one of the restaurant's two lounges. As the two elder Browns found a seat at the bar, the younger ones mingled, and a guy in the crowd—handsome, slim, and muscular—bumped into one of them.

"That was disrespectful," Bobby Brown's nephew, Shayne Brown, told him. "You need to say, 'Excuse me.'"

But the man didn't apologize. Instead, he and Shayne got into a shouting match, which escalated into the man pushing Shayne in the chest.

Shayne's cousin, Kelsey Brown, stepped in to try to break up the fight. But he was stopped in his tracks by a frighteningly large friend of the man who pushed Shayne. The big guy jumped over a table and struck Kelsey before he could do much to help.

The smaller of the men, the one who started the fight, told the cousins: "We kill niggas like you."

Bobby Brown's niece, who was standing in the middle of the brawl trying to pull Shayne away, started to cry. She called out for her uncle. Bobby Brown stood up on a chair at the bar. "What are you guys doing?" he yelled over the crowd. "That's my nephew!"

By the time he made it over to Shayne, Bobby Brown was too late. The men had fled. And Shayne's blood was everywhere. Kelsey was bleeding, too, though his injury wasn't so bad. He didn't realize he'd been cut until he saw his blood on his hands.

As the family screamed for an ambulance, Bobby Brown's niece ran outside, following her cousins' attackers. She watched as the two men and several others—one of whom she recognized as the rapper Fabolous—jumped into a Cadillac Escalade and made for the parking lot's exit. (Fabolous was never a suspect in the attack.) She raced over to the valet stand and asked the attendant to jot down the SUV's license plate number. The attendant got most of it, writing it down on the back of a blue valet ticket.

By the time she made it back inside, the police had arrived, and Shayne was gone. He'd been rushed to the hospital. One of the officers asked her to stay at Justin's and answer some questions, but she said she couldn't. She'd give her statement later. She handed the officer the blue ticket with the license plate number on it and told him she had to go to the hospital immediately. Shayne, she feared, was dead.

Doctors would later say that the stab wounds to Shayne's face, neck, and chest appeared to have been the work of an ice pick. Nerves, muscles, and glands had been severed. An artery had to be repaired. One of the punctures barely missed his jugular. Fortunately, he would live. But the twenty-year-old would be seriously disfigured. His injuries were so bad that he'd be incapable of normal facial expressions.

The following day, police brought a photo to Shayne's hospital room. The picture was of a man named Cleveland Hall, and it came from the department of motor vehicles. Based on the tag number provided by Brown's niece, police were able to pull the title of the Escalade that had fled the scene. It was registered to a sixty-two-year-old man who lived in a suburb just south of the city. And the man's twenty-three-year-old son, who stood six-foot-seven and weighed nearly 350 pounds, fit the description of one of the two attackers. Glancing at the photo, Shayne said the man definitely had been involved.

As for the other attacker, the one who started the fight, both Kelsey Brown and a witness who wasn't related to the family told police that he went by a nickname: Baby Bleu. The cops were aware of Baby Bleu, too. In a police report filed that morning, the incident was described as the "case involving Bobby Brown's family and members of BMF."

Less than thirty-six hours after the stabbing, police tracked down and interviewed Cleveland Hall. He told them he'd been at Justin's the night of the attack, and that he saw the fight break out between "Bobby Brown's nephew and some other individual." He said he tried to break it up—but after he saw the blood, he backed away, toward the exit. He then climbed into his Escalade, along with Fabolous, the rapper's manager, and three other men, and they bolted.

"Do you know any of the people involved in the altercation?" the investigator asked him two days after the stabbing.

"No," he answered.

"Was Fabolous or any of his companions involved in the altercation?"

"No," he said. "Nobody in my vehicle was involved."

"How do you know Fabolous?"

"I used to work in the clubs as security."

"Are you involved or affiliated with any type of gang in the city of Atlanta or elsewhere?"

"No."

The police weren't buying it. Based on the fact that Cleveland Hall drove the Escalade that was identified as the getaway vehicle— and that Shayne Brown identified him as one of his attackers—he was arrested shortly after his interview and charged with aggravated assault and party to a crime.

The following day, investigators were able to determine the real name of the second suspect. Baby Bleu was in fact Marque Dixson. They pulled his DMV photo, too, which Shayne Brown also identified. Shortly thereafter, a warrant was issued for his arrest, on charges of aggravated battery and aggravated assault.

That same day, Bobby Brown's twenty-year-old niece arrived at police headquarters to give her statement. She told the investigator how the fight started. She recounted the "We kill niggas like you" threat. And she described how she followed the two men into the parking lot and got the Escalade's tag number from the valet.

"Did the altercation start from just a push?" the investigator asked the young woman.

"Yes," she answered.

"Did you see who stabbed Shayne or Kelsey?"

"No," she said. But she knew it wasn't Fabolous.

"Are you able to identify the person that started the argument if you viewed a photo?"

"Yes."

"[Some of] the individuals that you saw get into the vehicle were the people that started the altercation with Kelsey and Shayne?"

"Yes."

In the ensuing week, as authorities hunted for Baby Bleu, local prosecutors believed they had a solid enough case against Cleveland Hall to present the evidence to the grand jury. At that point, the investigation seemed to be on solid ground. On June 3, 2005, the grand jury indicted Hall for aggravated assault in the attack on Shayne Brown.

Then, something strange happened.

Despite the fact that Cleveland Hall had been identified by the victim as one of the two attackers; despite the fact that the evidence firmly suggested he drove the getaway car; despite the fact that the investigation, at a month old, was still in its infancy; and despite the fact that a grand jury had just given the charges the green light, the case against Hall came to a screeching halt. One week after his indictment was handed up, Hall's charges were shelved at the request of the Fulton County District Attorney's Office. The government of-fered a succinct explanation of its decision to dead-docket the case. In fact, the reason for letting Hall off the hook boiled down to a single sentence: "Victims and witnesses in this case have been reluctant to come forward and cooperate with the State in its investigation, there-fore the State has insufficient evidence to proceed at this time."

At one point, Bobby Brown's family had been more than willing to assist in the investigation. Then, all of a sudden, they weren't.

NINE THE GATE

Dude is Meech.
—OMARI "O-DOG" MCCREE

The 500 block of Boulevard is one of the most incongruous blocks in Atlanta. It's not a ghetto, per se. A ghetto, by definition, is a place tucked away, pushed aside, disenfranchised, and disconnected from the rest of society. Boulevard's 500 block, on the other hand, sits in the middle of one of the most vibrant sectors of the city. Travel north or south on the thoroughfare, and you'll quickly hit upon vastly different landscapes. To the south, Boulevard is flanked on one side by historic Oakland Cemetery, the final resting place of *Gone with the Wind* author Margaret Mitchell and golf legend Bobby Jones, and on the other side by the artists' enclave Cabbagetown, named for the once-ubiquitous cabbage soup boiled by cotton mill workers who inhabited the neighborhood's shotgun shanties. (Those residents were mostly displaced after the mill was turned into high-end lofts, and the shanties became coveted real estate.) Beyond Cabbagetown to the south, million-dollar Victorians and historic Craftsman bungalows line the gentle green hills of Grant Park.

A few blocks north of Boulevard's 500 block, crossing over Ponce de Leon Avenue, the street changes not only in appearance but also in name. Several north–south thoroughfares assume new identities at Ponce de Leon, stemming from a pre-segregation attempt to distinguish the addresses of the mostly white neighborhoods on the north side of town from the mostly black ones on the south. Moreland Avenue transitions into Briarcliff Road. Courtland Street starts over as Juniper Street. And Boulevard reinvents itself as Monroe Drive, home to modern furniture stores, an art-house movie theater, and due to the proximity of Piedmont Park (Atlanta's equivalent of Central Park East), some of the highest-priced homes outside of Buckhead.

Driving from one end of Boulevard to the other, from Cabbagetown, say, to Piedmont Park, the stretch of road at the 500 block rudely interrupts the flow. On that block, even an act as mundane as parking the car is done with a flippant lawlessness. Vehicles are left in the outermost lanes of traffic, so that drivers unfamiliar with the practice must adjust at the very last second, swerving inward at the part of Boulevard where four lanes inexplicably narrow to two—a maneuver complicated by the fact that pedestrians tend to drift from the sidewalk into the street with little warning.

The common sentiment on the 500 block is that the outside world never cared about what happened there. Nobody ever succeeded in improving the schools or staving off the drug flow or fixing up the seven-hundred-plus units of subsidized housing that anchor the neighborhood. As a result, Boulevard is a world unto itself, and it flaunts its identity without a care for those who look down on it. Boulevard is brazen. In that way, Boulevard is much like one of its best-known inhabitants, who dropped off investigators' radar in late 2004 after losing ten kilos of cocaine that belonged to the Black Mafia Family. Omari "O-Dog" McCree and Boulevard were practically inseparable.

On June 8, 2005, Fulton County prosecutor Rand Csehy wasn't

looking for Omari. He'd gone down to Boulevard to give legal advice to a few Atlanta narcotics officers. The officers had noticed a car parked on Boulevard that they believed belonged to a local drug dealer, and they were hoping to secure a warrant to search it. Csehy advised them on the situation, and the warrant was obtained. With that out of the way, he was about to call it a day. It was sometime after 5 P.M., a warm and muggy Atlanta evening, and he walked the several yards back to his own car.

Boulevard is the type of place where any outsider, let alone a county prosecutor, would be on guard. And Csehy, being the vigilant type, kept tabs on his surroundings. He didn't notice anything out of the usual, though, just the older men and women lazing on the battered stoops of brick apartment buildings, and the younger ones kicking back on the littered sidewalks. Csehy started his car and pulled away.

He'd been driving for only a few minutes when he got the call. One of the officers told him he needed to turn around. Csehy had missed something. He'd walked right past it. Csehy, in fact, had walked right past *him*—the man who Csehy had worked tirelessly, for months, to build a case against, only to lose him just when the case seemed rock solid. Somehow, Csehy didn't even recognize Omari. But one of the officers did. The officer knew the players who populated the neighborhood he patrolled, and on Boulevard, Omari was a legend—a true BMF soldier, a man who had dealings with Big Meech himself, a former child of the streets who'd been memorialized by the rapper Young Jeezy. As any good cop working Boulevard would know, Omari was hot shit. And the cop told Csehy that, at that second, he had Omari in his sights.

Seven months earlier, Csehy had been faced with a choice. Omari's drug partner, Jeffery Leahr, and Jeffery's girlfriend, Courtney Williams, had been pulled over in a Porsche that had ten kilos stuffed inside a duffel bag sitting on the backseat. At the time, Csehy had plenty of evidence to take to the grand jury and indict all three. Even before that, Csehy believed he had enough to indict Omari and Jeffery. One of the men whom Jeffery and Omari supplied with dope, Decarlo Hoskins, had been caught on a wiretap setting up a sale of nine kilos to three men from out of town. The men were busted with the coke minutes later near the Georgia Dome. A month after that, Decarlo was arrested. And when faced with the prospect of investigators charging his wife, Decarlo offered up something that could save her: his suppliers. He admitted to investigators that Omari and Jeffery had fronted him the cocaine. And he was willing to testify to that in court.

But Csehy wanted to take it slow. He thought that if Omari remained free, he might lead investigators to someone higher up in BMF—perhaps even to Big Meech himself. And so instead of indicting Omari and Jeffery after Decarlo flipped on them, Csehy took another route. He helped HIDTA task force agents draft wiretap applications for Omari and Jeffery's phones, whose numbers came courtesy of their customer, Decarlo. The wiretaps, coupled with intense surveillance, culminated in the discovery of the ten kilos in the Porsche. And it brought local investigators closer than they'd ever imagine to the upper echelon of the Black Mafia Family. While listening to Omari's conversations, task force agents identified one frequent caller as a woman believed to be Meech's personal assistant, Yogi. Omari and Yogi chatted on the phone several times a day—and she was quick to describe how much access she had to Big Meech. Based on what she said, it appeared that Meech was willing to bend his own rule about talking on the phone, at least a little, in order to communicate with Yogi.

And so rather than charging Omari, Jeffery, and Courtney with the cocaine discovered in the Porsche, the investigators—advised by Csehy—held off. They focused on the bigger prize. After the raid on the Porsche, the investigators applied for a wire on two phones that belonged to Yogi. And once the investigators were up on her phones, they heard Meech's voice crackle over the wire. The snippets of conversation between him and Yogi were brief, and what he said wasn't exactly revelatory. But investigators finally had Meech's number. The next logical step was to get a wire on his phone, too.

Investigators began drafting Meech's wiretap application. It would be the zenith of months spent surveilling street-level drug dealers, tracking those smaller fish as they drifted closer to bigger catches, and filing wiretap application after wiretap application (six in all) for suppliers a step or two removed from the Black Mafia Family. All of it—the watching, the waiting, the listening—had been leading to this one thing: Meech's phone.

But the long-awaited wiretap never came to fruition. According to Csehy, the Fulton County District Attorney's Office didn't want to go after Meech. The office let the investigation into Yogi fizzle out, too. Instead, the local agency yielded to the feds, who were building their own case against Meech and the Black Mafia Family.

By June of 2005, it seemed to Csehy that all the hard work of the HIDTA task force had yielded virtually nothing. Close as they had been to Meech, he was now a distant memory. And Omari and Jeffery, who had once been such a sure thing, had turned to dust. For a while, the task force (and by extension, Csehy) had known every move Jeffery and Omari made. They knew the men's paranoia and fears, their weaknesses and inconsistencies. Now, the government knew nothing, not even where Jeffery and Omari lay their heads. For that, Csehy blamed himself. It was his decision to let Jeffery and Courtney walk on the ten kilos. He just didn't think that Omari, upon hearing about the bust, would disappear so quickly—or that the trail the investigators blazed toward Big Meech would be so coolly disregarded. Csehy was starting to think he'd made a bad call, that he'd blown the whole investigation—until Omari showed his face in the most obvious of places.

Once Csehy got the news that Omari was hanging out on Boulevard, he raced back to the 500 block. He called one of the HIDTA agents and told him to get a warrant ready. A county judge quickly signed off on the warrant, which accused Omari of trafficking the cocaine discovered on the backseat of the Porsche. By then, a small team of officers and investigators had formed on Boulevard. They surrounded their target. And they took Omari down.

Less than two hours later, Omari McCree was sitting in a HIDTA interview room with two Atlanta police investigators (who also were part of the HIDTA task force), Walter Britt and Bryant "Bubba" Burns. Britt went through the drill: "You have the right to remain silent. Anything you say can be used against you in court . . ."

When he finished, Britt asked, "Do you understand?"

"Yes," Omari answered.

"Are you willing to answer some questions?"

"Yes."

But first, Omari said, he wanted his attorney. Britt said go ahead and make the call. Omari dialed the attorney's number several times. No answer.

At that point, Britt told Omari he was being charged with trafficking cocaine, ten kilos of which had been discovered in a vehicle driven by Omari's "brother," Jeffery Leahr.

Omari piped up that Jeffery wasn't his brother. People just thought he was.

Britt asked again if Omari wished to speak with him and Burns. Omari said yes.

Britt told Omari that his willingness to cooperate would be relayed to the district attorney's office, which would look kindly upon his assistance when it came time to recommend a prison sentence. Britt then handed Omari a confidential-source agreement form. Omari signed it. And Britt launched into his questions.

"Are you familiar with BMF?"

"I learned about BMF back in 1999," Omari said. "They were not called BMF at that time."

"In 1999, whom did you know as members of BMF?"

"I knew of only Meech and Bleu DaVinci."

"When did you become a part of BMF?"

"In 2002."

"Have you ever heard of the Elevator?"

"Yes."

"Where is the Elevator located?"

"On Glenridge."

Investigators had not yet determined the exact location of the Elevator, though it was clear from the wiretaps that it was a BMF meeting place—the place where the crew gathered hours after Meech was released from jail on the Pin Ups arrest.

As for the next location Britt asked about, it, too, had been described over the wire, and investigators already knew where it was. They'd staked it out before. It had been one of Meech's distribution centers, later to be replaced by Space Mountain.

"Have you ever heard of the Gate?"

"Yes."

"Have you ever purchased or obtained drugs from the Gate?"

"Yes."

"How did you obtain the drugs?"

"I would call J-Bo, and then I would go and pick it up."

"Would anyone be there when you arrived?"

"Yes, J-Bo."

"Who is J-Bo?"

"He works for Dude."

"Who is Dude?"

"Dude is Meech."

With those three words, Omari became the first criminal suspect on record to implicate Meech as a cocaine boss.

"Who is responsible for the drugs getting to the Gate?" Britt said, hurrying to the next question.

"Dude."

"How much have you seen while at the Gate?"

"About fifty keys."

"Would you be willing to show me where the Gate is located?"

It was with that question, and not the one about Meech, that Omari began to backpedal. "Man, I ain't talking no more," he said. "These people know my family."

Omari's next words hinted at the fact that he thought he'd get off easier than he would.

"Will I walk?" he asked Britt.

"No."

Two days after Rand Csehy caught his lucky break, so did the bounty hunter Rolando Betancourt. A detective from L.A. called him with unexpected news, and Rolando liked what he heard. After he hung up, he made arrangements to return to California. It was time to resume the hunt for the fugitive Tremayne "Kiki" Graham.

Three months had gone by since Rolando was hired by the Atlanta bonding company Free at Last to track down Kiki. With each passing month that the fugitive remained on the lam, Free at Last had to pay the court thirty thousand dollars. If Kiki didn't turn up at all, the company stood to lose the entire $300,000 bond it had posted. Rolando's job was to stop that from happening. And he was racing against the clock.

Rolando had been the second bounty hunter Free at Last hired. The company chose him because he was considered one of the best in the country. But Kiki proved tricky prey. Rolando tracked him from Atlanta to L.A., where the focus of his investigation became a three-story house in the San Fernando Valley—a house that seemed to be at the epicenter of Rolando's web of clues. After exhausting every other possible lead, Rolando decided to put together a system of surveillance cameras, which would allow him watch the house in real-time from a remote location. The house sat so far back from the road that traditional surveillance—a car and binoculars—proved difficult.

Rolando decided to leave L.A. while the system was being built. But before he left, he made a few last stops. One of them was a well-tended four-story apartment building with boxy white balconies and chocolate-brown awnings. The building was the upshot of a tip that had to do with one of Kiki's suspected associates, Eric "Mookie" Rivera. Rolando didn't know much about Mookie—only that he'd written a down payment check for a Ferrari that Kiki had been driving. Still, it was a lead worth following. After a roundabout search of addresses that had been linked at one time or another to Mookie, Rolando ended up at the Studio City apartment building. Rolando hoped he'd find Mookie there. But the building manager didn't recognize a photo of Mookie, nor was his name on the apartment's lease. Rolando gave the manager his card, just in case something came up.

A month later, something did.

Rolando was in the midst of securing the high-tech snooping system when he got the call from Los Angeles. The detective on the line explained he'd gotten Rolando's name and number that very day from the manager of the Studio City apartment building. The manager told the detective that Rolando already had been by to talk to him. The bounty hunter had been looking for someone called Mookie.

The detective and his partner now knew where Mookie was. They'd just arrested him, and they were at the apartment to execute a search warrant stemming from the arrest.

The day before, on the afternoon of June 9, 2005, Mookie had shown up at Van Nuys Airport to board a private jet. He booked the seventeen-thousand-dollar flight the previous night and paid the five-thousand-dollar deposit in cash. But before he and his three pieces of luggage made it past security, he was stopped by several agents working for a local drug task force.

"Where are you going?" one of the agents asked Mookie.

"Atlanta," he answered.

"Business or pleasure?" the agent replied.

"Business," Mookie said. "I'm in the Internet raffle industry."

"Can we search your bags?"

"No," he replied. "I'm not comfortable with you searching my bags or me."

Another agent, drug dog in tow, joined the interrogation. The dog sniffed around Mookie's luggage. A moment later, it barked to the agents, signaling that there was something suspicious in all three bags.

The agents asked Mookie for his ID, and he handed over a fake driver's license with the alias Gary Rich. A moment later, they told Mookie that until they obtained a search warrant for his luggage and took a look inside, he wouldn't be allowed to board his plane.

While the task force agents waited on the warrant, Mookie's phone rang. Unbeknownst to the agents, their suspect wasn't planning on traveling alone. His associate, the federal fugitive Scott King, was supposed to meet him at the airport. Scott was calling to check in with Mookie. Out of earshot of the agents, Mookie told Scott not to come, to turn around. There was trouble at the airport.

Shortly thereafter, the search warrant was approved. The agents pulled Mookie's luggage aside and unzipped his bags. Inside, the agents found twenty tightly wrapped bundles. Each of the packages was bound in black plastic and topped with a flyer of a Hummer SUV. Peeling away the flyers and the packaging, the agents uncovered kilo after kilo of cocaine. All twenty keys had the word HUMMER pressed into the powder, branding the product to match the flyer.

Mookie was promptly arrested and fingerprinted, after which the agents learned his real name: Eric Rivera. The next day, they obtained a search warrant for the address on his fake driver's license, the apartment building in Studio City. And that's when the manager told them about the bounty hunter. One of the detectives gave Rolando a call, to let him know Mookie had been busted at Van Nuys Airport with a significant haul of cocaine.

Rolando told the detective that Mookie was a known associate of two federal fugitives, Scott King and Tremayne "Kiki" Graham. And considering the amount of coke that Scott and Kiki were known to have trafficked, the twenty kilos in Mookie's luggage was just the beginning of it. If the detectives were interested in additional drug seizures, Rolando said, just wait. The content of the suitcases would pale in comparison to what they'd find when they caught up with Kiki and Scott.

Four days later, Rolando flew to L.A. to chase down any clues Mookie might have left behind—clues that hopefully would lead to Kiki. Rolando met with the L.A. detectives, who handed over the few items found on Mookie's person: two dry-cleaning receipts and a business card from a local pool-cleaning company. Rolando perked up when he saw that both businesses were in the same part of L.A. where he'd narrowed his hunt for Kiki. He was sure that Scott and Kiki would turn up somewhere in that neighborhood—if they were still in the city, that is.

Rolando tried the dry cleaner first. It was a nondescript sort of place on bustling Ventura Boulevard, out in the western reaches of L.A.'s sprawling grasp. He showed the shop owner some photos of Mookie, Scott, and Kiki. The owner looked nervous. Glancing around, he motioned for Rolando to follow him into a side office. From the safety of the enclosed room, the shop owner told the bounty hunter that Scott had been by that very day. Scott's white Land Rover had pulled into a parking space, and the six-foot-five driver, a regular customer, climbed out. He had dry cleaning to retrieve. Had Rolando been a few hours earlier, in fact, he might have run into him. Instead, the bounty hunter received a small consolation prize. The shop owner fished Scott's dry-cleaning receipt out of the trash and handed it over.

Rolando gave the owner his card and told him to get in touch immediately if Scott or his friend Kiki (whose picture, unlike Scott's, the owner didn't recognize) showed their faces. Rolando then called deputy U.S. marshal John Bridge in Greenville, South Carolina. Bridge's office had been handling the federal investigation into the whereabouts of Scott and Kiki, both of whom had been indicted in U.S. District Court in Greenville and had been on the run since 2004. (Scott had skipped town early that year, to avoid arrest, while Kiki had cut his ankle monitor and jumped bond days before his November trial.) When Rolando was first hired onto the case, he'd met with Bridge several times to compare notes, and he'd kept the Greenville marshals' office in the loop as far as what his investigation revealed. Now, he was calling Greenville with good news. He told Bridge it might be a wise idea to get the U.S. Marshals Office in L.A. involved. Rolando felt he was just a step or two behind the two fugitives. A few more leads, perhaps, and he'd be right on top of them. For that, he'd need backup.

Later that day, Rolando followed up on the only other tip that the L.A. detectives had gathered from Mookie, the card for the pool-cleaning service. He drove out to the company and showed the man behind the counter the photos of Kiki, Mookie, and Scott. The man glanced at them and pointed at one. He said he'd cleaned that guy's pool. He was sure of it. He'd been to his house several times. It was out in Woodland Hills, on a street called Oso Avenue.

He was pointing at Kiki.

Rolando immediately drove to the address to check it out. Compared with the three-story house on Libbit Avenue, the one that seemed to be at the hub of Kiki's circle, this house was rather plain. The shoebox-shaped ranch had an attached two-car garage and was surrounded by an equally unremarkable middle-class neighborhood. Unlike the house on Libbit, it sat conspicuously close to the road. And its flat corner lot left it exposed on two sides—making it all the easier to surveil.

Rolando didn't think anyone was inside. All the shades were drawn and the driveway was empty. But Rolando did find trash on the curb, which led him to believe that someone had been there fairly recently.

He called the L.A. detective with whom he'd been in contact, and the two sat and watched the house together. At around 7:30 P.M., the garage door opened and a black Volvo pulled out. Someone had been home, after all. Rolando followed the car long enough to write down the tag number, and the detective ran a search on it. The Volvo came back as having been registered to Gary Rich—Mookie's alias. About an hour later, Rolando got a call from the U.S. Marshals Office in L.A. A supervisor said he'd have a team assembled the following morning, and they would meet him just off Oso Avenue.

The bounty hunter and detective kept an eye on the Oso house for a few more uneventful hours before calling it a night. Rolando wouldn't be gone long, though. He took a mere five-hour break before returning to the house at 7 A.M. When you're following a guy like Kiki, sleep is a luxury. To catch him, you have to work with half as much rest as he gets, and twice as much concentration as everyone around him.

In the morning, Rolando checked out the house from several vantage points, to make sure the team would have all sides covered. An hour later, he met with several U.S. marshals at a location around the corner. He briefed them on the situation and handed over photos of Kiki and Scott. Rolando and the marshals then retreated to various points around Oso Avenue. For four hours, they waited.

At 12:30 P.M., they watched as the Volvo pulled out of the garage. Rolando and a few of the marshals kept a tail on it, maintaining a safe distance while the rest of the team continued to watch the house. The Volvo meandered along several surface streets, rising up over the crests and dipping into the valleys of Woodland Hills. A few minutes later, it pulled to a stop in a parking lot. Rolando and the marshals watched as the driver of the Volvo stepped out of the car and ducked into a Subway sandwich shop. Rolando followed him inside and stood watch as the man ordered a sandwich. Rolando then gave the takedown signal to the marshals outside.

Once the man stepped back into the parking lot, he was quickly surrounded. The marshals asked for his identification. He handed over a very real-looking California driver's license. But he wasn't fooling anyone. His slender six-foot-five frame, his narrowed eyes and crooked grin, a style of dress more suggestive of a bank executive than of a cocaine kingpin—all of it was hard to deny. Rolando had his man. The search for Tremayne "Kiki" Graham was over.

As the marshals read Kiki his rights, he refused to acknowledge what he heard. He even sat mute when the authorities booking him into the county jail asked the usual questions: name, address, date of birth, social. Kiki wasn't talking, not at all.

Meanwhile, there was still work to be done on Oso Avenue. Though Rolando's job was finished, the marshals were holding out hope of finding Kiki's fellow fugitive, Scott King. Other law enforcement agencies had become interested in the house, too. If what Rolando had said was true—if Kiki and Scott had access to far more drugs than their associate, Mookie—then authorities were more than ready for an even bigger bust. The local drug task force that had arrested Mookie at the airport quickly filed for a search warrant for the Oso Avenue address, and they arrived at the house to join the marshals in their surveillance.

Two hours after the task force arrived, its agents were still waiting on the warrant when one of them noticed a silver Infiniti drive past the house several times. Finally, it pulled up to the curb a few houses down. One of the agents radioed the rest of the team and told them to keep an eye on the Infiniti. A few minutes later, the door to the house opened, and a man dressed in dark clothing walked out. He strode toward the Infiniti and was about to reach for its door when five task force agents jumped out of their cars, guns drawn. "Get on the ground!" they yelled.

The man did as he was told. He was cuffed, and the agents pulled his wallet and keys from his pocket. His Michigan driver's license identified him as Kevin Miller. The agents stuck him in a surveillance van and told him he'd have to stay there while they searched the house for a fugitive.

"Is there anybody else inside the residence?" one of task force agents asked him.

"Yes," he answered.

"How many?"

He wouldn't say.

At about that time, the surveillance team spotted another man walking away from the house in another direction, carrying a backpack. They stopped him and asked his name. "Richard Garrett," he told them, which was the truth—though he was known in BMF and Sin City Mafia circles as Baa, a former high-ranking lieutenant under the Flenory brothers who had jumped ship to become J-Rock's right-hand man. Baa told the agents he was walking to his girlfriend's place around the corner. The agents said they'd have to hold him while they searched the house he'd just left.

"Man, I didn't come from that house," Baa said. "I was just walking to my girlfriend's house."

"Which house is your girlfriend's?" one of the agents said.

"You can talk to my lawyer," he answered. "I know you guys try to get people to say things."

"If you give me the name of your girlfriend and where she lives," the agent offered, "I will contact her to verify your story."

"I know how you guys do things," Baa shot back. "I don't want you to raid her house."

He refused to say any more—except to tell the agents, who asked if he had any weapons or contraband in his backpack, "I just have some weed, man."

By then, a Los Angeles County Superior Court judge had signed off on the search warrant for the house on Oso Avenue. The agents marched the man in the van, the one with the Michigan ID, through the front door. They sat him down on the sofa and stood guard over him. One of the agents prodded the man for his real name.

"My name is Kevin Miller," the man said.

"If you're arrested, you'll be fingerprinted," the agent told him. "Your identity will be revealed."

The man looked down at his lap. "My name is Jerry Davis," he said.

As the agents combed through the house, they found that one of the bedroom doors was locked. Among the keys taken from Jerry "J-Rock" Davis's pocket, they found one that opened the door. Up to that point, the agents had come across a few things of interest strewn about the house. They'd discovered four handguns, three of which had their serial numbers scratched off, as well as a .223-caliber assault rifle. The agents also found mail addressed to Eric Rivera, which meant they had a more-than-direct link between him (and the coke they pulled off him at the airport) and the house on Oso Avenue. But the link was about to get stronger.

Inside the locked room, the agents came face-to-face with their prize: stacks and stacks and stacks of bricks—250 kilos of cocaine, to be exact, with a street value of approximately $25 million. Even at wholesale prices, a big-time distributor could expect to rake in $5 million on the haul. Also, like the coke at the airport, the bricks in the house were pressed with the word HUMMER.

It quickly became apparent to the agents that the house on Oso Avenue—better known to its inhabitants as Third Base—was a stash house. And whoever was running it had broken one of the major rules of the game. Usually, a drug trafficker keeps his product separate from his proceeds, because that makes it harder for authorities to prove he was selling the drugs. But behind the locked door, the agents found not only 250 keys, but also a large pile of money—totaling $1.8 million.

The marshals still didn't have Scott King. But thanks in large part to the bounty hunter, they had Kiki. They also seized a massive amount of cocaine, and an impressive amount of cash. And as an unexpected bonus, they had Scott and Kiki's boss, J-Rock.

Unlike the incident five weeks earlier in Atlanta—when J-Rock allegedly helped his friend Deron "Wonnie" Gatling place a hit on federal marshals who'd cornered him after he climbed into the attic of his girlfriend's house—the Sin City leader wouldn't be getting off so easy this time. Two months after his arrest in L.A., J-Rock's name was added to the indictment that had charged Scott King, Tremayne "Kiki" Graham, and the late Ulysses "Hack" Hackett with trafficking cocaine. J-Rock was facing twenty years to life. And he was no longer untouchable.

With the arrest of Kiki, Rolando was ready to head home. But there was one more favor he was willing to do. A few hours after the day-long showdown on Oso Avenue, one of the L.A. detectives called the bounty hunter. Since Rolando had been so thorough in his investigation of Kiki, the detective was wondering if he might be willing to offer any insight into their fresh catch, J-Rock. The Infiniti, for instance, the one in which J-Rock almost fled the scene. Did Rolando have any clue to whom it might belong? Obviously, considering the volume of the drugs and cash discovered in the house on Oso, the government would be interested in seizing any cars or property that could be linked to the suspected kingpin.

Rolando told the officer that he'd seen the Infiniti before. It was pulling out of the driveway of a three-story home at the other end of the Valley, in a far more posh neighborhood south of Ventura Boulevard. That house, in fact, had seemed to be a hub for Kiki and his associates. Rolando gave the detective the address of the home on Libbit Avenue.

The detective assembled a small team to scope out the house. They climbed up its long, steep driveway and peered through its glass doors. Inside, the detective saw several empty duffle bags, similar to ones that were inside the locked room on Oso. He also noticed boxes and packing materials, multiple security cameras, a monitor in the kitchen into which the cameras fed, and food left sitting out, as if the occupants had up and left in a hurry. The detective knocked on the door. No answer. He and the rest of the team dipped inside.

All over the house, the detectives found family photos of J-Rock and his children. There was a checkbook in his wife's name, and her name was on a bill from the Communion Christian Academy of Arts & Sciences, too. In the master bedroom, the detectives checked out the drawers of both nightstands. In one, there was a .40-caliber Glock, with ammo. In the other, there was a book: *The Power of a Praying Wife*.

Just like that, the detectives had found First Base, too.

Before the month of June 2005 was up, another of J-Rock's associates was picked up, this time by authorities in New Jersey. The arrest would have broad implications. Though the suspect was nabbed on a three-year-old drug-trafficking warrant, his capture was a small but reassuring step in an unrelated homicide investigation nine hundred miles away.

Back in 2002, Jamad "Soup" Ali was indicted in Florida on federal drug-trafficking charges, and he'd been a fugitive ever since. Authorities considered him dangerous. He'd been convicted of manslaughter in the early '90s and had served nearly four years in prison. And in 2001, he was connected to another violent crime. Soup was questioned in a fatal shooting that rocked the streets of D.C. the weekend of the NBA All-Star game. After the interrogation, authorities let Soup go and arrested one of his friends, Michael "Playboy" Harris. But the case remained unsolved. Playboy's murder charge was dismissed that summer for lack of evidence.

The night of the D.C. shooting, Soup, Playboy, and several of their friends had been riding around in a limo. But after someone in the limo fired at a pedestrian who'd crossed the limo's path, two of Soup's friends hopped out—just in time to avoid getting pulled over and hauled in for questioning. Scott King had abandoned the limo first, and when Kiki called him moments later, Scott advised that he do the same. Had Scott stuck around for questioning, though, authorities would've been interested to hear his side of the story. According to Scott King, it was Soup, not Playboy, who shot the man dead in the street.

In the years following the D.C. shooting, Soup had maintained a low profile. Even after the Florida indictment, he stayed off of the feds' radar. But in June of 2005, the feds had a pretty good idea of where he was. And by then, catching Soup had become more urgent.

The information the feds had pieced together on Soup led to a ritzy neighborhood in Livingston, New Jersey, called Chestnut Hill. Soup supposedly was hiding out in a big white modern house with a three-car garage and a teardrop-shaped driveway. On the evening of June 29, 2005, a team of twenty U.S. marshals, DEA agents, and local police officers set up surveillance outside the home. They watched as several cars came and went, and several men walked in and out of the house with duffle bags slung over their shoulders—a likely sign that drugs and money were changing hands inside.

At 9 P.M., the agents saw Soup pull up in a Cadillac Escalade and disappear behind the set of double doors that opened into the foyer. The agents then spread out to form a perimeter around the property. Two sides of the house were flanked by broad balconies, which could offer an easy escape route. Several agents kept an eye on them. Some of the other agents knocked on the front door to announce their presence.

Almost immediately, the sliding-glass door to one of the balconies opened, and two men started to climb over the railing. As soon as they noticed the agents, though, they scampered back inside. On the other side of the house, Soup opened an upstairs window and was about to jump when he, too, noticed the agents. He dipped back into the house. Seconds later, the lights on that side of the house switched off. Throughout the house, in fact, lights began clicking off.

The federal warrant for Soup's arrest allowed the agents to enter the house, if necessary. And at that point, the agents determined that Soup wasn't going to give up willingly. The agents stationed at the front of the home tried the front door. It was unlocked. As they stepped inside, they saw Soup and one of his associates walking out of the upstairs master bedroom. The agents told the two men to show their hands and walk down the stairs. They complied. When they reached the bottom of the steps, the agents cuffed them.

As the agents made their way from room to room, they detained another of Soup's associates in the kitchen, where a loaded handgun was sitting on the counter. A fourth man was handcuffed in the dining room, and two more in the garage (they were hiding between the cars). The last man to be found in the house was hiding out in the laundry room closet. Upstairs, the agents discovered two more guns: a .40-caliber semiautomatic in the master bedroom, and a loaded 9 mm machine gun in the bedroom's closet. Since Soup was spotted walking out of that room, authorities in New Jersey were able to press gun charges against him—possession of a firearm by a convicted felon.

The agents also found a single kilo of cocaine—and a far more impressive amount of cash. Bundles of shrink-wrapped bills were stacked throughout the house and were secreted away in hidden compartments built into two of the cars parked in the driveway. Between the cash in the house and the vehicles, the search team turned up more than $1 million.

Soup was held without bond on the New Jersey gun charges. The older drug charges in Florida—which carried a minimum sentence of ten years—were still pending. Basically, Soup wasn't going anywhere. And that gave investigators down in Georgia some much-needed time.

In Atlanta, local and federal agents were trying to piece together a murder investigation, but it was slow going. The crime seemed like a fairly professional job. No prints or fibers were left behind. A getaway car had been idling at the curb. And the assailants struck in the predawn hours, when most people, including the victims, were asleep.

Someone was still awake, though—a neighbor. He saw two men leave the scene of the crime. As they stepped away from the town house, the one where Misty Carter and Ulysses "Hack" Hackett had just been shot to death in her bed, the neighbor caught a good glimpse of the second man.

DEA agent Jack Harvey, who was leading the Atlanta investigation into the Black Mafia Family, was called in to assist the murder investigation. He sat down with the neighbor and showed him a bunch of photos. There were eight photos in the lineup. All of them were mugshots, showing the faces of similar-looking men.

When the neighbor made his choice, he didn't hesitate. He pointed straight at Jamad "Soup" Ali.

TEN THE GAME DON'T STOP

I can sleep when I die.
—YOUNG JEEZY

hen Eric "Slim" Bivens saw the flashing blue lights rushing up behind the rental car, he knew it meant trouble. The car reeked of weed. Plus there was a shitload of jewelry in the rental, which might look a little suspicious. But Slim wasn't sweating it. As far as he knew, this was a run-of-the-mill traffic stop. He didn't think for a second that the stop was anything but a minor inconvenience. His boss, Terry, who was beside him in the car, would know how to handle it.

As Terry's right-hand man, Slim traveled nearly everywhere with him. They'd met back in 2000, and in five short years, Slim had climbed the ranks from entry-level drug distributor to BMF under-boss. His position in Terry's drug organization was almost as lofty as Meech's had been before the brothers split. Slim wasn't an equal part-ner to Terry, but he was still way up there. His primary responsibili-ties were to keep track of BMF's drivers as they hauled cash and cocaine across the country, and to make sure the couriers got paid—and the distributors paid up. Most important, though, Slim could be counted on to do as Terry told him. Slim was a yes-man. And on July 11, 2005, when Slim and Terry were pulled over in the rental car, that trait came in handy.

Slim knew that most of the jewelry in the car was from Terry's personal collection, and that it had been bound for a Young Jeezy video shoot in St. Louis. Terry claimed to be tight with Sean "P. Diddy" Combs, the owner of the label that had signed Jeezy's rap collective. (Jeezy's solo deal was with another label, Def Jam.) At the very least, the kingpin was indirectly linked to the music mogul in several ways. Terry employed Diddy's cousin, Darryl "Papa" Taylor, who'd been hired under the pretense of working at 404 Motorsports, the company belonging to "Kiki" Graham in which Terry had invested a quarter of a million dollars. Rather than work for 404, though, Papa became one of Terry's drug couriers—and recently had been promoted to a major distributor. Another of Terry's cocaine associates was the man who'd introduced Papa to Terry: Diddy's chief of security, Paul Buford. Paul held the job under Diddy that once belonged to Wolf Jones, who was killed behind Club Chaos. So it was nothing out of the ordinary for one of Diddy's guys to call Terry and request a favor—and in this case, it was Paul requesting the use of his impressive array of diamond-encrusted watches and multiple-carat pendants. Paul asked Terry if he'd travel to St. Louis from L.A. and bring whatever bling he could spare. Young Jeezy needed a little more sparkle for his shoot.

In July of 2005, Terry and Slim, carrying $5 million in jewelry, boarded a private jet in L.A., where they both lived, and flew to their hometown Detroit, where they had one of their cocaine couriers pick them up in a BMF van. From there, the three of them drove nine hours to St. Louis.

Once they arrived, however, they learned the video shoot had been canceled. Hoping to prevent the trip from being a total waste,

Terry made other arrangements. He decided that he and Slim would drive to Cleveland to meet up with Corey Fuller, the former NFL defensive back. The plan was to do a little gambling. So they left the van and the courier behind and had another drug associate rent them a car in St. Louis. A third associate was enlisted to drive them to Cleveland.

They were barely out of the St. Louis suburbs, crossing through Bond County, Illinois, when the patrol car's blue lights flashed in the rearview mirror. The trooper asked about the strong smell wafting from the vehicle. Terry and Slim admitted to smoking weed in the car. He asked for their licenses, and they handed over fake IDs. He searched them and found twenty-one cell phones—and, in Terry's pocket, four thousand dollars in crisp fifty-dollar bills. Finally, the trooper discovered nearly two dozen pieces of wildly opulent jewelry. Terry needed to come up with a story about the origin of the bling, fast. He couldn't claim it as his own. How could he explain why he, with no verifiable income, possessed a fortune in diamonds?

The jewelry was confiscated, and the three occupants of the car were driven to the sheriff's office. After sitting down with the trooper, Terry agreed to give a statement. He admitted that the licenses were fakes. He said they only carried the false ID to distance themselves from his brother, Demetrius "Big Meech" Flenory, who tended to attract trouble. Terry said he didn't want anything to do with his brother, from whom he'd been estranged for more than a year. Terry also said the jewelry wasn't his. He said his friend in L.A., a successful music producer named Damon Thomas, had bought or rented all the pieces. Terry went so far as to tell the cops where Damon had gotten the jewelry: the ritzy New York boutique Jacob & Co., owned by celebrity's king of bling, Jacob Arabo. Jacob was known in hip-hop and Hollywood circles as, simply, Jacob the Jeweler. And his iconic designs—big, flashy, and colorful—were one of high society's ultimate status symbols. In fact, Terry told his interrogator, the pieces of jewelry in question were to be props in a video shoot. He said he was merely delivering them to the set on behalf of their actual owner.

After Terry's interrogation was over, he instructed Slim to repeat the story he just told, with a few extra flourishes. Terry told Slim that he needed to present himself as a music producer, a colleague of Damon Thomas's. Tell them you make beats for a living, Terry said. Tell them you earn $150,000 per year. That might help deflect attention away from Slim and Terry's true profession. Slim had no problem following his boss's orders. And he wasn't at all worried about what would happen if he lied. No way, he thought, was the government on to them. They were just going through the motions of a traffic stop.

Slim and Terry's story appeared to have convinced the cops. Once the questioning was over, the troopers acted satisfied with what they heard. They kept the jewelry, to be sure the story behind the diamonds checked out. And they let the men go.

Once they were back on the road to Cleveland, Terry called his friend Damon Thomas in L.A. He told Damon that he needed him to jump through a few hoops. Terry wanted Damon to create a fake paper trail to support the illusion that the jewelry belonged to him. That way, Terry could send Damon to Illinois to claim the bling. Terry already had laid the foundation for the ruse. Terry's assurances to the officers, coupled with Slim's story about being a music producer himself, would make the whole incident seem less suspicious.

Of course, to produce the kind of paperwork showing that Damon was the actual owner of the diamonds, Jacob the Jeweler had to be involved. That meant a trip to New York. Terry asked Damon if he could fly to the city for a meeting with Jacob the following day. The two of them would need to sit down with the jeweler and come up with a plan. Damon said he'd be there.

Slim and Terry spent the night in Cleveland. The next day, they flew by private jet to New York and booked a room at the Swissotel on Park Avenue. The meeting with Jacob would take place at the hotel, because Jacob's wife wasn't crazy about Terry showing up at

Jacob's Upper East Side jewelry store. After Damon and Jacob arrived at Terry's suite, Slim stepped out of the room to give them some privacy. Once the meeting was over, Terry filled him in on the details. He said Jacob had agreed to help him and Damon retrieve the $5 million in bling that the authorities had taken.

Jacob and Damon said they'd handle the paperwork. After the meeting, the two of them headed over to Jacob's home to figure out how they could lay claim to the twenty-two pieces of confiscated jewelry. They decided that the documentation for the majority of pieces should show that the jewelry had been purchased by Damon. A few of the other pieces would be portrayed as loaners—items that, though consigned to Damon, technically belonged to Jacob. That way, Damon could request the return of most of the jewelry, and Jacob could claim the rest.

With the details hashed out, the two men left Jacob's house and went to his Upper East Side store, where Jacob drafted a memo dated June 21, 2005—three weeks earlier. The memo stated that Jacob & Co. had lent five pieces of jewelry to Damon Thomas on that date, and that each of the pieces was valued between $95,000 and $420,000. As further "evidence" that Damon owned the jewelry, Jacob pulled copies of six checks that Damon actually *had* written him over the past year. On those occasions, as with this one, Damon had come to Terry's aid. Federal law requires that retailers file a form with the IRS any time they conduct a cash transaction over ten thousand dollars. Terry wasn't cool with the forms being in his name; he didn't want to draw the feds' attention to his spending habits. So he had given Damon the cash for a few pieces he wanted for his collection, and Damon wrote several personal checks to Jacob—checks that Jacob now would use in his effort to fool the authorities.

Several weeks after Jacob the Jeweler drafted the fake memo, he had it on hand when two DEA agents called on him at Jacob & Co. The

DEA had arranged the meeting, with Jacob's consent. They told him that authorities in Illinois had confiscated some jewelry during a traffic stop, but they didn't get into any details. So the agents were surprised when, upon arriving at the super-slick jewelry store fashioned to look like the inside of a space-age diamond mine, Damon Thomas's file was sitting on a table, waiting for them. One of the agents asked Jacob how he knew which file to pull.

Jacob—always cool, always collected—told the agent he'd received a phone call from Damon Thomas shortly after the jewelry had been seized on an Illinois highway, and that Damon was eager to get his diamonds back. So Jacob figured he'd help speed things along. Jacob pulled from Damon's file the fake memo dated June 21, 2005, and handed it to the agents.

Jacob then handed over several other documents from the file. He gave the agents invoices for nine of the twenty-two pieces of confiscated jewelry. Those invoices showed that Damon had purchased the pieces in 2004 and early 2005. Jacob also produced the six cleared checks written to him by Damon over the past year, totaling over $700,000. The checks were the clincher. They'd been written to Jacob months earlier and were drawn from Damon's account— evidence that the bank would be able to verify.

The agents asked Jacob if he'd ever sold any pieces to Terry Flenory. Jacob told them that he was in fact familiar with Mr. Flenory, a heavyset black gentleman who typically accompanied Damon when he came by the shop. But he said he'd never sold any jewelry to him. Certainly not.

The agents sat back and let Jacob try to convince them of his story. But they already knew something was up. A year earlier, in August 2004, the feds intercepted several phone calls between Terry Flenory and Damon Thomas. Over the wire, the agents heard the two men discussing a jewelry deal. Terry had asked Damon if he could write a few checks in Terry's behalf to Jacob the Jeweler. So when the DEA began investigating the jewelry that the troopers found in the rental car, they suspected Terry was trying to trick them. And now it appeared that both Jacob and Damon were in on it, too.

In addition to the intercepted phone calls, the feds had other evidence pointing to the cover-up. Federal banking records showed that in the summer 2004, two weeks before the first intercepted call, Damon Thomas deposited $215,000 cash into his checking account. Judging from what was said on the phone, the cash came from Terry. Sure enough, three days after the money was deposited, Damon wrote Jacob the Jeweler a check for the same amount: $215,000. A short time later, Damon deposited another $150,000, presumably from Terry, and wrote Jacob another check—for $150,000.

Now, Jacob was presenting those checks to the agents—trying to pass them off as something they weren't. Little did he know that, far from helping Terry, he was strengthening the federal investigation into Black Mafia Family.

On July 26, 2005, two weeks after Slim and Terry's traffic stop, Young Jeezy's major-label debut, *Let's Get It: Thug Motivation 101*, was released—and the Atlanta rapper was met with instant mainstream success. In its first week, *Let's Get It* sold 172,000 copies, earning it a number-two spot on *Billboard*'s top-selling albums chart. It eventually would go platinum. And in the eyes of music critics across the country, Jeezy was pure gold. In the months following the release, Jeezy was called "a great rapper," "your favorite rapper's favorite rapper," and "a first-rate narrator, lovable although never quite trustworthy." The praise was equally effusive for *Let's Get It*: "mesmerizing," "brilliantly simple," "endlessly entertaining."

"This is sly, insinuative music," according to a flattering review in the *New York Times*. The newspaper later christened *Let's Get It* the best album of the year.

With *Let's Get It*, Jeezy made good on his promise to acquaint the masses with the perils and poetry of street life. The album made frequent and unapologetic references to the drug game, and T-shirts emblazoned with Jeezy's mascot, a menacing snowman, were selling like crazy—thanks in part by the publicity they generated when several school districts across the country banned them for being a blatant reference to cocaine.

That summer also saw the release of BMF Entertainment's lifestyle magazine, *The Juice*, which hit the streets with far less hoopla. Though stylish, there was little substance to the publication, and virtually no advertising. The glossy, dual covers (Meech was featured on one side, Jeezy on the other) mostly served as a prop in photo shoots, promotional DVDs, and music videos, including the one for Jeezy's hit single, "Soul Survivor."

The song has a chilly, stoical quality. Over the backdrop of tinny synthesizers, Jeezy's dark and breathless rasp is offset by the more ethereal flow of guest rapper Akon, the Senegalese MC who delivers a chorus that rivals the rawest of street anthems: "Everybody know the game don't stop; tryin' to make it to the top 'fore your ass gets popped." The lyrics paint a grim and realistic picture of the drug game that Meech all but perfected. And as with virtually every other line of the track, it could just as well have been Meech speaking.

The video for the song follows a narrative in which Jeezy, earning a living at a dry-cleaning business, stumbles upon a drug deal gone bad. He snatches a backpack full of cash belonging to the gunned-down distributor. He then begins slinging full-time, only to end up the victim of a fate similar to the backpack's original owner—the difference being that Jeezy survives the attack on his life.

Toward the end of the video, the camera pans over a crowd congregating on a bleakly lit street corner. All of a sudden, the camera pauses. It fixates on a man wearing a white T-shirt and white baseball cap, a telltale diamond cross swinging from his neck. As Big Meech turns slowly to face the camera, he seems to be gazing far beyond his surroundings. His distant expression appears to be locked on what lies ahead—as if he knew, at that moment, that the spotlight would be shining on him for the last time.

Meech knew that, for years, investigators had been following him. And he always believed he was one step ahead of them. Stay off the phone. Don't get caught with a package. Surround yourself with associates who would always remain loyal. Those were his rules. But they weren't enough. By the fall of 2005, the FBI and IRS had joined the DEA in its investigation into the Black Mafia Family. And they were keeping a closer watch on Meech than ever. At that point, Meech knew he was putting on a show. He realized he was guilty of living too large. But he didn't think it mattered. He still thought he was invincible.

As 2005 wore on and Jeezy began performing at larger and larger arenas, for crowds that began to number in the thousands, he paid frequent homage to one source of his inspiration. Before launching into the first verse of "Soul Survivor," he'd press his lips to the mic and shout out a dedication to Big Meech. All the while, the song climbed higher and higher in the charts, debuting at a modest eighty-four before rising all the way to the top 10—including a number-one spot on *Billboard*'s Radio Monitor. And as Jeezy's career began to soar, Meech's started to implode.

The investigation into the Black Mafia Family didn't hinge on a certain pivotal event. It wasn't precipitated by one dramatic bust, or a single miscalculated move, or a particular lapse in judgment. Rather, it was brought on by years of painstaking surveillance, fastidious police work, and incremental victories. As the alphabet boys' investigation neared its conclusion, the hunt was drawing to a close. But the game was far from over. Meech and Terry's influence remained strong. And BMF's myth was only just beginning.

In October 2005, a team of federal agents that included members of the DEA; the Bureau of Alcohol, Tobacco and Firearms; and the U.S.

Marshals Service traveled from Atlanta to Texas on the trail of a wanted man. The agents had received a tip that their suspect was living in a $1.7 million home in a wealthy Dallas suburb. The 6,500-square-foot modernist mansion was a big blockish expanse of asymmetrical windows and angular rooflines—a home as ostentatious as its suspected occupant. Upon their arrival at the house, the agents set up surveillance outside. They didn't have to wait long to see if their tip checked out. They watched as the man they were hunting arrived at the house and disappeared inside.

The team kept an eye on the house late into the night and early the next morning, staking it out from several angles. Sometime before 10 A.M., they noticed the suspect emerge from the back door and step into the yard. Standing next to the shimmering pool, he lit up a blunt and took a few deep, morning drags.

Minutes later, the team made its move.

Agents burst through the front door of the house and announced their presence in a rapid-fire series of exclamations. "Police!" "Don't move!" "Search warrant!" "You're under arrest!" They swept through the home, footsteps pounding from room to room. There wasn't much chance for the three occupants to run. Two of them didn't need to. The agents were interested in only one person inside the house: Demetrius "Big Meech" Flenory.

Meech had been arrested several times before, and for the most part, he didn't give up easily. When police went looking for him after the Chaos killings, they caught up with him only because he was stuck at the hospital, being treated for a bullet wound to the buttock. When he'd been snared in a roadblock outside the strip club Pin Ups, he gave a fake name to throw the police off his trail—and, after he was detained, took a piss on the interrogation room's wall. Another time, when he and J-Bo were pulled over in his Bentley in the parking lot of his club, Babylon, J-Bo was asked to step out of the vehicle, and Meech jumped into the driver's seat and hit the gas.

But this arrest was different. This time, Meech submitted quietly, and he let the tide take him. As a team of agents swarmed the house—a sure sign that the feds meant business—Meech kept his composure intact and his mouth shut. He would soon have other battles to fight.

After Meech was cuffed, more investigators were called to the house to help conduct a search. The mansion had been equipped for a battle that never happened. Guns were strategically placed in several locations: a loaded .40-caliber in the kitchen cabinet next to the stove, tucked alongside a stack of business cards with Meech's name; a semiautomatic with bullets that could breach a Kevlar vest, secured in a safe in the master bedroom closet; two more pistols stashed in the attic, which would have been a decent hiding place had Meech decided to secret himself away.

The two dozen law enforcement agents also uncovered bags of weed in the upstairs closet and in the kitchen, a heap of diamond jewelry on the kitchen counter (four necklaces, two watches, two pairs of diamond earrings, and a bracelet), ten thousand dollars in cash and a handful of ecstasy pills in the nightstand drawer of the master bedroom, and Meech's silver Bentley in the garage.

Meech ostensibly was arrested on a warrant filed a week earlier in Atlanta. The warrant charged him with possession of a firearm and possession of marijuana—offenses stemming from the year-old search of Space Mountain. It seemed doubtful, however, that a team of federal agents would track him to his Texas retreat on such low-key allegations—especially ones that investigators sat around and waited a year to file.

No, there definitely was something bigger at play. And Meech would have to sit in a Texas county jail for eight days before he learned what was really going on.

A week after Meech's takedown, a team of DEA agents and U.S. marshals descended on a quiet middle-class suburb ten miles north of

St. Louis. They approached an unpretentious home at the end of a curving driveway on Jamestown Farm Road. The house sat in the middle of a clearing bordered by dense woods on one side and a sprawling wheat field on the other. The homeowner was Danny "Dog Man" Jones, a suspected BMF drug distributor in St. Louis.

Even from outside the house, the federal agents could smell the weed. They knocked on the front door—and heard what sounded like a crowd of people scurrying from room to room, yelling that the police were outside. The agents didn't wait for an answer. They busted through the door, interrupting what appeared to be a party. A table to the right of the door was strewn with playing cards and cash, evidence of a gambling game rudely interrupted. In the bedroom, the agents found even more money: $600,000 stacked in neat piles.

In addition to Dog Man, who was hosting the gathering, the agents caught up with fifteen other BMF members: Terry's childhood friend and trusted Detroit manager, Benjamin "Blank" Johnson; another of Terry's top managers, Derrick "Chipped Tooth" Pegeuse; his girlfriend's grown son, Marlon "Lil Dog" Welch, whom Terry treated as one of his own; three of the organization's drivers and drug couriers; and nine other associates.

The agents also came face-to-face with Terry "Southwest T" Flenory.

The day after Terry's arrest, on October 28, 2005, a twenty-eight-page, eleven-count indictment was unsealed in federal court in Detroit. The case had been filed in Detroit partly for symbolic reasons. Though Meech and Terry had moved the heart of their operation to L.A. and Atlanta, Detroit was the birthplace of their Black Mafia Family. It was the brothers' childhood home.

Meech was charged with seven counts and Terry with nine. The most serious of them was the allegation that the Flenory brothers ran a continuing criminal enterprise. Like the more commonly used

RICO statute (Racketeer Influenced and Corrupt Organizations), the CCE law was created to tackle organized crime. Both RICO and CCE charges are used to target long-term, elaborate criminal enterprises that operate like businesses. The difference is that a RICO case is brought against leaders of organizations who oversee a number of activities, including gambling, prostitution, bribery, and counterfeiting. A CCE case, on the other hand, can be brought only against drug traffickers. And the charge is reserved for the most serious of them. Of all the drug cases the feds investigate, only 1 percent ends up being a CCE prosecution. To get a CCE conviction, prosecutors must prove that the defendant was the boss of at least five subordinates, that he oversaw at least three related drug offenses, and that he earned a "substantial" amount of money from the organization.

The other major difference between a RICO and CCE charge is that while a RICO conviction is typically punishable by a maximum twenty-year sentence, a CCE conviction guarantees twenty years to life.

In addition to the Flenory brothers, twenty-three of their associates were indicted on lesser chargers—most of them on Terry's side. Eleven distributors and ten drivers were charged with conspiracy to distribute cocaine, as was Terry's longtime girlfriend, Tonesa Welch. Many of the defendants also were charged with money-laundering. Among the indicted were Chipped Tooth Peguese and Blank Johnson; Blank's brother, Arnold "A.R." Boyd, who had replaced Blank as Terry's Detroit manager; Calvin "Playboy" Sparks, who'd been caught on a wiretap in early 2004 talking with Terry about his recent roadside arrest on nine kilos of cocaine; Christopher "Pig" Triplett, who'd been arrested along with Playboy, and whom Playboy had complained about during the wiretapped call; and Jabari Hayes, who'd been pulled over days after Pig and Playboy in an RV loaded with more than 100 kilos of cocaine, worth an estimated $2 million wholesale and $10 million on the street.

Because investigators were able to get a wire up on several of Terry's phones, he was charged with three counts of using a cell phone in violation of the U.S. Controlled Substance Act. Meech mistakenly was charged in one of those counts, too. When Terry and Playboy had talked on the phone that day in May 2004, Terry had pretended to hand the phone over to Meech. (In fact, he'd handed it to his right-hand man, Slim, who did his best Meech impersonation.) The feds, who were listening in on the call, believed that it was actually Meech on the phone. That charge was soon dropped.

Surprisingly, Slim wasn't charged in the indictment. William "Doc" Marshall, BMF's chief financial officer and one of the few employees who continued to have contact with both Meech and Terry, was mentioned only in passing. And despite their lofty positions, none of Meech's top associates were indicted, either. There was no mention in the indictment of Chad "J-Bo" Brown, Meech's second-in-command; Fleming "Ill" Daniels and Martez "Tito" Byrth, who were directly below J-Bo; or the rapper Barima "Bleu DaVinci" McKnight, one of Meech's most trusted confidants and cocaine distributors. Nor was there any indication that the feds thought Jeezy might be involved in Meech's criminal enterprise.

The evidence laid out in the indictment was enough to provide a glimpse of the organization. But it did not provide the full picture. The document describes eight cocaine busts that took place over the course of six years. A collective 500 kilos were seized. But one of those busts—the 250 kilos discovered inside the house on California's Oso Avenue, where Tremayne "Kiki" Graham had been arrested—didn't have anything to do with BMF. Though the coke likely came from the same supplier, that shipment belonged to Jerry "J-Rock" Davis's Sin City Mafia. The feds later struck that information from the indictment. That reduced the amount of cocaine mentioned in the indictment by half.

None of the drugs was seized from Meech or Terry directly. And of the $3.9 million in cash that the feds claim to have confiscated from BMF, none of that was seized from the Flenory brothers either. As with the cocaine, the amount of cash seized paled in comparison to what the feds believed the Flenorys' had pulled in. Even by conservative estimates, Meech and Terry are believed to have earned, in the course of a decade, $270 million.

As for the brothers' assets—proof that they'd seen "substantial" income from BMF—the evidence in the indictment stacked up much higher against Terry. Though both brothers had driven Bentleys, Lamborghinis, and Maybachs, the cars weren't registered in their names. But Terry did buy three cars using an alias the feds cracked: a Mercedes, a Range Rover, and a Chevy van. Terry also was linked, through his girlfriend, to three homes—the White House and two of his three California residences. According to the indictment, the homes were titled to Tonesa, and she made $840,000 in payments on the California mortgages over four years. That averages out to $17,500 per month. Though Tonesa owned her own business—a high-end car shop that the feds believed was one of Terry's fronts—she didn't make the kind of money to pay those mortgages. The feds believed she had help from Terry.

The only asset the indictment linked to Meech was the house he'd rented in South Beach. But the lease wasn't in Meech's name, making it harder to prove that he was the one paying the thirty-thousand-dollar monthly rent.

Terry had been the understated brother, the careful one, the one who admonished the other for his extravagance. But in the end, the feds' case against Terry was far stronger than the one against Meech. The feds had Terry, not Meech, on a wiretap. They'd indicted many of Terry's associates, and few of his brother's. Terry appeared to have substantial assets, while Meech had none.

All of which meant that in order to build their case against Meech, prosecutors needed witnesses willing to take the stand against him. And they were hoping Terry would be one of them.

ELEVEN **BREAKING THE CODE**

Really, in a lot of ways Mr. Flenory is his own worst enemy.

—FEDERAL MAGISTRATE JUDGE STEVEN WHALEN

A Few years before Meech and Terry were arrested, their chief financial officer, the preppy and charismatic Doc Marshall, ran into DEA agent Jack Harvey at the Atlanta airport. Doc was traveling on BMF-related business, weaving through the world's busiest terminal when the slender, soft-spoken agent approached him. Harvey had a question for the CFO—one that had been a long time coming.

Starting in the late '90s, Harvey had begun fielding rumors about Big Meech, and he'd spend the next five years shadowing various members of BMF. Through confidential sources, Harvey heard about Meech's alleged ruthlessness as a cocaine kingpin and his supposed role in the highway shooting of a federal informant. Years later, Harvey staked out the sprawling White House, watching as the iron gate at the foot of the road admitted select guests to Meech's thirty-fifth birthday party. Within a few months, Harvey found a way inside the house—as part of a law enforcement team armed with a search warrant for the weapon used in a shootout behind Club Chaos. The search didn't turn up the gun, but it did yield documents that linked the Flenory brothers to a company called XQuisite Empire and to its owner, William "Doc" Marshall.

Doc was under investigation at the time by another member of the White House search team, Atlanta Police detective Bryant "Bubba" Burns. For nearly a year, Burns had been working undercover to infiltrate a white-collar crime ring that Doc oversaw. By posing as a would-be "straw borrower," Burns determined that Doc's brokerage firm, XQuisite, was getting loans for high-end cars and homes in the names of willing participants such as himself, then passing them along to drug dealers. In the midst of the undercover sting—and two months before the White House search—Burns's investigation got an unexpected boost. Doc Marshall shot and killed a home intruder inside a posh town house. When Burns searched the house, he found a pile of documents that listed XQuisite's roster of workers and its illegal deals. Investigators also discovered a room-sized safe that held a single kilo of cocaine. Once Burns and Harvey linked the documents in Doc's town house to others discovered in the White House, the two investigators concluded that Doc was closely tied to the Flenory brothers. In fact, Burns and Harvey believed that Doc had been guarding a BMF stash house.

From that point on, Doc became a highly desirable target. Judging from the paperwork in the White House, he was integral to the Flenorys' organization. And though he hadn't been charged in the incident at the town house (the shooting of the armed intruder appeared to be self-defense), investigators could still dangle the threat of a few major felonies over his head. The kilo in the safe and the mortgage fraud ring were plenty incriminating. But investigators wanted more.

When Harvey caught up with Doc at the airport that day, he had a good idea how high his target ranked in the Black Mafia Family. Harvey also believed that the well-dressed, deep-voiced businessman might be open to negotiating. He pulled Doc aside and said he wanted to show him some pictures. He wanted to know what he might be willing to say about a few members of the Black Mafia Family. Doc's reply was succinct: "I'm not saying anything." But if he *were* to say something, Doc asked, would his cooperation prevent him from being charged with a crime?

"No," Harvey answered.

"Am I going to be arrested?"

"Yes."

"Well," Doc said, issuing a not-so-subtle challenge, "let's get it going."

In the years since the encounter in the airport, Doc became more intertwined with BMF. He also was one of the few associates who maintained close contact with both Flenory brothers after they split—a factor that would make him an invaluable witness. Though Doc had begun to align himself more tightly with Meech's crew, he continued to do the books for the two separate sides of the organization. As CFO, he kept track of all the income, debts, and expenses for both Meech's and Terry's crews. Through XQuisite, he obtained cars, homes, and jewels for the brothers. He set up a fake travel company so that he could procure airline tickets for BMF members. He even created fake W-2s for the agency's fictitious "employees" so that BMF members could show legitimate income.

Doc also began to traffic BMF's cocaine. He sometimes picked up kilo-stuffed duffel bags from Terry at the White House in Atlanta, where he witnessed the boss in the presence of a hundred bricks at a time. Though Doc couldn't say the same of Meech (Meech didn't handle his cocaine shipments personally; J-Bo did), Doc paid plenty of visits to Meech's Atlanta stash houses, too: the Gate, the Elevator, and Space Mountain. Doc also tagged along with Meech and his entourage when they descended on the city's clubs. In fact, Doc had been hanging out with the crew the night a few of its members got into a deadly fight behind the Velvet Room.

Doc hadn't been indicted along with the Flenory brothers. But he was named in a related federal indictment filed under seal the same day in Orlando. The indictment charged eight defendants with helping BMF obtain luxury cars outfitted with secret traps for hauling cash and cocaine. And it described Doc as both the leader of the car ring and BMF's chief financial officer. Eight days after the indictment was filed, on October 28, 2005, Doc was heading home to Atlanta from a meeting in Miami with Slim, Terry's right-hand man. (Terry required that Doc and Slim meet once a month in person, because the fiscal reports Doc prepared couldn't be discussed over the phone.) Before Doc made it to his house, he was surrounded by a federal task force. Agents arrested him, and the indictment against him was unsealed. The feds hinted that more charges would be coming. And they immediately began to discuss with him the benefits of cooperating with the government.

To investigators, the difficulty of any BMF probe boiled down to the crew's strict code of silence. Crew members lived by it, and they often pressed the importance of the code upon outsiders who'd witnessed their crimes. The silence was infectious. It was common for police to begin interviewing witnesses, only to find that, once the witnesses learned the identity of the suspects, they'd go south. That had been the problem in the Chaos investigation, after Sean "P. Diddy" Combs's former bodyguard, Wolf Jones, and Wolf's childhood friend, Riz Girdy, were killed. The same issue plagued the investigation of the Velvet Room incident, during which Rashannibal "Prince" Drummond was severely beaten and then shot to death. The attack at P. Diddy's Atlanta restaurant, Justin's, was no different. Two nephews of R&B superstar Bobby Brown were brutally stabbed—and Brown's family quickly clammed up.

But once a potential witness is under indictment, convincing them to talk gets easier. That's because the authorities have a powerful bargaining chip: the possibility of a shorter prison sentence. Defendants who cooperate typically get 20 percent of their sentence shaved off, sometimes more. If a defendant decides to assist the government, the information he shares often leads to more indictments and additional defendants, which means a larger pool of potential witnesses from which to draw. That was the government's strategy in its case against the Flenory brothers. And by the time the brothers were arrested, the feds had leads on several insiders who they thought could help build their case.

One potential witness on Meech's side seemed particularly promising. Three months before the Flenorys' indictment and minutes before his cocaine-trafficking trial was set to begin, Omari "O-Dog" McCree surprised a number of people—including Rand Csehy, the assistant district attorney working his case—and decided to plead guilty. For Csehy, the plea was the end of an exhausting wiretap investigation in which he and a handful of Atlanta's best law enforcement officers (including his close friend, detective Burns) had come within a breath of getting a wire up on Meech's phone. With Omari's guilty plea, that local investigation into BMF was nearing its conclusion.

The feds had taken over the broader investigation, and Csehy wasn't entirely happy about it. He felt that the Atlanta-based officers were the real heart of the BMF investigation. His disenchantment over the case led to him leaving the DA's office for private practice—but not before Omari was sentenced to fifteen years in state prison.

Following the sentencing, the feds swooped into the DA's office to pull Omari's file. Omari already had given a statement that implicated Meech. Now, the feds were hoping he'd be willing to make the same claim on the witness stand. In the statement, which Omari delivered to detective Burns and a fellow investigator, he laid out in no uncertain terms that he was part of Big Meech's cocaine ring. He said he regularly picked up kilos from Meech's right-hand man, J-Bo, at two locations: the Gate and the Elevator. But at that point in the interview, he got spooked. He refused to say anything else, and he soon would try to distance himself from what he did say. Omari didn't want to be known as a snitch. His attorney worked, unsuccessfully, to have the statement stricken from the court record. But even though the document was ruled fair game, Omari was hesitant to cooperate further. For that and other reasons, the case against Meech wasn't shaping up as well as prosecutors had hoped.

As for Terry's side of the organization, at least one high-ranking crew member quickly turned. In November 2005, Terry's trusted Detroit manager Arnold "A.R." Boyd was the first to flip. A.R. had grown up a block away from the Flenory brothers in southwest Detroit and got his start in the organization as Terry's personal driver. He later assumed the top post in Detroit after his older brother, Benjamin "Blank" Johnson (who'd been a part of the Flenorys' drug ring since it operated out of their childhood home on Edsel Street), was busted with a kilo of coke. A.R. was part of Terry's innermost circle. He'd been exposed to many of the most intimate details of Terry's side of the organization, and he was extremely familiar with his boss's manipulative managerial style. It appeared to have left A.R. somewhat bitter. He didn't need much time to decide what he should do. He made a deal with the feds a month after he, the Flenory brothers, and twenty of their associates were indicted. For his cooperation, he'd have four years shaved off his eight to twelve-year sentence.

A.R. gave the feds a rundown of how he helped Terry shuttle cash and cocaine across the country, in the secret compartments of BMF's vans and limos. He illustrated how the kilos were processed in the Detroit lab. He described how Terry circumvented the IRS to buy millions of dollars in diamonds from Jacob "the Jeweler" Arabo. He mentioned how, during a trip to Atlanta, he visited the White House—and saw Terry and his top-ranking associates Slim Bivens, Chipped Tooth Peguese, Lil Dog Welch, and Texas Cuz Short, hanging out in the basement where stacks and stacks of kilos were secreted. He described how, during another White House visit, he helped Terry load $250,000 in drug money into the vehicle of Terry's

business partner, Tremayne "Kiki" Graham. The money, A.R. said, was an investment in Kiki's high-end car dealership, 404 Motorsports.

Basically, A.R. had a lot to say about Terry. But he hardly had anything to say about Meech. Because he'd been on Terry's side of the organization, A.R.'s knowledge of Meech's business was minimal. He was familiar with the basics: that Meech ran the rap label BMF Entertainment; that he oversaw the organization's Atlanta headquarters; that J-Bo was his second-in-command; and that his close friend, the rapper Bleu DaVinci, had helped out in his cocaine ring. But A.R. didn't have any firsthand knowledge of those things. As with the majority of witnesses to come, A.R. had plenty of info to share about the quieter, more reserved Flenory brother—and hardly a thing to say about the flashier, more flamboyant one.

On January 4, 2006, DEA special agent Bob Bell stood before a federal magistrate in Detroit and laid out the government's case so far against Demetrius "Big Meech" Flenory. Prosecutors were trying to convince the judge that Meech was a flight risk and a danger to the community, and therefore should be locked up without bond. To ensure that Meech remained behind bars, they'd have to show there was a sufficient amount of evidence against him. And so the testimony of agent Bell, who worked out of the DEA Detroit office and swapped information with agent Harvey out of Atlanta, was crucial. Bell told the judge that the DEA had interviewed more than twenty-five witnesses in the multi-state investigation into the Black Mafia Family. And ten of them, he claimed, could link Big Meech to the drug trade.

Drew Findling, the Atlanta lawyer who'd represented Meech for several years (he helped Meech avoid indictment after he was charged with the Chaos double-homicide), wasn't buying it. He drilled into Bell. Findling wanted to know who these ten witnesses were, and

what they'd said. "Is there anybody you've interviewed that says they've sat down with Demetrius Flenory and discussed the sale and distribution of cocaine?" he asked.

"I don't know if they said it just like that," agent Bell replied. "But one witness comes to mind who says that he or she distributed multiple kilograms of cocaine for Demetrius Flenory. And there's another witness who says that he or she witnessed cocaine being handed back and forth between Demetrius Flenory and others." Bell didn't name those witnesses, though. When the judge asked if their identities needed to be kept secret, for safety reasons, Bell said they did.

Moving on from the subject of confidential witnesses, Bell's testimony switched gears. He was questioned about Meech's lifestyle. And on that topic, there was no shortage of detail. The DEA—both Bell in Detroit and Harvey in Atlanta—had conducted an exhaustive inventory of Meech's excess. Bell began by describing the biggest, most brazen of Meech's displays. "There are billboards up in the Atlanta, Georgia, area with Demetrius Flenory's and other folks' photos on them, advertising BMF Entertainment," he said. He then gave an account of Meech's thirty-sixth birthday bash a year earlier. An entire Atlanta mega-club was rented out, half-naked models were hired, and $100,000 in exotic animals was brought in. Then there were the videos that Meech had commissioned in an attempt to draw the attention of big-time record execs. "I'm aware of a DVD in which Demetrius Flenory says he was signing one artist and going to put large volumes of money behind him," Bell testified. "It was during the time frame when Demetrius Flenory was on house arrest in the Atlanta area for the double-homicide."

"Did Demetrius Flenory indicate that his organization, BMF Entertainment, was putting all their money behind Bleu DaVinci?" assistant U.S. Attorney Dawn Ison asked.

"Yes," Bell said.

"And did he mention a specific amount that they were putting behind this one artist?"

"He at one point mentioned five-hundred-thousand dollars. At another point, he mentioned a million dollars."

Toward the end of the three-hour bond hearing, Ison told the judge that Meech had all the markings of a big-time drug trafficker. She claimed he hadn't filed taxes in years and had no verifiable income. She cited as many as ten aliases, many of them with corresponding fake driver's licenses. She said he certainly partied like a kingpin. She pointed out that his brother, Terry, in a wiretapped phone conversation, complained that Meech's lifestyle was spiraling out of control. And though Meech hadn't been caught with cocaine in hand, Ison said that the sheer quantity of kilos the organization was believed to have trafficked should be incentive enough to deny bond. "Based on the amount of drugs involved," Ison said, "this is probably the highest-volume drug conspiracy in this district, ever."

Findling was quick to admit that his client very well might be guilty of decadence. He also pointed out that decadence is not a crime. "What strikes me not only about this indictment, Your Honor, but about the testimony today, is we essentially heard that Demetrius Flenory lives a flamboyant lifestyle," Findling said. "There is no specific reference in the testimony to Demetrius Flenory participating in a singular act of the distribution of cocaine. It's just the aura of Demetrius Flenory. It's the aura of homes. The aura of cars. The aura of money. The aura of rap."

Magistrate Judge Steven Whalen quickly hinted that he might be willing to grant Meech bond—in part because Meech's ego seemed too big for him to escape. "Really, in a lot of ways Mr. Flenory is his own worst enemy," Whalen said from the bench. "The magazine articles, the billboards, the big mouth, the lavish lifestyle. The positive side of that is he's an individual who does have a high profile, and in a perverse kind of way, that works to his benefit in terms of assuring that he's going to appear."

Whalen said Meech's ostentatious behavior, though not illegal in and of itself, was somewhat incriminating. He also said that compared with the case against his brother, who'd been denied bond at a hearing a few weeks earlier, the case against Meech seemed more weak. "There is a lot of evidence that he's sort of around this organization," the judge said. "His brother certainly is portrayed as a leader of this organization. But as far as what he actually did, that remains pretty ambiguous to me. And although there's probable cause, I don't think there's necessarily overwhelming evidence based on what I've heard today. And that's all I have to rule on, what I've heard today."

Over the outcry of the prosecutor, Judge Whalen ruled to release Meech on a $100,000 unsecured bond, meaning there'd be no asset, such as a home, offered as collateral in the event he fled. Meech would be required to wear an ankle monitor, the judge said, and to live under house arrest with his mother in Detroit. A month later, another judge ruled to allow bond for Terry—even after the court's initial determination that he was too great a flight risk. Terry was ordered to pay his $150,000 bond up front, and he was to be released to the custody of his father.

The prosecution launched a vigorous battle against the rulings to allow the Flenory brothers to walk. In Terry's case, the U.S. Attorney's Office claimed the defendant could easily skip out on his bond. He likely had cash secreted away that far exceeded the $150,000 bond. To Terry, the bond money could be viewed as the price of freedom—a ticket he could easily afford. "BMF members are known to be hiding in Mexico or have been intercepted talking about fleeing to Mexico," prosecutor Ison wrote in paperwork she filed to reverse Terry's bond. Terry Flenory, Ison claimed, "has the ability to become a real, international fugitive."

Terry's wealth was far more tangible than Meech's. Terry had been caught on a wiretap talking about his recent purchase of a $195,000 Bentley. The feds were able to prove that he lived in a $3 million house on L.A.'s Mulholland Drive. He'd been pulled over in Illinois with $5 million in jewelry. And at the house in St. Louis where he'd been arrested, agents found $600,000 cash.

Within a month, before either brother was allowed to post bond, a different judge reversed the earlier rulings. Neither Meech nor Terry would be allowed to leave jail after all. The court proceedings would progress slowly, with both brothers forced to spend years in separate county lockups. And the stakes in the case were about to get higher.

Doc Marshall knew what he'd be looking at if he were convicted: twenty years. Even if he were to plead guilty and spare the feds the trouble of a trial—an act that likely would be rewarded with the dismissal of a charge or two, and a low-end sentence on the charges that remained—he'd still be locked up for well over a decade. His situation was grim, but he did have options. He also had one of the best lawyers in Atlanta. Doc's attorney, Steve Sadow, had helped Baltimore Raven Ray Lewis beat a highly publicized murder rap stemming from a Super Bowl 2000 after-party. Years later, Sadow would be part of a legal dream team that snared a mere yearlong sentence for hip-hop superstar T.I., who faced a decade in prison on federal machine gun charges. Sadow arguably was the best defense money could buy. Yet in the end, there wasn't much the lawyer could offer Doc. The CFO already had made up his mind. He was going to cooperate. And for that, Doc didn't need a high-priced attorney. Once Sadow negotiated the plea deal, he gave Doc the only advice he'd need: Tell the truth.

Doc first met with the feds on March 7, 2006, less than two months after Meech's bond hearing. Over the course of the year, he laid out the details of his involvement with no less than seventy of BMF's major players. He also confessed to how much coke he'd moved himself. The number startled his interrogators, including agent Harvey and detective Burns. They knew Doc to be the moneyman, a numbers cruncher. But they didn't realize he was a major drug distributor, too. Not until he told them that he moved nearly two thousand kilos in three years did they come to realize how significant Doc truly was.

Doc described how in late 2003 and early 2004, he'd go to the White House once a week to grab ten kilos or more. By then, he said, Terry had wrenched control of the house from Meech. Meech had nothing to do with the mansion anymore. During most of Doc's visits, he picked up his shipment from one of Terry's top managers, Michael "Freak" Green. On other occasions, he'd get the coke from Slim, Texas Cuz, or Terry himself. Doc also met regularly with Terry, both at the White House and elsewhere, to advise him on his finances. Terry wanted to move his drug money into his girlfriend's bank accounts, since she had a company (set up for her by Terry) in her name. Doc helped Terry funnel the cash to her in such a way that avoided federal detection. He also helped Terry find legitimate investments in which he could safely sink his drug money. Any company that made a profit would suffice. At one point, Doc even laundered Terry's drug money through a daycare.

Doc conducted business separately with Meech. As with Terry, he prepared spreadsheets for Meech that itemized his spending. In any given month, there were tens of thousands of dollars in first-class airline tickets for his crew; a similar amount to cover the car notes on the Maybachs, Ferraris, Lamborghinis, and Porsches that he and his associates drove; and a seemingly exorbitant fifty thousand dollars to cover a month's rent at a Miami mansion, which actually amounted to less than putting up crew members in individual hotel rooms.

Doc also described what went on inside Meech's stash houses. At the Gate, a handsome traditional home that sat well off the road in a wooded, residential part of Buckhead, kilos of cocaine were stuffed into duffel bags and passed out in the common room, in plain view of the pool table where BMF's customers congregated. Doc said the house held two hundred or so kilos every ten days—until Meech, wary that the feds were close at hand, ordered that the operation be moved to Space Mountain.

Doc never knew Meech to set foot inside the Gate. The boss was too careful to get that close to his shipment. Yet Doc did visit with Meech at the brick town house where he lived, the Elevator. Doc had helped Meech procure the home in the name of a straw purchaser. The Elevator was considered a safe, insulated place. Meech held regular meetings there for his most trusted crew members. And Doc was in a better position than most to describe to the feds, with authority, the rank of Meech's crew—most of whom hadn't yet been charged. Doc told the feds that Chad "J-Bo" Brown was right under Meech, followed by Meech's top-level managers Fleming "Ill" Daniels and Martez "Tito" Byrth. He also said that Meech's drug associates included the rapper Bleu DaVinci. In all, Doc identified more than a dozen BMF members who hadn't yet been indicted—but soon would be. In the years to come, he'd take the stand in front of juries and grand juries in Detroit, Orlando, Nashville, and Greenville. Doc was polite and confident on the stand, and nothing he said was discredited. As a result, he was sentenced to only eight years in prison. Even after his sentencing, he continued to offer information to the government—and to find himself on the receiving end of threats including a razor blade slipped into his plate of jail food.

Doc's first testimony was in front of a federal grand jury in Detroit. Terry's high-ranking associate, A.R., testified, too. The grand jury had been called in the spring of 2006 to decide whether more charges should be filed against the Flenorys, and whether evidence of several specific drug deals should be added to the indictment. The grand jurors agreed that the charges and evidence had merit. Due in part to Doc and A.R.'s testimony, Meech and Terry faced a few extra counts of cocaine distribution, and the indictment was enhanced with a lengthy description of the hundreds of kilos the brothers allegedly trafficked on specific occasions.

The new allegations seemed minor compared with the charges the brothers already were facing. But there was one catch. Due to the amount of cocaine now alleged to have been trafficked by BMF, the case surpassed an important milestone in federal law. The sheer volume of drugs was enough to increase Meech and Terry's mandatory prison sentence. If convicted, they'd no longer have the option to get the minimum twenty years. If convicted, they'd be sent to prison for life. And in the federal system, there is no parole.

Of all the information Doc fed investigators, there was one area in which his assistance would be of little use: the aftermath of the gruesome fight at Sean "P. Diddy" Combs's Atlanta restaurant, Justin's. During the brawl, Bobby Brown's nephews were stabbed, and BMF member Marque "Baby Bleu" Dixson was arrested on aggravated assault charges. Yet Fulton County prosecutors were having a hard time getting the witnesses, including Brown's family, to cooperate. Though a few of them provided statements shortly after the incident, they later backed away from what they said. Prosecutors then dropped the case against the other man allegedly involved in the attack: a six-foot-seven, 350-pound member of Baby Bleu's entourage named Cleveland Hall. The DA's office believed that without the cooperation of the victims and witnesses, Hall's charges wouldn't stand. But prosecutors were still plowing ahead with the case against Baby Bleu.

As Doc would later explain to Harvey, the hush fell over the witnesses for a reason. Doc told the federal agent that a message from BMF's top brass had quieted the Browns. Apparently, Meech had gotten through to them. "J-Bo told me that Meech contacted their family members and said, 'Well, let's just squash this thing,'" Doc recalled to Harvey. "'We are prepared to take this to another level.'"

Baby Bleu initially was denied bond on his aggravated assault charges. Detective Burns, who testified at the bond hearing, tried to ensure that he stayed locked up. But in the fall of 2005, Baby Bleu's attorney convinced a judge to release him pending trial. Had the attorney failed, Baby Bleu's life might have been spared.

Doc was friendly with Baby Bleu, a young, handsome, and heavily tattooed member of BMF. He passed himself off as Bleu DaVinci's younger brother, and though the two weren't actually related, they did have a few things in common. They both had relocated from Southern California to Atlanta. They both had matching tattoos on their forearms bearing BMF's motto, DEATH BEFORE DISHONOR. And both were highly visible members of Meech's entourage—Bleu DaVinci because his songs, along with Jeezy's, were BMF's club anthems, and Baby Bleu because he was a perfect specimen for the spotlight. He had a slender, muscular build and the perfectly chiseled features of a statue.

After Baby Bleu was released on a fifty-thousand-dollar bond, he immediately went to visit Doc. He said he didn't feel like he should have to go down for the stabbings. He said he intended to beat the charge. He'd just graduated from Talladega College, in Alabama. At age twenty-seven, he said, it wasn't too late for him to turn this mess around.

The following spring—two days after Doc had his first debriefing with the feds—Baby Bleu and his girlfriend were hanging out at a Buckhead club called the Living Room when he ran into an ex-girlfriend. The two women got into a fight, after which Baby Bleu asked his ex to meet him in a nearby parking lot. At the lot, they got into a screaming match. His current girlfriend stayed in the car. His ex called her friends for backup. Within minutes, they pulled up in a black BMW. Baby Bleu told the driver that he'd kill him if he didn't back off. Moments later, Baby Bleu approached the driver's side window. For once, he didn't have the protection of the foreboding entourage to which he'd grown so accustomed. This time, he was on his own.

When Baby Bleu pulled on the door handle, the driver panicked. He pulled a gun, fired twice, and peeled out of the parking lot. With his girlfriend standing by helplessly, Baby Bleu collapsed on the pavement. He was dead by the time police arrived. And the investigation into the brutal stabbings at Justin's was closed.

• • •

Later that month, federal agents in Greenville, South Carolina, reached what they thought was the end of a two-year investigation into Tremayne "Kiki" Graham. A year had passed since a bounty hunter and a team of U.S. marshals surrounded the unsuspecting fugitive outside a Subway sandwich shop in suburban Los Angeles. For months after, Kiki held his tongue. But on March 27, 2006, his change of heart arrived—a week before he and his boss, "J-Rock" Davis, were scheduled for trial on cocaine-conspiracy charges. The last time Kiki was about to face a jury, back in November 2004, he'd cut his ankle monitor and fled across the country. This time, though, he decided to take what seemed to be a less resistant route. Kiki pleaded guilty to his charges and immediately agreed to cooperate with the feds.

DEA special agent Jay Rajaee, out of Greenville, South Carolina, interviewed Kiki that very afternoon. There were a couple of things the government was eager to know, and one of them had to do with a man Rajaee had interrogated two years earlier: Kiki's codefendant, Ulysses "Hack" Hackett. During the interrogation of Hack, Rajaee had been surprised to find that Hack was defending Kiki. Hack denied to the agent that Kiki had much of anything to do with the cocaine trade—and at that point, Rajaee cut the interview short. He didn't believe what he was hearing, and he didn't want to continue an interview with someone who was lying to protect another suspected drug dealer.

Within months, Hack and his girlfriend, Misty Carter, were dead. Six months after Hack met with Rajaee, he and Misty were gunned down in the middle of the night as they lay in bed. It appeared that someone thought Hack said too much, and the DEA was left wondering if Hack had been intentionally silenced. Nearly two years later, as Rajaee began asking questions of Kiki, he felt he was interrogating one of the few witnesses who could offer any insight into the double-homicide.

But when Rajaee asked about Hack and Misty's deaths, Kiki said he had no idea who was behind the killings. He said he'd been scared when he heard about what happened. He pointed out that he was under house arrest at the time, and he said he immediately called his mother-in-law, Atlanta mayor Shirley Franklin, upon hearing the news. He said she confirmed the killings through her police department. She then allowed Kiki to stay at her house—for his own safety, he claimed. Less than two months later, he went on the run.

Kiki told agent Rajaee that while he was a fugitive, he didn't want to leave his wife, the mayor's daughter, destitute. So he funneled cash to her through his associate, Eric "Mookie" Rivera, who'd ferried Kiki's drugs and drug proceeds across the country in private jets. Kiki wanted to make sure Kai Franklin Graham had enough money to cover the couple's mortgage and bills. He also said that he never had any direct contact with her while he was on the run, which was consistent with what Kai herself had told authorities—though quite inconsistent with what others would say.

Before Kiki was caught, his wife filed both for bankruptcy and divorce. In court documents, she claimed her husband had abandoned her. She claimed she was destitute and couldn't afford to pay the bond Kiki had broken, let alone her five-thousand-dollar monthly mortgage and her everyday expenses. The eighty-thousand-dollar salary she'd earned while working for her father at his airport concessions company had dried up, too. David Franklin's business was failing, and he could no longer afford to pay his daughter. (In fact, the company would declare bankruptcy and be shuttered a year later.) Kai was making a successful case for bankruptcy protection. Court documents described her as subsisting off a two-thousand-dollar monthly handout from family and friends, having received no other contributions in the past two years.

Shortly thereafter, Kiki's associate Mookie was arrested at the Van Nuys airport with a suitcase packed with cocaine. He eventually agreed to cooperate with investigators—several months before Kiki did. As a result, Kiki's revelation about funneling money to Kai didn't come as a surprise; Mookie already had told the agents about the deliveries. However, there was one part of the narrative where their stories didn't match up: Mookie described conversations Kiki had with his wife, letting her know the cash was coming. Yet Kiki insisted that Kai had no knowledge of what was going on. He told agent Rajaee that not once, during his three years of marriage, did he tell Kai he earned nearly all his cash from cocaine. "If she knew about it," Kiki said during the interview, "it's not because I told her."

Rajaee would later testify that he was skeptical of Kiki's denial. It would have been a crime for Kai to harbor her fugitive husband. It also would have been illegal for her to pay her bills with known drug money. Regardless of what went on between the couple early in the marriage, Rajaee thought Kai would have a hard time claming ignorance about the origin of the money that showed up on her doorstep. After all, by that time her husband was a federal fugitive wanted on major drug charges. Back in 2004, agent Rajaee suspected that Hack was lying to protect his friend Kiki—a plan that appeared to have tragically backfired. Now, Rajaee believed he was being fed another line of bullshit, and he would later testify that he believed Kiki was lying to protect his wife.

In the end, Rajaee's interview with Kiki was far from revelatory. Even after Kiki was given a list of names and asked to divulge what he knew about each one, he didn't exactly elaborate. When Rajaee asked about Terry Flenory and Demetrius Flenory, Kiki said they were the leaders of BMF, but he didn't delve much further than that. It was the same deal when Rajaee brought up Jamad "Soup" Ali—the man who'd been spotted by an eyewitness leaving Misty Carter's town house the night she and Hack were killed. Again, Kiki was vague. And the feds reached the conclusion that Kiki was lying to protect Soup, too.

But Kiki did help the feds in one substantial way. He agreed to testify in the impending trial of his boss, Jerry "J-Rock" Davis. The following day, after learning about the recent development, J-Rock followed Kiki's lead and entered a guilty plea. Unlike Kiki, J-Rock wasn't interested in sharing info with the feds in exchange for a lighter sentence. The reason: J-Rock's lawyer claimed his client didn't want to expose his loved ones to retribution from his associates in the Black Mafia Family.

Six weeks after the two pleas, Kiki sat down to a lie-detector test. The polygraph was a condition of his plea deal. Federal prosecutors expected full and truthful information from him, and they intended to make sure they got it. If they didn't, Kiki's guilty plea would still stick—but the feds would be allowed to withdraw their offer of a reduced sentence and push for the maximum. There were two things that polygraphers planned to ask Kiki about, both of which agent Rajaee already had gone over. First, they wanted to find out if he knew anything about the murders of Misty and Hack. They also wanted to know if he'd ever told his wife that his income came from the cocaine trade.

During the polygraph, Kiki's interrogator asked several "relevant" questions ("Did you shoot those people?"), each of which were sandwiched between ten nonrelevant ones ("What is your shoe size?"). That way, the test could determine whether he reacted differently to the controversial versus the noncontroversial inquiries. His reaction was measured by any change in his breathing rate, heart rate, and sweat gland activity. Over and over, in the midst of all those mundane statements, the polygrapher would let slip the loaded questions:

"Did you shoot those people?"

"Did you participate in shooting those people?"

"Do you know for sure who shot those people?"

"Did you tell your wife that any of that money came from drug proceeds?"

It took six hours to plow through the test. Each set of questions had to be repeated several times, and the questions themselves had to be asked slowly, with a twenty-second pause between each one to give the machine ample time to gauge Kiki's reaction. His attorney peeked in on him several times, and he complained about how cold it was in the stark room. He said he hadn't eaten all day. (His interrogator eventually brought him an apple.) The experience was exhausting.

After the test was over, the polygrapher gave Kiki a rough idea of how he did. The results weren't final; they'd first have to be vetted by the DEA. But the polygrapher was able to draw a few broad conclusions. He said Kiki's reaction to the questions about the murder was "positive," indicating he was telling the truth. But the DEA later determined the results were inconclusive. The questions were not asked in the proper sequence, the agency ruled. His reaction to the questions about Kai, on the other hand, showed he was being deceptive, the polygrapher said. The DEA would rubberstamp those results.

After hearing the results, Kiki turned away from the table. His hands flew to his face several times. He laughed a tired laugh. And he told the polygrapher that the test was wrong. He repeated to him what he'd told agent Rajaee: that he never, ever let Kai know that his money came from the drug trade.

Two weeks after the polygraph, the holes in Kiki's story got a lot more pronounced. The U.S. Marshals Service finally fielded a tip as to where Kiki's close friend and business partner, Scott King, might be hiding out. Scott had been a fugitive for more than two years now. Somehow, when the feds caught Mookie, Kiki, and J-Rock in L.A. the year before, Scott managed to slip away. From then on, he remained a step or two ahead of the feds, even after a high-speed police chase during which he crashed his SUV and fled the scene by foot. But on June 6, 2006, the game was up. Investigators finally cornered Scott, who was hiding out at a friend's house in the L.A. suburbs. The marshals found him in the closet, under a pile of clothes.

Within weeks, Scott agreed to tell investigators everything, and to tell it in great detail. Unlike Kiki's version of events, Scott's story made sense to the feds. It also was consistent with the information

Mookie provided. Scott said that while Kiki was on the run, he spoke regularly to his wife. In fact, he had a special phone that received her calls, a phone Kiki referred to as "the Kai phone."

Scott also described an event that he and Kiki witnessed in D.C. in 2001. He said they were riding around in a limo with a bunch of friends when one of the guys, Jamad "Soup" Ali, shot a man dead in the street. Scott said Kiki clearly saw what happened—yet Kiki hadn't mentioned it during his debriefing. Nor did Kiki mention a man named Ernest Watkins, whom Scott described as an integral part of his and Kiki's drug ring. Scott said Ernest helped ship kilos of cocaine across the country using an inside source at the United Parcel Service. According to Scott, Ernest also played a crucial role in the murders of Misty and Hack, perhaps without knowing it. Ernest allegedly provided Kiki with the murder weapon, which Kiki in turn passed along to J-Rock. Yet when Kiki met with agent Rajaee, he never so much as brought up Ernest's name. The feds didn't think that was an oversight. They thought Kiki was trying to protect Ernest for the same reason he might want to protect Soup: It was in his best interest to keep investigators in the dark about the details of Misty and Hack's deaths.

Agent Rajaee, with the help of agent Harvey, quickly tracked down Ernest in Atlanta. He'd not yet been charged with a crime, but he was told he might be soon. As a precautionary measure, Ernest agreed to speak with the agents. He told them that Kiki was an acquaintance of his. He said he wouldn't call him a friend. When shown a photo of Kiki's codefendant, Mookie, Ernest said he didn't recognize him. (Mookie, on the other hand, had told investigators that he and Ernest had worked closely together.) "Are you sure?" the agents prodded Ernest. "Yes," he said, "I'm sure." The agents then asked if Ernest, an admitted gun collector, ever had a weapon stolen. No, he said. The agents asked if he'd ever traded in a gun. No, he replied. Ever given one away? No. Finally, the agents asked Ernest if he was willing to take a polygraph test. He said he wasn't.

A month later, Ernest was served with a subpoena to appear before a Greenville grand jury. At that point, some of his answers changed. Once under oath, Ernest said that he did know Mookie after all. He also said that in 2003 his home had been burglarized, and three guns were stolen.

Meanwhile, investigators continued to hunt for evidence against Kiki. Even though he'd already pleaded guilty, there was still a case to build. The prosecution wanted to convince the judge that Kiki had fed them lies when they'd bargained for truth. By October 2006, the government had amassed two hundred pages of new allegations, most of them raised by Scott King. The following day, Scott pleaded guilty to cocaine and money-laundering charges. Also on that day, Greenville U.S. Attorney Reginald Lloyd sent a letter to Graham's attorneys. Kiki's guilty plea would stand, the letter stated, but the government's promise of a reduced sentence was null and void. Prosecutors would now aggressively pursue the maximum punishment. According to the letter:

> The United States intends to present evidence as to the defendants' involvement in various crimes and acts of violence (including but not limited to the brutal murder of Ulysses Hackett and Melissa Carter) in support of its request for a life sentence.

On June 15, 2006, near the Upper East Side corner of Fifty-seventh Street and Madison Avenue, federal agents slipped behind a pair of heavy etched-glass doors. Above the entryway, silver letters mounted against a white tiled background spelled out JACOB & CO. Unlike the last time the agents traveled to Manhattan to visit Jacob "the Jeweler" Arabo, this time they arrived unannounced. And they were carrying a search warrant.

The agents stepped into the brilliant space-agey showroom, moving purposefully across the glossy floor. Built-in jewelry cases glowed a purplish blue against gleaming white walls. The cases held chunky sixty-carat pendants, glimmering chandelier earrings, a one-of-a-kind canary-yellow diamond ring worth nearly a million dollars, and in the roped-off VIP section, Jacob's signature diamond-encrusted "Five Time Zone" watches.

The agents were on the hunt for documents pertaining to the Flenory brothers. And they had a search warrant that granted them better-than-VIP access to Jacob's surreal jewelry salon. After passing rows upon rows of bling, they headed to Jacob & Co.'s office, where they went straight for a file marked "Damon Thomas." Damon, an L.A. music producer who'd worked with the likes of Justin Timberlake and Aretha Franklin, was an integral part of the feds' investigation into the possibly criminal connection between Jacob the Jeweler and the Black Mafia Family.

The previous summer, Damon had claimed to be the owner of most of a whopping $5 million in jewelry confiscated from Terry Flenory during a Missouri traffic stop. Jacob himself had claimed the six remaining pieces. It was part of a plan they'd hatched with Terry. It could never be known that the jewelry belonged to the cocaine kingpin. That would draw way too much attention.

After claiming the jewelry, Jacob went so far as to tell the DEA that he'd never sold Terry Flenory a single diamond. To back up his claim, he produced a document showing that all the jewelry seized in the traffic stop either had been purchased outright by Damon Thomas or consigned to him. Even after Terry and Meech were indicted, Jacob continued to press the government for the return of the six pieces he supposedly lent Damon. On November 28, 2005, Jacob went so far as to send a letter to the U.S. Attorney's Office, through his attorney, that stated: "Please make arrangements to have the jewelry in question returned to my client as soon as possible." Attached to the letter was the fake document Jacob had created, purporting that the jewelry had been consigned to Damon. Basically, Jacob was delivering to the feds evidence that would later incriminate him.

On June 13, 2006, two days before the DEA showed up at Jacob & Co. with their search warrant, Jacob sent yet another letter, again through his attorney, to the government: "It has now been seven months since my first telephone conversation with you concerning my client's jewelry that was seized by the government. My client is quite perplexed and frankly does not understand what he must do to get his jewelry returned."

Little did Jacob know, Damon had already cooperated against him. Damon didn't give in easily. He'd been subpoenaed to testify about the jewelry before a federal grand jury in Detroit the month before. Through his attorney, he invoked his Fifth Amendment right against self-incrimination and attempted to keep his mouth shut. The feds then filed a compulsion order to force Damon to testify, and he relented. He described the plan hatched by him, Jacob, and Terry. The feds then took a trip to New York's Upper East Side. At Jacob & Co., DEA agents found in Damon's file a photo of Terry and his girl-friend, Tonesa. They also recovered receipts showing that jewelry had been shipped to two Atlanta addresses with ties to the Flenorys: 404 Motorsports, the business owned by Scott and Kiki in which Terry Flenory was a silent partner; and the home of Yogi, Meech's assistant.

A month later, in July 2006, sixteen more people were added to the Flenory brothers' indictment. Jacob was among them. He faced one count of money-laundering, for allegedly circumventing the IRS so that the Flenorys could spend their drug money on his jewelry— and for lying to the feds about the true owners of the bling. The indictment also nabbed Meech's second-in-command, J-Bo; Terry's right-hand man, Slim; his girlfriend's son, Marlon "Lil Dog" Welch; Meech and Terry's longtime associate Wayne Joyner (the one who'd allegedly introduced them early on to their Mexican cocaine connection); Paul Buford, who was chief of security for Sean "P. Diddy" Combs; and, most surprisingly, Meech and Terry's father, Charles Flenory.

Meech believed the feds were trying to rattle him by charging his fifty-eight-year-old father, who'd never been in trouble with the law before. Charles's alleged crime: handing envelopes stuffed with Terry's cash to a contractor working on the White House. It didn't matter that neither the money nor the home belonged to Charles, and that he appeared not to benefit in any way from the transaction. The alleged act still constituted money-laundering. Considering the insignificance of the allegation, Meech felt the government was targeting his father as a way to pressure him and his brother into pleading guilty. Perhaps if the brothers fessed up, the feds would spare Charles a trip to prison.

But neither Meech nor Terry took the bait. Their father didn't want them to. As the brothers neared the one-year anniversary of their indictment, each seemed determined to beat their charges—while faced with two very different sets of challenges. Terry's problems were more immediate. By the summer of 2006, his relationship with his Detroit-based attorney, Steve Fishman, had deteriorated. Terry requested that Fishman be removed from the case. He also claimed that he was destitute and therefore unable to retain a lawyer on his own. Terry asked that the court appoint him an attorney, and the judge obliged. The appointment of a public defender marked a precipitous fall for a man who was accustomed to driving Bentleys and Maybachs and dropping fifty thousand dollars on Lakers' tickets.

Meech, on the other hand, was doing his best to keep up appearances while behind bars. His well-respected legal team—Findling, out of Atlanta, and James Feinberg, out of Detroit—worked aggressively to challenge the hundreds of motions filed by federal prosecutors and to investigate the government's voluminous evidence. In the meantime, Meech wanted everyone to know that his current situation wouldn't derail his dreams. From behind bars, Meech kept BMF's publicity machine humming. He even attempted to keep his year-old magazine, the *Juice*, afloat—despite having published only one issue the summer before.

On his MySpace page, where well-wishers left comments that proclaimed BMF 4 LIFE and FREE BIG MEECH, the boss posted letters to his followers. One of them, dated August 30, 2006, suggested that he'd be out soon—and that he expected those on the outside to behave accordingly:

> As you can see they can lock up my body, but not my mind! So I just want everyone to know that this is the "Real Big Meech" MySpace web site, and I appreciate everyone for logging on sending your pictures, music and comments. Everything gets forwarded to me in St. Clair County jail where I'm temporarily being held. . . . The world is still BMF's. We still here and we're not going anywhere! . . . Even though I'm locked up I'm still focused on my "vision," making my challenges temporary but my "vision" permanent. So understand that nothing disturbs the trials of the present like the expectations of the future!!! I will be back in black soon, so until my pencil meets my paper again remember *loyalty* is not just a word, it's a *lifestyle*.

By the time Meech's MySpace letter was posted, Doc Marshall had been holed up in an Orlando jail cell for nearly a year. He'd been allowed out on several occasions, to travel to no less than three states to assist authorities in their BMF investigations. He testified in front of grand juries in Atlanta and Detroit. He showed up in Greenville, South Carolina, to take the stand against Kiki and J-Rock (though he was relieved of having to testify after the duo entered last-minute guilty pleas). He met on numerous occasions with detective Burns and agent Harvey in Atlanta, to help them identify specific members of BMF. And in early 2007, he agreed to sit down with another Atlanta lawman—one who'd toiled through three BMF-related murder investigations in as many years.

Despite a couple of promising leads, Atlanta homicide detective Marc Cooper had made no arrests in a string of brazen killings: a shootout that left two men dead behind Club Chaos, a vicious brawl that took the life of a man behind the Velvet Room, and the apparent revenge killing of a drug defendant and his girlfriend. But in one of those cases, Cooper was about to get the break he'd been waiting for. Near the end of 2006, the detective got a call from the DEA. Doc Marshall, who was under federal indictment in Florida, had information he was willing to share about a murder he'd witnessed. He wanted to come clean about what happened behind the Velvet Room.

A month later, on January 15, 2007, detective Cooper traveled to Orlando to interview Doc. The former CFO was at ease with the detective, and he chatted comfortably. He filled Cooper in on some of the people who were part of Meech's entourage that night. He said Meech's right-hand man J-Bo was there, of course. So was Meech's close friend, the rapper Bleu DaVinci, and his third-in-command, Fleming "Ill" Daniels—who was jokingly referred to as Ill Pesci, because his short stature and tough-guy attitude brought to mind the actor Joe Pesci. Omari "O-Dog" McCree was part of the crew, too, as were several other midlevel players: Baby Bleu, Deron "D-Shot" Hall, Martez "Tito" Byrth, and Ameen "Bull" Hight. "Just regular guys that we hang out with," Doc told Cooper.

After asking Doc to describe where everybody was situated in the parking lot, Cooper got to the point. "Let me ask you this," he said. "Was the guy laying on the ground when he was shot?"

"Yes," Doc said. "He certainly was."

Cooper then asked Doc to slow down and start from the beginning.

"Ill was backing his vehicle up, and he didn't see the guys behind him," Doc recalled. "So the guys start banging on the window. One of them said, 'Hey, look man, you about to run us over.' So at that point, Ill was like, 'Y'all motherfuckers don't ever touch my car again.'" By then, Doc said, Meech and his bodyguard were gone. J-Bo was pulling out of the lot himself. And those who were left jumped into the fight. "It starts out to be about five on three, and they are beating the guy pretty decently," Doc said. "One of them slips out and leaves, then about five minutes later you hear 'bang, bang, bang.' He just shooting up in the air and everybody drops."

Doc said that it was clear to everyone involved that one of the guys who was getting beat up had squeezed off a few warning shots. It wasn't a big deal, he claimed. The fight appeared to be winding down, anyway. Then, he said, one of Meech's guys snapped. "At that point, Ill goes to the car. I seen his weapon when he pulled it out. Now, the guy is already beat down good. So Ill goes 'bang, bang, bang.' Then he waited, and in another second—pow! He dropped the last one."

"So you actually saw him?" Cooper asked.

"Yeah," Doc said. "This is something where you hook me to a polygraph, and I'm right there with it. It's not no third-party or hear-say."

"You definitely didn't see the victim with a gun or anything?"

"No. He was whooped up. It didn't make any sense. The guy was busted. I don't know if that was just a retaliatory thing that Ill did. He was off the chain most of the time."

A week later, Cooper obtained an arrest warrant for Fleming "Ill" Daniels, charging him with the murder of Rashannibal "Prince" Drummond. Ill already was jailed on a minor probation violation charge. As soon as he finished serving that time, he'd be transferred to another jail to deal with the far more serious accusation.

Debbie Morgan had been waiting nearly two years for an arrest in the murder of her son. She'd been in regular contact with detective Cooper and special agent Harvey. Early in the investigation, she'd tried to help investigators by convincing Prince's friends to tell police about what happened that night. She'd also rebuffed an offer, sent to her through people she assumed were Meech's minions, to handle this whole ordeal "the street way." Instead, she sought out a distraction— something that might help her forget that there'd been no closure in Prince's case. She found a small space for rent inside a tattered shopping center just off Boulevard, along the gritty but hip stretch between the Atlanta neighborhoods Old Fourth Ward and Cabbagetown. She would open a Jamaican restaurant there, called One Love.

But before the restaurant opened, Debbie's world fell apart again. Her eldest child, Rasheym, was gunned down in broad daylight by two men on Martin Luther King Drive. At first, she thought Rasheym's death was retaliation for the heat drawn to BMF over Prince's murder. But she was mistaken. The killings were unrelated. Nonetheless, agent Harvey responded to the crime scene himself, just to be sure. Rasheym's suspected killer was arrested the following day. It was a small consolation, but consolation nonetheless.

Of course, Rasheym's death was an excruciating reminder of the loss she'd already suffered. After the second of her three sons was killed, Debbie needed closure for Prince more than ever. Doc Marshall helped deliver that. After he agreed to talk to detective Cooper, Debbie finally had a clearer picture of what happened that night. And she was relieved to know that the man believed to be her son's killer was finally locked up. From the beginning, she felt that the Black Mafia Family was responsible for Prince's death. She'd been looking for validation for three years. In fact, her quest had started with a letter she wrote to the Atlanta mayor days after Prince was killed.

Dear Mayor Shirley Franklin,

On July 25, at approximately 4 A.M. in the parking lot of the Velvet Room, my son Prince and my nephew were jumped on, stomped and beaten by a group of men. Prince was shot and died in the parking lot. I believe the detectives involved will do a thorough job. However, this is a gang of drug dealers and murderers who have set up shop in most major cities—and make no mistake, business is booming. They travel under the guise of a promotions and record company. Ms. Franklin, I appeal to you not as my mayor, but as a mother who knows the pain of childbirth and would understand the loss of a son. You have seen your son grow to manhood, and your dreams of seeing your grandchildren may have already come through. My son died without a child. My dream of seeing his seed grow has been shattered.

These individuals drive around this city in luxury cars, doing what they please, living by the motto, "We rule the world." My question, Ms. Mayor, is do they rule Atlanta?

Within months of Ill's arrest, another seemingly dormant murder investigation would be revived. And another mother who lost a child would be left wondering how, under the watchful eye of the government, such a terrible thing could happen.

Nearly three years after Misty Carter's death, her town house on Atlanta's Highland Avenue was just as she'd left it. Katie Carter wanted it that way. To Katie, the mere thought of the town house was excruciating at times. She imagined the police trudging into the bedroom that had become a crime scene. She imagined the paramedics carrying Misty out. But the town house also was a source of solace. Katie kept it for as long as she did because, at other times, it helped convince her—if only for a second—that Misty was still there. Katie could visualize her daughter surrounded by all her things, breathing and laughing and alive. She didn't believe she was crazy to think that. She believed she had to do what she could to keep going. Her only child, the joy of her and her husband's life, was gone. So it was okay to pretend. When she stopped pretending, then she'd have to admit to herself that Misty was truly and forever gone.

After Misty died, Katie began to work long hours at her husband's medical practice. The work took her mind away from things. At home, the pain was constant. Plus, being away from the house gave Katie another chance to make believe. She'd often call home from the office to check her answering machine. One of the messages would always be from Misty. It was the last message Katie got from her daughter. She couldn't bring herself to erase it.

By the spring of 2007, three years had passed since that terrible night, and time had done little to ease the pain. But there was one small source of solace. In April of that year, Katie and her husband, Dr. Paul Carter, traveled from their home in Fayetteville, North Carolina, to a federal courthouse four hours away. They wanted to be sitting in the courtroom when the judge read the prison sentences of Tremayne "Kiki" Graham, Scott King, and Eric "Mookie" Rivera.

The hearing in Greenville, South Carolina, would be unusual as far as sentencings go. Prosecutors were hoping to prove that Kiki had lied to the feds, thereby breaking his "contract" for a reduced sentence. To prove that he'd misled the government, his associates Scott and Mookie would be testifying against him. If the judge believed them, Kiki could be sentenced to life without parole on his cocaine charges. Still, there was a chance the judge wouldn't buy their stories—and Kiki was willing to gamble on that. The possibility of a life sentence hadn't been his only option. Even after he failed his polygraph, Kiki got one last offer from the government. The prosecution was willing to go as low as thirty-five years—five years less than the sentence his boss, "J-Rock" Davis, received. But Kiki turned the deal down. Despite the fact that prosecutors intended to bring up evidence of his alleged role in the murders of Misty and Hack, he was willing to risk it all.

When Scott King took the stand on the morning of April 17, 2007, he spared no detail. In front of a room full of onlookers, including the families of both Misty and Hack, he methodically laid out the history of his friendship and business relationship with Kiki. He described how the two met, back when Kiki was still a student at Clemson University. He talked about how they both fell into the local cocaine trade. He mentioned that Kiki helped him get back in the drug game after he finished a three-year stint on a cocaine charge. By that time, Scott recalled, they'd both ended up in Atlanta. He said

Kiki was clearly doing well for himself. Soon, he said, they combined forces. They found a big-time dope supplier in J-Rock. They opened a high-end car dealership to help their drug income seem legit. They each dated one of the mayor of Atlanta's daughters. They pulled their friends, including Ulysses "Hack" Hackett, into their drug ring. Then, the cocaine operation they so carefully pieced together began to crumble. Scott described his decision to flee to California after he learned he'd been indicted. He said Kiki, who would be added to the indictment a little later, decided to stick it out in Atlanta. Scott claimed that, even then, Kiki was suspicious about Hack.

"Did y'all discuss any particular concerns about Mr. Hackett?" assistant U.S Attorney Mark Moore asked Scott.

"Yes. Tremayne told me he felt that Hack was cooperating, and that we might need to take care of him."

"When you say, 'Take care of him,' what did that mean to you?"

"Kill him."

"How did you feel about that, Mr. King?"

"I didn't want no part of it. He was like my brother. But to Tremayne, he was just somebody who could finger him and get him convicted."

"Did you agree to assist Mr. Graham in doing something to Mr. Hackett?" Moore continued.

"No," Scott said.

"Did Mr. Graham let it die at that point?"

"No."

"What, if anything, did he say to you?"

"That he was going to find somebody to take care of him."

According to Scott, that person was J-Rock. Kiki had convinced the boss that Hack could incriminate him, too. "So if Jerry didn't want to get fingered in our indictment," Scott testified, "maybe he needed to think about taking care of Hackett."

"Did you have any other discussions with Mr. Graham about doing something to Mr. Hackett?" Moore asked.

"Yes. He discussed getting a gun from Ernest Watkins to take care of the murder. He told me that Ernest had come across a gun and gave it to him."

"And did he tell you what, if anything, he did with that gun?"

"He told me that he passed it along to Jerry Davis."

Scott said Kiki was out on bond and under house arrest one morning several months later, when he was roused from sleep by a ringing phone. He said Kiki was on the line, and he had news to share: "Stupid and the girl are dead."

Within weeks, Kiki jumped bond and joined Scott in L.A., Scott recalled.

"During the time period that he was living as a fugitive in California with you," Moore continued, "did y'all have any other further discussions about what happened to Ulysses Hackett and Misty Carter?"

"Yes," Scott said. "Tremayne told me that Jerry and him had went over to T's house."

"Who is T?"

"Big T from BMF."

"Is that Terry Flenory?"

"Yes."

"Did you know Mr. Flenory?"

"Yes."

"And where did you meet him?"

"In Atlanta at my place of business."

"Why did you meet him in Atlanta at your place of business?"

"Because he invested in the business."

"So Tremayne told you about an occasion where he and Jerry Davis went over to Terry Flenory's house?"

"Yes. And somehow Hack's name came up, and Jerry boasted that he had took care of it."

Under cross-examination, Kiki's attorney hinted that Scott might be saying whatever he could to make sure he served the least possible sentence. "You obviously don't want to spend any more time than you have to in prison, correct?" the attorney, J. Bradley Bennett, asked.

"I'm saying, I done the crime, so I'm going to do the time," Scott replied.

"Do you have a desire to spend less time in prison?" Bennett reiterated.

"I have a desire to tell the truth," Scott shot back.

After Scott wrapped up his lengthy testimony, U.S. District Court Judge Henry Herlong called a short break. When he returned to the bench, one of the prosecutors approached him with an alarming bit of information. She said the government's next witness, Eric "Mookie" Rivera, had just been threatened by Kiki.

"May it please the court, Your Honor?" prosecutor Regan Pendleton interjected. "Mr. Rivera, the government's witness and codefendant in this case, was brought in the courtroom by the marshals service and placed in that chair, at which time the court was in recess and everyone was standing around talking. And I glanced over and I observed Mr. Graham make a threatening gesture toward Mr. Rivera. He pointed his fingers as if shooting a gun and then put the gun to his heart. Mr. Rivera observed it and I observed it. And Mr. Rivera is very concerned about it."

The judge said he would get to that in due time. But first, a somewhat shaken Mookie launched into his testimony. Like Scott King, he gave a sprawling narrative of his history as Kiki's friend and drug associate. Mookie described himself as a courier-for-hire who transported kilos of coke and huge shipments of cash across the country on private jets. He recalled meeting Kiki through their mutual employer, J-Rock. He said he continued to do business with Kiki while he was under house arrest, and that the two became friends. Mookie said Kiki opened up to him.

"Did you have a conversation with him about Ulysses Hackett's death?" prosecutor Moore asked.

"It came up," Mookie said.

"How did it come up?"

"I was over there. We were discussing our next trip. And out of curiosity, I asked him how the case was going. And he says, 'Oh, it's looking good right now.' I said, 'What's going on?' He said the one guy that could say anything about him got murdered. He just said that the guy is gone. He can't say anything about him."

Mookie testified that after Kiki became a fugitive, he traveled to the East Coast to pick up drug money for him—and that while he was in Atlanta, Kiki had him deliver bundles of the cash to his wife. Mookie said he also met with Kai Franklin Graham to pick up Kiki's son. He said he transported the child across the country so that Kiki could spend time with him. Mookie then returned the boy to Kai, in Atlanta.

At the end of his testimony, the judge asked Mookie to describe what had just happened between him and Kiki in the courtroom.

"He, um, made eye contact, and then he shot one time," Mookie said, pointing with two fingers the way children do when mimicking a gunshot.

"And what did you take that to mean?" the judge asked.

"That, you know, they're going to try and kill me."

Later in the hearing, Mookie took the opportunity to address some of the people seated in the courtroom: "I want to apologize for the loss that the Hackett family received, and the Carter family. I hope that they do get justice."

The judge then sentenced Mookie to three and a half years in federal prison.

As for Scott King, his situation was more serious. Scott was a higher-level dealer, one who'd spent two years as a federal fugitive. What's more, he'd brought his friend Hack into the fold—eventually leading him to his death, even if Scott didn't have a hand in the murder. After Mookie's testimony, the judge asked Scott if he had anything more to say before his sentence was read. "I would like to apologize to the Hackett family and the Carter family and let them know that I loved Misty and Hack like a brother and sister," he said. "I'm just so sorry."

Despite Scott's extensive cooperation, his punishment was severe. Judge Herlong gave him twenty-four years.

Neither Mookie's nor Scott's sentence was all that unexpected. The real barometer of the government's success would be Kiki's prison term. Right away, the judge hinted that he was impressed with the evidence the government laid out—and with the broader investigation. "I have handled some very serious drug cases," Herlong said. "This is the biggest one I have ever seen."

Then, it was Kiki's turn to speak. He tried to strike a conciliatory tone, perhaps with a poor choice of analogies. "I assure you, I have many, many regrets," he told the judge. "And if I could take them back, I would in a heartbeat. But unfortunately, life is not like golf, so you can't take a mullet."

He, too, asked for mercy and forgiveness. He also tried to diminish the testimonies of Scott and Mookie. "I learned that as long as you've got life, you have a chance to turn your life around, Your Honor," Kiki said. "That's what I've been trying to do. And I feel I've been truthful, Your Honor. And I'm sorry that my story wasn't embellished or sensationalized enough to the agents' liking. But my plea agreement didn't require that. All it required was for me to be truthful, Your Honor, and I was truthful."

Last of all, he denied ever threatening anyone tied to the case—let alone wanting them dead: "I just want it on the record that there was no way I would threaten a witness or anyone in the courtroom," Kiki said. "I mean, it just don't make sense. And for the record, me and Rivera was very close. Actually, it broke my heart to see him get on the stand and testify against me, Your Honor, because I have never did anything wrong to Rivera. I wouldn't want him dead or anyone dead. And I played no part in Misty Carter or Ulysses Hackett's murder. And that's all I want to say."

It would seem, based on what happened next, that the judge was not moved to sympathy.

"I am familiar with life sentences that have been imposed in this district," Judge Herlong said. "And there certainly have been life sentences imposed for crimes of this nature and less than this nature. And as far as being compared to other major drug dealers, he ranks right up there at the top.

"It is therefore the sentence of the court that the defendant, Tremayne K. Graham, is hereby committed to the custody of the Bureau of Prisons to be imprisoned for a term of life."

If Kiki wasn't officially a suspect in the murders of Misty and Hack before he was sentenced on cocaine charges, his status became official afterwards. But prosecutors still had a long way to go before they'd be ready to indict him for the killings—if they were ever to make such a move. By the summer of 2009, no charges had been filed in the five-year-old double-homicide. Still, in the year-and-a-half following Scott and Mookie's testimony, the government began lining up several potential witnesses. The idea, as with the Detroit-based case against the Flenory brothers, was to bring charges against potential witnesses, then offer them plea deals in exchange for their cooperation. And there were two witnesses in particular whom federal prosecutors were eyeing.

On the surface, it might have seemed pointless to investigate Kiki on a murder charge when he'd just been sentenced to life in federal prison. But in addition to holding someone accountable for the deaths, there was another reason the government might be inclined to prosecute. Killing a federal witness is a capital offense.

Even before the feds tracked down the two witnesses they'd been circling, one person central to the investigation already had landed in federal custody: Jamad "Soup" Ali. Soup had been snared in a sting operation at an upscale home in New Jersey suburb. He almost escaped through the window of the huge modern house, but a team of agents quickly surrounded the property. After storming the house, task force agents found a loaded machine gun in the closet of the master bedroom. As a result, Soup was charged with felony firearm possession. Two months after Kiki's sentencing, Soup was sentenced to nearly seven years in prison—giving the feds plenty of time to focus on the double-homicide investigation without having to worry that the suspected hit man would slip away.

With Soup behind bars, investigators turned their attention to the man who was believed to have supplied the murder weapon: Ernest Watkins. At first, Ernest had been hesitant to cooperate with the feds. He was cagey in initial interviews, and the investigators believed that when he was called to testify in front of a grand jury, he misled jurors, too. Scott King had an explanation for Ernest's behavior. He said Ernest had been kidnapped and tortured by drug-dealing acquaintances of Kiki—and that Ernest had the scars to prove it.

In the fall of 2007, Ernest was indicted for cocaine trafficking, obstruction, and giving false statements to a grand jury. Months later, the government hired a specialist to examine the scarring on his back, which he claimed was the result of a motorcycle accident. On the second day of his trial in federal court, he cut the testimony short and entered a belated guilty plea. He signed an agreement to cooperate with the government. He later received the same sentence that Scott King did: twenty-four years.

By then, the feds had another potential witness in the bag. In December 2007, Kai Franklin Graham struck a deal with the government and agreed to plead guilty to "structuring financial payments." The feds decided not to seek the more serious charge of money-laundering. Her crime: Visiting seven post offices and buying fourteen postal money orders, totaling one thousand dollars each. She admitted that she bought the money orders in smaller increments to avoid drawing the attention of the IRS.

The government had collected additional evidence that showed Kai Franklin Graham had been handling lots of cash. The feds claimed to have tracked down not just those fourteen, but *sixty* money orders that she'd bought while her husband was on the run. A prosecutor alleged that she used the money orders—all of which were just shy of the three-thousand-dollar minimum that draws the IRS's attention—to pay her credit card bills and mortgage. It appeared to investigators that Kai wanted to keep the government from finding out where that cash was coming from. However, Kai denied that the money came from Kiki—or that she was trying to evade the IRS in order to throw the feds off her then-husband's trail. She claimed the money came from her father. That also had been her defense when the bonding company that sprang Kiki, Free at Last, sued her.

The company accused Kai of misleading the government about both her financial situation and the whereabouts of her husband. Free at Last was still hoping to recover $185,000 it had lost—a debt that Kai, who'd filed for bankruptcy, was trying to avoid. In a signed affidavit, Kai repeated her claims that she'd had no contact with Kiki after he fled, and that he'd left her destitute. (Kai eventually prevailed in the lawsuit; Free at Last settled the case for a paltry five thousand dollars.)

At her plea hearing, held in the same courtroom where her ex-husband received a life sentence eight months earlier, assistant U.S. Attorney Moore contradicted her affidavit: "The government could show, if required to at trial, that she assisted her husband in structuring other transactions on other dates, and that on a couple of occasions she received drug money from her husband's associates while he was fleeing." The government recommended that Kai serve thirty months of probation, in exchange for her full cooperation in the U.S. Attorney's ongoing investigation.

After Kai entered her plea and returned to her seat, her mother greeted her with a warm smile. Atlanta mayor Shirley Franklin had traveled to South Carolina as a testament of her love and support for her daughter. She was a protective mother, and she was incensed that the case would later see a flurry of media attention. The scrutiny placed on the Franklin family was more than its matriarch was willing to endure. Months later, in an interview with National Public Radio, Franklin said the publicity surrounding her daughter had turned her off to politics altogether.

"When you run for public life, you fully expect your own life to be evaluated," the mayor said during the interview. "I did not expect that my children's lives would make the front page or NPR. And I'm not sure I would have run if I had known that. The truth of the matter is, I won't run again for that reason. I will not put my children, my grandchildren, or any of my family members in the spotlight again. The public can decide whether that's good or bad. It's great for me."

Yet it wasn't Kai's case—or the break in the three-year-old investigation into Hack and Misty's murders—that got the lion's share of public attention in 2007. Instead, the fallout from the death of a ninety-two-year-old woman named Kathryn Johnston mesmerized Atlanta that year. The case brought much criticism to Franklin's administration and the Atlanta Police Department—and drove a wedge between two local law enforcement agents who'd once been consumed by the investigation of the Black Mafia Family. The bond that the lawmen had enjoyed while working on the BMF case was destroyed by what happened in the Johnston one.

When three Atlanta police officers showed up at Johnston's house, on the fringe of the open-air drug zone called the Bluff, they believed they were serving a no-knock warrant on a drug dealer. The problem was, they'd lied to obtain the warrant. And it turned out that by cutting corners, they were targeting the home of an elderly woman who had nothing to do with the drug trade. Two of the officers, Gregg Junnier and Jason Smith, pried open Johnston's burglary bars and took a ram to her front door. Johnston heard them trying to break in. Scared for her life in the sketchy neighborhood, she grabbed her rusty revolver. As the officers barged in, she fired and missed. Junnier and Smith returned fire, squeezing off thirty-nine rounds and striking her a half dozen times. She was cuffed and left to die in her front hallway. Minutes later, Junnier and Smith realized that there were no drugs, or drug dealers, in the house.

One of the officers tried to cover up their mistake by planting a few baggies of weed in the basement. But in the days to come, officer Junnier caved. He told the FBI the whole story of the ill-fated day, from cutting corners on the warrant to planting drugs to cover up the killing of an innocent woman. But that wasn't all. Junnier also described the allegedly unethical and illegal practices he'd witnessed at the Atlanta Police Department. He said that officers routinely lied under oath to obtain warrants, and that supervisors turned a blind eye to the practice so long as officers hit their arrest numbers. Junnier shifted the blame away from his own actions and toward a more pervasive climate of corruption. He did so in order to serve the least possible sentence. And to represent him in his plea deal with the feds, he hired a tough former prosecutor and longtime friend to many of the officers who staffed the APD's now-disgraced narcotics unit, a guy who'd always bonded more easily with cops than with his fellow lawyers. He hired Rand Csehy.

The same month that Kiki was sentenced to life in prison, Junnier—with Csehy at his side—pleaded guilty to voluntary manslaughter. The fallen cop didn't wish to address the court, so Csehy spoke for him. He ripped into the police department, blaming the top brass for the corruption that had trickled to the rank and file. "It's a case where the fish rotted from the head down," Csehy told the judge. "Hopefully, this will reverberate through the police department."

The plea did reverberate, in more ways than he anticipated. The officers with whom he'd worked so closely now considered him an outsider. His close friend, detective Bryant "Bubba" Burns—who'd served as Csehy's best man when he married his third wife (a gutsy fellow prosecutor) the year before—was stunned by the position Csehy had taken. In some ways, it wasn't all that different from Junnier's decision to turn against his former cohorts, or, for that matter, Doc Marhsall's or Scott King's or Mookie Rivera's. Tradition was tradition. Honor was honor. Rules were rules. Csehy, like the others, had broken the code.

TWELVE THE EVIDENCE

*Most of the witnesses are specifically aimed at either one
brother or the other. Very few are aimed at both.*
—ATTORNEYS JAMES FEINBERG AND DREW FINDLING,
IN A SEPTEMBER 2007 COURT FILING

In an early August morning in 2007, a fleet of bulldozers rolled through the desolate streets that once encompassed the rowdiest nightlife district Atlanta had ever known—and the most poorly placed. The two dozen bars in Buckhead Village had long been at odds with the blue bloods who wielded the real power in the neighborhood. In the end, the blue bloods won. A mall developer from the suburbs swooped in and bought every last property in Buckhead Village's eight-block radius. The once-legendary nightclubs Tongue & Groove, World Bar, Mako's, and Chaos were reduced to a pile of bricks. And Atlanta, a city tirelessly committed to reinventing itself, was smitten with what the seven-acre plot would one day become. A Rodeo Drive–styled shopping mecca would rise from the rubble. The raucous celebrity playground would fade from memory. And the crime scene where Big Meech unwittingly stepped into the public spotlight would disappear forever.

Buckhead had been Meech's primary stomping ground. It was the neighborhood where a billboard for his record label proclaimed: THE WORLD IS BMF'S. It was home to his swanky town house, the Elevator; his two stately stash houses, the Gate and Space Mountain; and the clubs and high-end boutiques where he easily dropped fifty grand in a single visit. It was where he took a bullet during a gun battle behind Club Chaos, setting into motion a sputtering police investigation and cementing Buckhead's reputation as a destination as dangerous as it was glamorous. At one time, the existence of the Black Mafia Family in Atlanta had seemed as entrenched as those Buckhead nightclubs. Then, suddenly, everything changed.

In the summer and fall of 2007, as Buckhead Village was being demolished, two more federal indictments were handed up in Atlanta and L.A. The government snared the few stragglers who hadn't been busted in Detroit, where the Flenory brothers and an eventual sixty coconspirators were charged; in Orlando, where Doc Marshall was nabbed; in Greenville, where J-Rock's crew was dismantled; or in Nashville and St. Louis, where a handful of lower-rung associates were swept up. The two new indictments brought the total number of defendants charged in the nationwide BMF investigation to 150. Every significant player now faced a major felony. In Atlanta, three of Meech's crew members and a dozen of Terry's were indicted. The most noteworthy on Terry's side was Darryl "Poppa" Taylor, a BMF cocaine courier and the first-cousin of Sean "P. Diddy" Combs. On Meech's side, the indictment charged his third-in-command, Fleming "Ill" Daniels, who'd already been indicted for the Velvet Room murder in a separate, state case; Deron "D-Shot" Hall, a drug associate of Meech's who popped up on the feds' radar after he boarded a private jet with the kingpin; and Barima "Bleu DaVinci" McKnight, the beloved rapper on whom Meech had pinned his hope for mainstream success.

Bleu had been running Meech's floundering record label in the two years that the boss was locked up. Now that Bleu was indicted, too, the label was done for. Yet despite putting an end to BMF's hip-hop aspirations, the indictment was a blessing for Bleu. It squashed speculation that he'd been spared by the feds because he'd broken ranks and snitched on Big Meech. In fact, after the indictment was filed, Bleu gave his street rep a boost by becoming a fugitive. Even after the U.S. marshals tracked him down five months later in Las Vegas, Bleu adhered to the code of silence espoused by Meech—at least for a while.

It would seem that with the Atlanta and L.A. indictments, BMF's forced departure from the drug trade would have left a power vacuum in the cities where the crew dominated the cocaine trade. But that wasn't the case in Atlanta, BMF's largest market. Meech and Terry's organizations were responsible for the vast majority of coke that landed on Atlanta's streets. From the ten-dollar crack rocks hawked on Boulevard to the hundred-dollar grams of powder passed around the most posh of clubs, the lineage of most of Atlanta's cocaine was just a few steps removed from Meech or Terry' stash houses. Yet with Atlanta's main cocaine supplier knocked out, there was little in the way of a drug war waged for the territory. In fact, the midlevel dealers who'd relied on BMF were, by the summer of 2007, enjoying an unprecedented heyday.

Following the police shooting the year before of ninety-two-year-old Kathryn Johnston, Atlanta's narcotics unit had been disbanded, and it had yet to be reassembled. As a result, many of the dealers who'd once feared the APD's heat had little to worry about. In the absence of a narcotics squad, the dealers could relax. Their drug houses—which were a notch or two closer to the streets than BMF's cocaine warehouses—were practically warrant-proof. In the six months leading up to the narcotics unit's dissolution, the APD had served nearly two hundred search warrants on the dealers' suspected drug houses. In nearly the same time period after the Johnston shooting, only fourteen drug-house warrants were served. By the summer of 2007, the number sank to a measly *one*. "Do they know we're not doing the enforcement we were before? Yes, they do," Deputy Chief Carlos Banda told the *Atlanta Journal-Constitution* in the summer of 2007. "The drug dealers aren't that stupid."

In addition to the carte blanche handed to Atlanta's midlevel dealers, the problem of finding a new supplier was easily solved. Since at least 2000, an organization that was far bigger than BMF had been putting down roots in the city. As had long been the case on the West Coast, in Texas, and in certain pockets of the East, Mexican cartels were infiltrating Atlanta. The predominant cartel in Atlanta was the Federation, a crew that originated in the coastal state of Sinaloa— called the "Sicily of Mexico" because of its concentration of crime bosses. Mexican cartels already imported 90 percent of the cocaine sold in the United States, including the tens of thousands of kilos BMF moved. At its height, BMF had distributed several thousand kilos a month. But compared with the Mexican cartels, a couple thousand keys was nothing. One of the cartels in Atlanta had *sixteen thousand* kilos seized. The feds also accumulated $22 million of the cartel's cash, setting a record for the amount of drug money confiscated from a single crew in the city. As one federal officer put it, the Mexican cartels "could wipe their feet on BMF." In the end, the dismantling of the Black Mafia Family in Atlanta was merely the eradication of the middleman, an opportunity for Mexican cocaine importers to extend their ever-expanding reach.

The situation was a bit different in Detroit, BMF's second-largest distribution hub. In the Flenorys' hometown, BMF, as a brand, had trickled further down the food chain, to midlevel and street-level dealers who claimed allegiance to the crew. Those dealers held the same positions that Meech and Terry occupied more than a decade earlier. (Atlanta had known BMF only as the city's top players; thus Atlanta's lower-tier guys, while in awe of the BMF, had less personal connection to the crew.) The young Detroit dealers clashed over who would step into the Flenorys' void. It stood to reason that every Detroit dealer aspired to be the next Big Meech or Southwest T. But the battle to succeed BMF's top players was messy and unorganized. While the myth of BMF was still strong, the organization itself—the cocaine-processing labs and fleets of tricked-out limos and handsome stash houses and piles and piles and piles of cash—had withered away. BMF's army of couriers and distributors had fractured, and the lieutenants who'd directed them were AWOL. It was no surprise, then, that no successor emerged. There was no real infrastructure to inherit. One of the only tangible signs of the Flenorys' fading empire were three spray-painted letters—B-M-F—that graced the highway overpasses on Detroit's South Side.

Detroit was where Meech and Terry's cocaine enterprise started, and Detroit would be where it came to an end. By the fall of 2007, nearly all the defendants who'd been indicted along with the Flenorys had pleaded guilty. (Another twenty-three had been charged in a second Detroit indictment, most of whom eventually would plea as well.) Charles Flenory, Meech and Terry's father, fessed up to a money-laundering charge, and New York's Jacob "the Jeweler" Arabo admitted to lying to federal agents. Both men received less than three years in prison. Most everyone else received far stiffer sentences—the longest of which went to Meech's second-in-command Chad "J-Bo" Brown. J-Bo, who pleaded guilty in the summer of 2007, refused to cooperate with the feds. He got fifteen years. Ultimately, a mere five of the forty-plus defendants indicted with the Flenorys, including the brothers themselves, were still standing when the November 2007 trial date approached.

The trial, which was expected to last two months, would be complicated by the fact that Meech and Terry faced two different stacks of evidence—and planned on raising two, often contradictory, defenses. Unlike Terry, Meech hadn't been caught on a federal wiretap, nor had he been busted with an exorbitant amount of cash. Then there was the matter of witnesses. "Most of the witnesses are specifically aimed at either one brother or the other," Meech's attorneys wrote in a document filed weeks before the trial, "and very few are aimed at both." In fact, most of the witnesses that had been identified would be testifying against only one of the brothers. Judging from what had been divulged in the discovery phase of the case, witnesses against Terry were stacking up, and that didn't bode well for him. More than a half dozen of Terry's associates had pleaded guilty and cut deals, and that wasn't counting those who'd stepped up in other jurisdictions. Most significant, Terry's second-and third-in-command, Eric "Slim" Bivens and Arnold "A.R." Boyd, both agreed to take the stand against their former boss. So did a minimum of five of Terry's drivers, distributors, and money-launderers. But of everyone who agreed to cooperate, none—aside from "Doc" Marshall—appeared to have any substantial dirt on Meech. J-Bo, one of the few people under indictment who could provide real insight into Meech's operation, held his tongue. Ill would do the same. Yet there was still one defendant who could nail the feds' case against Meech. He hadn't cooperated yet, but he might find it worth his while. After all, he had more animosity toward Meech than anyone did. He also had more to gain than the other defendants, seeing as how he was facing a mandatory life sentence. By turning on his brother, Terry could save himself.

At the time, Meech didn't know about the feds' attempts to turn Terry against him. In fact, there was much that Meech and his attorneys didn't know about the government's case. Prosecutors successfully relied on a federal law that allows witnesses' statements and identities to remain a secret until the very eve of their testimony. As for everything else, the evidence kept rolling in. Less than two months before the trial, the government introduced a heap of new discovery: eight hundred pages of documents, five hundred pages of photographs, and thirty-three CDs of taped phone calls that both Meech and Terry made from jail. Meech's attorneys began sifting through the last round of what, in the end, amounted to a total fourteen thousand pages of discovery. It was the last step in a case for which the lawyers had spent two years preparing. Meech's attorneys appeared to be confident about their client's odds—right up until they finished sifting through the last stack of evidence.

Something in the pile of photos and pages of DEA notes and hours upon hours of tape recordings changed Meech's mind. Whether it was the culmination of so many small but damaging insinuations, the burden of his outsized lifestyle and inexplicable spending habits, or simply the fear of the unknown, Meech was no longer willing to risk it. He felt the hope of escaping the mandatory life sentence slip away. Less than a week before his trial was set to begin, he set his sights on a guilty plea. Only later would he learn that the government had tried to convince Terry to testify against him—and that Terry had refused.

By pleading guilty, Meech knew there was a good chance that he'd receive the sentence recommended by the feds: thirty years. Yet he held out hope that the judge would go as low as twenty, perhaps out of appreciation for sparing the government the time and expense of such a complicated trial. It was a calculated risk on Meech's part, but a worthwhile one. And he wanted to convince Terry that he should do the same.

The week before the trial, Meech's lawyers made an unusual though compelling request to the judge. They asked that the Flenory brothers be allowed to meet face-to-face. Meech wanted to talk Terry into pleading guilty. The judge agreed to the meeting, which would take place at the federal courthouse in downtown Detroit. It would be the first time the brothers spoke in nearly three years. If all went according to plan, Terry would accept the same deal as Meech.

But once the brothers were in the same room, it wouldn't be so simple as that. Apparently, Meech overestimated his diplomatic skills. Terry didn't take too kindly to his big brother's advice that he cop a plea. The peace talk quickly devolved into a shouting match. As assistant U.S. Attorney Dawn Ison later would say, the meeting between the Flenory brothers "was disastrous." Meech's attorneys agreed with her characterization. But they also believed Meech planted a seed in Terry's head. The following morning, Terry would stand before the judge and say he wasn't interested in pleading guilty; he was ready to go to trial. After he was escorted out of the courtroom, however, Terry would have second thoughts. He would ask to be allowed back in the courtroom. Like his brother before him, he would reach the conclusion that his best path was the one of least resistance.

For Meech, pleading guilty was easier. On the afternoon of November 19, 2007, he was led, shackled and smiling, down a long linoleum-tiled hallway. He passed through a set of double doors and was steered toward the defendant's table. The marshals uncuffed him and he slid into a chair. He glanced over his shoulder at the near-empty courtroom and paused on two familiar faces: Charles and Lucille. He locked eyes with his parents and flashed a wide grin. They nodded in return.

Before pivoting back to face the judge, Meech offered one last gesture of solidarity to the two people who'd seen him through it all: the years of yearning, the slow and steady hustle, the meteoric rise, the precipitous fall. He turned around in his chair as far as he could and gently, deliberately shook his fist. It was a message to his parents that it was he who'd triumphed over this situation, not the other way around. He'd known all along that none of it could last forever. The game, for him, had run its course. But for longer than most people could begin to imagine, the world had been his. And that was enough to make everything worth it.

EPILOGUE: 2008

Twenty sounds bad. But it's doable.
—DEMETRIUS "BIG MEECH" FLENORY

In a way, Big Meech believes his brother saved him from a lifetime behind bars. Sure, the feds had amassed more evidence against Terry Flenory—and perhaps without that evidence, Meech wouldn't have been busted when he was. But in the end, Terry stood his ground. For that, Meech remains grateful.

Cooped up in a suburban Detroit jail, pushing three years in lockup while awaiting his sentencing, Meech is quick to point to the deal the feds dangled in front of his brother. "He was offered twenty years to snitch on me," Meech says. "He didn't."

I don't even have the chance to ask if he was approached with a similar deal. "They didn't offer *me* that," he says, seated comfortably on the ledge opposite a glass partition. "They know that goes against everything I stand for." One thing does bother him, though: "He had a public defender," Meech says of Terry, with a laugh, "and he got the same deal I did."

As for the time he'll serve, he's banking on the judge's mercy. He doesn't even bring up the possibility of thirty years. "Twenty sounds bad," he says. "But it's doable." As long as he lands in a federal pen near Orlando or Atlanta, he'll be satisfied. He wants to be close to his friends and family. He wants to keep tabs on the progress of his son Demetrius Jr., the child of a girlfriend he met soon after moving to Atlanta—a woman with whom he maintained ties, despite the demise of their relationship. He also wants to make sure, somehow, that his parents will be okay. "The hardest part about this situation is my kids and my mother and father," he says. "I just hope to come home before they pass away."

Then there's his crew, the guys whom he believes will still stand up for him—even as their cases continue to unfurl in courts across the country. After all, he says, it was Terry's guys who turned on their boss. Not his. "You can tell, by my close circle, that everybody had the same values," he says. "No one who was close to me said anything." He brings up only one of them by name: "It's not like Bleu went against me."

No matter how things turn out at sentencing, he doesn't have much in the way of regrets. "At the end of the day, I had a beautiful life," he says. "I have a lot of memories. I wouldn't trade them for nothing."

In the fall of 2008, all of BMF's big-time players would see their cases come to close. By that point—with the bosses' guilty pleas behind them—crew members got a bit more relaxed about cutting deals with the government.

In Atlanta, a parade of BMF affiliates were sentenced in federal court. As the two-day hearing rolled along, it became apparent that of the ten BMF associates, only Deron "D-Shot" Hall had refused to talk to the feds.

Darryl "Poppa" Taylor, the first cousin of New York–based music mogul Sean "P. Diddy" Combs, provided substantial assistance in the government's investigation, in exchange for which he received a three-year sentence reduction. Poppa's superstar attorney, Steve Sadow, told the judge that his client—in addition to info he shared about Terry Flenory—might also be able to offer the government some insight into "activities going on in the Northeast."

Though he had faced ten years, Papa got seven.

None of the other deals that were cut that day were all that surprising, with one exception: Barima "Bleu DaVinci" McKnight. Bleu was sentenced to five years and four months—a punishment that was reduced, in part, for his willingness to cooperate with the feds.

Assistant U.S. attorney Robert McBurney told the court that Bleu, by debriefing "fully and truthfully" with the government, qualified for a federal "safety valve," which allows the judge to hand down a sentence that's lower than the mandatory minimum. By the time Bleu was debriefed, however, the government already had built most of its case against BMF. As Bleu's lawyer David MacKusick told the court, "He would have liked to cooperate if he could. But unfortunately, he did not really have any useful information."

A tearful Bleu then told the judge that he got involved in BMF's record label as a rapper—and took a detour into BMF's cocaine syndicate. "I didn't look at them as a big drug ring," Bleu said. "Demetrius did not show me that part of his world when I met him. I got into a big brother–little brother relationship with this guy. I came to know this man without even knowing the other side of his life. I did get in above my head. He ordered me to stay away from anything illegal that they were doing. And that's what I did."

Bleu wasn't the only rapper tied to BMF whose name came up in federal court that year. During the cocaine-conspiracy trial for Bleu's codefendant and Meech's third-in-command, Fleming "Ill" Daniels, another revelation concerning a rapper was made.

One of the witnesses who took the stand against Ill was Ralph "Ralphie" Simms, who'd been a regular at Meech's stash houses. Ralphie had been indicted the year before in a related federal drug case out of L.A., and he told the jury that in exchange for his truthful testimony against Ill, he hoped to receive a reduced sentence.

Ralphie said his job was to unload BMF's cocaine from the limos outfitted with secret compartments. He said he piled as many as a hundred bricks at a time in the basement of Space Mountain. And he said that on one occasion, in the fall of 2004, he was ordered by BMF managers Chad "J-Bo" Brown and Martez "Tito" Byrth to set aside multi-kilo shipments for two customers.

When U.S. attorney McBurney asked who those customers were, Ralphie gave two names: William "Doc" Marshall, who'd testified earlier in the trial, and "Jeezy."

"The musician named Young Jeezy?" McBurney asked.

"Yes," Simms answered.

Jeezy hasn't been charged with a crime in relation to Ralphie's allegation, and the Justice Department declined to comment on whether there's an open investigation into the rapper. Scott Leemon, the New York–based lawyer who represented Jeezy on weapons charges out of Miami in 2006 (charges that were later dropped), also declined comment.

As for Ill, he was convicted of a cocaine-conspiracy charge and sentenced to twenty years. Meanwhile, the murder case against him— the one stemming from the shooting death in the Velvet Room parking lot of Rashannibal "Prince" Drummond—was repeatedly postponed. Part of the delay had to do with Ill's lawyer recusing himself from the case—after NFL star Adam "Pacman" Jones, a friend of Ill's who'd been covering his attorney fees, quit making the payments.

On September 12, 2008, inside a small courtroom on the second floor of the Theodore Levine federal courthouse in downtown

Detroit, an anxious crowd gathered to witness the symbolic end of the government's investigation into the Black Mafia Family.

One of the bailiffs barked a succinct order. "No outbursts." A moment later, a team of U.S. marshals escorted into the courtroom a slender man gazing straight ahead through rimless glasses. "That's your Uncle T," one of the onlookers, Lucille Flenory, whispered to her grandson, sitting next to her. The bespectacled man, Lucille's son, was hardly recognizable as he made his way to the defense table. From the time he was locked up three years ago, Terry "Southwest T" Flenory had lost close to a hundred pounds.

Shuffling close behind him, in a matching orange jumpsuit, was Terry's older brother. Meech's hair was pulled back in a ponytail, and the tattooed letters BMF peeked above his collar on the left side of his neck. He scanned the courtroom, turned to his supporters, and flashed a wide smile.

With the two Flenory brothers seated in front of him, U.S. District Court Judge Avern Cohn called the sentencing hearing to order. He asked to hear from Terry first. The fallen kingpin spoke in a quiet, steady voice. He said he was sorry he wasted the feds' time. "I'd like to apologize to the government for my ignorance and for them having to spend countless hours working this case," he said. "I'd like to apologize to the many families hurt by the result of this ignorance."

Judge Cohn's response was sharp: "I think you're a very lucky man that it took the government this long to build a case against you." He sentenced Terry to thirty years.

As Terry was cuffed and led out of the courtroom, Meech and his attorneys were asked to approach the bench. They were hopeful that the judge would treat them differently. Meech's Atlanta-based lawyer, Drew Findling, reminded the judge that Meech had requested a meeting with Terry shortly after Meech decided to enter a guilty plea. During the meeting, Meech advised his brother to do the same—an act that would spare the government a lengthy, expensive trial.

Assistant U.S. attorney Dawn Ison then piped up that Meech shouldn't be credited for Terry's contrition. Ison said it wasn't Meech who persuaded Terry to plea. She said it was Terry's father, Charles Flenory, who was about to start on a short prison stint of his own.

When it came time for Meech to address the judge, he, too, apologized. "I don't think 'I'm sorry' is really the right words to say, because most people is only sorry they get caught. So I just ask that you show me as much leniency as possible, so that I can get on and do my time."

The judge quickly gave Meech the same sentence he'd handed Terry: thirty years. Under current law, Meech will be at least sixty-one, and Terry fifty-nine, when they're released from prison.

ENDNOTES

PROLOGUE

"As bad as they wanted me, there was no winning." Interview with Demetrius "Big Meech" Flenory, March 4, 2008.

ONE: CHAOS

"Everybody moves like brothers." Demetrius Flenory, in vol. 8 of DVD magazine *Smack*, January 2005: "Everybody move like brothers, and then everybody is from different places—Milwaukee, St. Louis, Detroit, Texas, Atlanta, Cali. You know what I'm saying? We got people from everywhere in our mob. Everybody move as one."

"The big one." Buckhead resident, quoted in a Nov. 12, 2003, *Atlanta Journal-Constitution* article: "Several years ago, I was talking to detectives and officers and they said there was going to be, quote, 'the big one.' This, I guess, you would call a big one."

Confrontation in the club. (a) Atlanta Police Investigator Louis Torres described the incident in an affidavit filed in Fulton County, Ga., Superior Court. (b) A Nov. 13, 2003, *Atlanta Journal-Constitution* article states: "Anthony 'Wolf' Jones confronted his longtime girlfriend because she had arrived with a group of men for 'hip-hop night' at Chaos." (c) According to a May 2006 *Vibe* story, "Mo' Money, Mo' Problems,"

"Wolf staggered through the BMF-heavy crowd inside the club and began chatting up an ex-girlfriend, a stripper who had been partying with Meech that night. When Wolf groped her in full view of the other clubgoers, Meech warned him to back off, and Wolf responded by choking her." (d) Meech Flenory described the confrontation similarly during a March 2008 interview.

Searching the White House. (a) *Affidavit and Application for a Search Warrant for 6086 Belair Lake Drive, Lithonia, Ga.; Return of Search Warrant and Inventory*, Magistrate Court of DeKalb County, No. 03-W-05357. (b) *U.S. v. Terry Flenory, et al*, United States District Court, Eastern District of Michigan, No. 05-CR-80955.

T-Stuck's storied past. U.S. v. Thelmon Stuckey, United States Court of Appeals for the Sixth District, No. 97-CR-80625.

Calling for backup. An account of Anthony "Wolf" Jones' call to his friend was published in the May 2006 issue of *Vibe*: "Outside Chaos, the humiliated thug called for backup. Minutes later, Lamont Girdy, a boyhood friend from the Bronx, arrived at the scene."

The witness. (a) At a Nov. 26, 2003, hearing in Superior Court of Fulton County, Ga., Atlanta Police Investigator J. K. Brown testified that a call from a woman was transferred from 911 to him. (b) According to an affidavit filed in Fulton County Superior Court by Atlanta Police Investigator Torres, "A witness who knows [Flenory] stated that she saw him with a gun, running after Girdy and Jones and shooting at them. Both Girdy and Jones were also shooting." (c) In a November 2006 interview, Flenory's attorney, Drew Findling, said of the witness: "There was never a name, [and there was] no evidence that there was anybody accompanying her to corroborate her presence there. The whole thing was just comical."

The inner workings of XQuisite Empire. (a) *U.S. v. William Marshall, et al*, United States District Court, Northern District of Georgia, No. 06-CR-306. (b) *U.S. v. Dionne Beverly, et al*, United States District Court, Northern District of Georgia, No. 07-CR-233.

TWO: THE FLENORY BROTHERS

Melvin and "Playboy" Sparks. Melvin Sparks was not charged with a crime in relation to the BMF investigation. His brother, Calvin "Playboy" Sparks, pleaded guilty to misprision of a felony, for falsely denying to federal officers his knowledge of the Flenory brothers' cocaine enterprise.

Details of the brothers' formative years. (a) *U.S. v. Terry Flenory, et al*, United States District Court, Eastern District of Michigan, No. 05-CR-80955. (b) Interviews with Demetrius Flenory, March 4 and March 5, 2008.

Sin City Mafia's connection to BMF. U.S. v. Tremayne Graham, et al, United States District Court, District of South Carolina, No. 03-CR-1092.

THREE: PUSHING JEEZY
The race to legitimatize. Demetrius Flenory described his aspirations during a March 2008 interview.

"We can do all kinds of things if we start from Bleu DaVinci." Meech, as quoted in DVD magazine *The Raw Report,* vol. 2, released in October 2004.

BMF Entertainment enters the music scene. Meech's push to legitimize BMF is chronicled in DVD magazines *Smack,* vol. 8, and *The Raw Report,* vol. 2.

Jeezy rising from the streets. DVD magazine *The Raw Report,* "Trap or Die."

Pushing Jeezy. (a) *The Raw Report*'s "Trap or Die." (b) Interview with Demetrius "Big Meech" Flenory, March 5, 2008.

Surveilling Meech's birhtday party. From testimony offered in the case *U.S. v. Dionne Beverly, et al,* United States District Court, Northern District of Georgia, No. 07-CR-233.

Terry's wiretap. U.S. v. Terry Flenory, et al, United States District Court, Eastern District of Michigan, No. 05-CR-80955.

A drug dealer advertising on a billboard? Interviews with Fulton County Assistant District Attorney Rand Csehy, October 2006 and March 2008.

FOUR: FALLEN PRINCE
Prince's backstory. Interviews with Debbie Morgan, August 2004, January 2005, October 2006, and March 2008.

The Velvet Room incident. State of Georgia v. Fleming Daniels, Fulton County, Ga., Superior Court, No. 07-SC-56450.

FIVE: STUPID AND THE GIRL
Scott and Kiki's crew. (a) *U.S. v. Tremayne Graham, et al,* United States District Court, District of South Carolina, No. 03-CR-1092. (b) *U.S. v. Richard Garrett,* United States District Court, District of South Carolina, No. 06-CR-986.

"There is so much that I would like to say about my daughter." Interview with Katie Carter, May 2007.

NBA All-Star shooting. (a) *U.S. v. Tremayne Graham, et al*, United States District Court, District of South Carolina, No. 03-CR-1092. (b) From the Feb. 11, 2001, *Washington Post*, story, "Shots ring amid crowd in Dupont, killing man."

Playboy beats his charge. From the Aug. 29, 2001, *Washington Post* story, "Charge is dropped in slaying on NBA weekend."

"We must let the legal system run its course." Atlanta Mayor Shirley Franklin, in an April 27, 2004, Associated Press story.

"He is the mayor's former son-in-law." Mayor Franklin's aide, speaking to the Associated Press, June 18, 2005.

SIX: SPACE MOUNTAIN

O-Dog's wiretap. *State of Georgia v. Omari McCree, et al*, Superior Court of Fulton County, Ga., No. 05-SC-31397.

Meech's roadblock arrest. *State of Georgia v. Demetrius Flenory*, Superior Court of DeKalb County, Ga., No. 05-CR-3947.

Closing the Gate. *U.S. v. Dionne Beverly, et al*, United States District Court, Northern District of Georgia, No. 07-CR-233.

Searching Space Mountain. (a) *Affidavit and Application for a Search Warrant for 4363 Mount Paran Road*: Fulton County, Ga., Superior Court, Nov. 23, 2004. (b) *U.S. v. Dionne Beverly, et al*, United States District Court, Northern District of Georgia, No. 07-CR-233.

Climbing the food chain to get to O-Dog. (a) *State of Georgia v. Omari McCree, et al*, Superior Court of Fulton County, Ga., No. 05-SC-31397. (b) Interviews with Fulton County Assistant District Attorney Rand Csehy, October 2006 and March 2008.

SEVEN: THE BOUNTY HUNTER

Kiki's plan. *U.S. v. Tremayne Graham, et al*, United States District Court, District of South Carolina, No. 03-CR-1092.

"We have no suspect, no motive and no arrest at this time." From the Sept. 7, 2004, *Atlanta Journal-Constitution* story, "Pair slain in home invasion."

Hiring the bounty hunter. (a) *U.S. v. Tremayne Graham, et al*, United States District Court, District of South Carolina, No. 03-CR-1092. (b) *Free at Last Bail Bonds v. Kai Franklin Graham*, United States Bankruptcy Court for the Northern District of Georgia, No. 05-6585.

Kai's money woes. (a) United States Bankruptcy Court for the Northern District of Georgia, No. 05-91520. (b) *U.S. v. Tremayne Graham, et al*, United States District Court, District of South Carolina, No. 03-CR-1092. (c) *Franklin & Wilson Airport Concessions, debtor,* United States Bankruptcy Court for the Northern District of Georgia, No. 06-69773. (d) *U.S. v. Kai Franklin Graham*, United States District Court, District of South Carolina, No. 07-CR-517.

Firing on the marshals. *U.S. v. Tremayne Graham, et al*, United States District Court, District of South Carolina, No. 03-CR-1092.

Calling "Magic" for backup. *U.S. v. Deron Gatling, et al*, United States District Court, District of Missouri, No. 04-CR-1499.

"Do I believe that Tremayne Graham runs his mouth to Scott King about how much influence he has? Yes." Interviews with assistant U.S. Attorney Mark Moore, April 2007, July 2007, and December 2007.

EIGHT: STAY STRAPPED

The Space Mountain warrant. (a) *Affidavit and Application for a Search Warrant for 4363 Mount Paran Road*: Fulton County, Ga., Superior Court, Nov. 23, 2004. (b) *U.S. v. Dionne Beverly, et al*, United States District Court, Northern District of Georgia, No. 07-CR-233.

"We appreciate Miami. We appreciate the hospitality." Ill, in the January 2005 DVD magazine *Smack*, vol. 8.

"I don't see no one to come after us, either. None. Nobody will ever do this again." Meech, in DVD magazine *Smack*, vol. 8.

"Two hundred thousand mixtapes later." DVD magazine *The Raw Report*, "Trap or Die."

Jeezy's praise. (a) *The Montgomery Advertiser*, March 17, 2005. (b) *The New York Times*, April 24, 2005. (c) *The Macon Telegraph*, May 6, 2005.

"When my album comes out, all the dots will connect." Jeezy, quoted March 12, 2005, in *Billboard*.

The Gucci–Jeezy beef. (a) "At the video shoot of Gucci Mane's 'Icy,'" April 14, 2005, *Atlanta Journal-Constitution*. (b) "Big Cat CEO Jacob York talks Gucci Mane arrest, says hip-hop cops gathering info," July 25, 2005, AllHipHop.com. (c) Jeezy's July 2005 interview with AllHipHop.com. (d) Interviews with attorneys Dennis Scheib and Ash Joshi, November 2006.

Club Money's George "G. Money" Willis. (a) "The Year of Young Jeezy," Jan. 1, 2006, *The Macon Telegraph.* (b) "Record label offering reward in shooting death of Macon rapper," May 24, 2005, *The Macon Telegraph.*

Pookie Loc's death. (a) DeKalb County, Ga., Department of Public Safety incident report, No. 05-064545. (b) "Record label offering reward in shooting death of Macon rapper," May 24, 2005, *The Macon Telegraph.* (c) "Slain rapper was no stranger to law enforcement," May 26, 2005, *Atlanta Journal-Constitution.*

"I know they did it." Radric "Gucci Mane" Davis, quoted by AllHipHop.com.

Gucci's arrest. (a) "Rapper wanted in slaying turns self in," May 20, 2005, *Atlanta Journal-Constitution.* (b) "Rapper in jail for weekend," May 21, 2005. *Atlanta Journal-Constitution.*

"They put out a contract on him." Dennis Scheib, Gucci's attorney, quoted May 25, 2005 in the *Atlanta Journal-Constitution* story "Rapper facing murder charge freed from jail."

"Here's the situation: Five guys came in. They were BMF." Interviews with attorney Dennis Scheib, November 2006.

History of Loccish Lifestyle. Interviews with Carlos "Low Down" Rhodes, November 2006.

The birthday party stabbings. State of Georgia v. Marque Keimon Dixson, Superior Court of Fulton County, Ga., No. 05-SC-34097.

NINE: THE GATE
Catching O-Dog. (a) *State of Georgia v. Omari McCree, et al,* Superior Court of Fulton County, Ga., No. 05-SC-31397. (b) Interviews with Fulton County Assistant District Attorney Rand Csehy, October 2006 and March 2008.

"Dude is Meech." From the statement given by Omari in the investigation *State of Georgia v. Omari McCree, et al,* Superior Court of Fulton County, Ga., No. 05-SC-31397.

Catching Kiki and his crew. (a) *U.S. v. Tremayne Graham, et al,* United States District Court, District of South Carolina, No. 03-CR-1092. (b) *Free at Last Bail Bonds v. Kai Franklin Graham,* United States Bankruptcy Court for the Northern District of Georgia, No. 05-6585. (b) *U.S. v. Ernest Watkins,* U.S. District Court, District of South Carolina, No. 0-962.

Catching Soup. (a) *U.S. v. Jamad Ali,* U.S. District Court, Middle District of Florida, No. 02-115. (b) *Affidavit in Support of a Search Warrant,* filed June 30, 2005, in Essex

County, N.J. (c) *U.S. v. Jamad Ali*, U.S. District Court, District of New Jersey, No. 05-906. (d) *U.S. v. Tremayne Graham, et al*, United States District Court, District of South Carolina, No. 03-CR-1092.

TEN: THE GAME DON'T STOP

The traffic stop. (a) *U.S. v. Terry Flenory, et al*, United States District Court, Eastern District of Michigan, No. 05-CR-80955. (b) *U.S. v. Dionne Beverly, et al*, United States District Court, Northern District of Georgia, No. 07-CR-233.

"A ruthlessness no one can touch and a weariness no one can cure." From the Dec. 25, 2005, *New York Times* story, "The year's best albums and songs."

Jeezy climbs the charts. From the Oct. 21, 2005, Billboardmonitor.com story, "Jeezy's 'Survivor' story ends at No. 1."

Closing in on Meech. (a) *Affidavit for a search warrant for 5173 Brandywine Lane, Frisco, Texas*, filed Oct. 20, 2005, in Collins County, Texas, Magistrate Court. (b) *Affidavit for a search warrant for 5173 Brandywine Lane, Frisco, Texas*, filed Oct. 20, 2005, in United States District Court, Eastern District of Texas, No. 05-M-166. (c) *U.S. v. Demetrius Flenory*, United States District Court, Eastern District of Texas, No. 05-213.

Closing in on Terry. *Terry Flenory, et al*, United States District Court, Eastern District of Michigan, No. 05-CR-80955.

Tonesa Welch. Welch, who was charged with conspiracy to distribute cocaine and to launder money, ultimately pleaded guilty only to the money-laundering charge.

ELEVEN: BREAKING THE CODE

Tailing Doc. (a) *U.S. v. Dionne Beverly, et al*, United States District Court, Northern District of Georgia, No. 07-CR-233. (b) *U.S. v. William Marshall, et al*, United States District Court, Middle District of Florida, No. 05-CR-188.

Disenchantment with the BMF investigation. Interviews with Fulton County Assistant District Attorney Rand Csehy, October 2006 and March 2008.

O-Dog gets cold feet. State of Georgia v. Omari McCree, et al, Superior Court of Fulton County, Ga., No. 05-SC-31397.

Terry's guys talk. U.S. v. Terry Flenory, et al, United States District Court, Eastern District of Michigan, No. 05-CR-80955.

"This is probably the highest-volume drug conspiracy in this district, ever." Assistant U.S. Attroney Dawn Ison, at a January 2005 hearing for the case *U.S. v. Terry*

Flenory, et al, United States District Court, Eastern District of Michigan, No. 05-CR-80955.

Doc's debriefings. (a) *U.S. v. William Marshall, et al*, United States District Court, Middle District of Florida, No. 05-CR-188. (b) *U.S. v. Dionne Beverly, et al*, United States District Court, Northern District of Georgia, No. 07-CR-233. (c) *Terry Flenory, et al*, United States District Court, Eastern District of Michigan, No. 05-CR-80955. (d) *State of Georgia v. Fleming Daniels*, Fulton County, Ga., Superior Court, No. 07-SC-56450.

Death of Baby Bleu. (a) Atlanta Police Department incident report, No. 06-068-0226. (b) *State of Georgia v. Marque Keimon Dixson*, Superior Court of Fulton County, Ga., No. 05-SC-34097.

Kiki's deception. *U.S. v. Tremayne Graham, et al*, United States District Court, District of South Carolina, No. 03-CR-1092.

Catching Jacob. *U.S. v. Terry Flenory, et al*, United States District Court, Eastern District of Michigan, No. 05-CR-80955.

"Ill goes 'bang, bang, bang.'" Statement of William "Doc" Marshall, *State of Georgia v. Fleming Daniels*, Fulton County, Ga., Superior Court, No. 07-SC-56450.

Two mothers' grief. (a) Interviews with Debbie Morgan, August 2004, January 2005, October 2006, and March 2008. (b) Interview with Katie Carter, May 2007.

Sin City's sentencing's. *U.S. v. Tremayne Graham, et al*, United States District Court, District of South Carolina, No. 03-CR-1092.

The case against Ernest. *U.S. v. Ernest Watkins*, U.S. District Court, District of South Carolina, No. 0-962.

Kai's guilty plea. *U.S. v. Kai Franklin Graham*, United States District Court, District of South Carolina, No. 07-CR-517.

"Hopefully, this will reverberate throughout the department." From the April 27, 2007, *Atlanta Journal-Constitution* story, "Deadly Deception: Two Atlanta cops plead guilty in woman's death, blame pressure from police brass."

TWELVE: THE EVIDENCE

Atlanta and L.A. indictments. (a) *U.S. v. Dionne Beverly, et al*, United States District Court, Northern District of Georgia, No. 07-CR-233. (b) *U.S. v. Kenyan Terrance Payne, Sr., et al*, United States District Court, Central District of California, No. 07-CR-1215.

Atlanta's changing cocaine landscape. (a) Interview with Fulton County Assistant District Attorney Rand Csehy, March 2008. (b) Interview with Jack Killorin, director of the Atlanta branch of the U.S. High Intensity Drug Trafficking Area task force, July 2008.

"Drug dealers aren't that stupid." From the Oct. 14, 2007, *Atlanta Journal-Constitution* story, "Drug dealers beware: After hands-off year in wake of botched raid, APD's reborn narcotics squad is ready to roll."

"Most of the witnesses are specifically aimed at either one brother or the other." Drew Findling, in a court document filed in *U.S. v. Terry Flenory, et al*, United States District Court, Eastern District of Michigan, No. 05-CR-80955.

Change of heart. (a) *U.S. v. Terry Flenory, et al*, United States District Court, Eastern District of Michigan, No. 05-CR-80955. (b) Interview with Demetrius "Big Meech" Flenory, March 5, 2008.

The brother meet. (a) *U.S. v. Terry Flenory, et al*, United States District Court, Eastern District of Michigan, No. 05-CR-80955. (b) Interview with Demetrius "Big Meech" Flenory, March 5, 2008.

EPILOGUE

"It's not like Bleu went against me." Interview with Demetrius "Big Meech" Flenory, March 5, 2008.

Atlanta sentencings. *U.S. v. Dionne Beverly, et al,* United States District Court, Northern District of Georgia, No. 07-CR-233.

Bleu's debriefing. *U.S. v. Dionne Beverly, et al,* United States District Court, Northern District of Georgia, No. 07-CR-233.

Allegation against Jeezy. Trial of Fleming "Ill" Daniels, June 12, 2008, *U.S. v. Dionne Beverly, et al,* United States District Court, Northern District of Georgia, No. 07-CR-233.

The Flenorys' sentencings. Sept. 12, 2008 sentencing hearing, *U.S. v. Dionne Beverly, et al,* United States District Court, Northern District of Georgia, No. 07-CR-233.

INDEX

IRS investigation into, 214, 226
Jeezy and profile of, 68
loyalty to, 45, 246
as medallion, 21, 52–54, 55
Morgan offer by, 83, 248
myth of, 73, 214, 267
partying by, 52, 64, 69, 113, 161, 166, 179–80, 191, 215, 223
Pookie Loc murder and, 178–79
publicity by, 67, 71, 73, 162, 228, 245, 264
raining cash by, 67
rumors about, 71–72
Sin City Mafia alliance with, 89
St. Louis cell for, 43, 57–58, 132, 217, 230, 264
stash houses of, 47, 50, 70–71, 114, 125, 127, 138, 139–41, 150–51, 161–62, 191–92, 216, 223, 225, 232, 233, 264, 267, 274
succession to, 267
surveillance of, 11, 23, 100, 117–21, 124–26, 133–35, 138, 156, 159, 188, 192–93, 198–99, 203, 214
as tattoo, 16, 45, 52–53, 275
wiretapping of, 11, 58, 73–74, 98, 117–18
"Blank." *See* Johnson, Benjamin
Blazin' Saddles (club), 176
"Bleu DaVinci." *See* McKnight, Barima
bling
    Arabo for, 53–54, 56, 172, 208–9, 226
    "icy" as, 172
    for Jeezy video shoot, 207–9
    for rappers, 169–70
    transportation of, 101–2, 106, 147, 148, 207, 237, 254
Blood Raw (rappers), 172
Bloods (gang), 52
the Bluffs, drug trade in, 21, 50, 116–17, 260
BMF. *See* Black Mafia Family
BMF Entertainment
    billboards for, 71, 73, 162, 228, 264

Bleu DaVinci for, 61–65, 67, 69, 71, 73, 84, 97, 162–67, 180, 213, 227–29, 245, 264–65, 273
    The Juice by, 213, 245
    McKnight running of, 264–65
    by Meech, 62–63, 97, 227
    at Velvet Room, 84
    "We Still Here" by, 61, 67, 69, 97, 163–67, 180
bodyguards
    for Meech, 5
    for "P. Diddy," 8, 224
Bogard Records, 97, 150. *See also* Platinum Recording
bonding company, 103–5, 124, 145–46, 151, 152, 153–54, 192–98, 227–31, 259. *See also* Free at Last Bail Bonds
Boom, Benny, 61
Boulevard, in Atlanta, 50, 65–66, 116–17, 131–32, 185–86, 265
Boyd, Arnold ("A. R.")
    as government witness, 226, 233, 268
    indictment of, 218
    in Terry's crew, 42, 54, 55–56, 96, 150, 218, 226
    at White House, 55, 226–27
Boyz N Da Hood, Jeezy and, 66
Brantley, Damonne, 23
Bridge, John, 154, 156, 196
Britt, Walter, 140–41, 190
Brown, Bobby, 179–83, 224, 234
Brown, Chad ("J-Bo")
    at Babylon, 215
    birthday party for, 164–65
    code of silence by, 268
    Derrek Williams as alias for, 141
    Doc's negotiations with, 44
    docu-video with, 163–67
    at the Gate, 70–71, 140, 191–92, 225
    indictment for, 244
    as Meech's second-in-command, 41, 44, 60, 64, 125, 131, 219, 225, 227, 233, 234, 247, 274

drug, ecstasy as, 6, 67–68, 216
Drug Enforcement Administration
    (DEA)
  arrests by, 216–17
  B. Burns in, 73
  Harvey as investigator under, 11, 69,
    73, 115, 117, 159, 221, 227, 231,
    241, 246, 248
  information for, 3
  investigation of BMF by, 214–15
  Jacob & Co. and, 210–12, 243
  at the Jump, 150–51
  Meech investigation of, 13, 214–15
  raid/arrest of Terry by, 151, 216–17
  search warrant by, 215
  surveillance by, 11, 215
  wiretapping by, 11, 58
drug trade, American dream and, 46–47
drugs. See also cocaine; Graham Method
  from Colombia, 38, 116
  investment in, 44
  market for, 21
  from Mexico, 28, 37, 38, 42–43, 47,
    100, 116, 266
  through UPS, 102–3, 105
Drummond, Raschaka ("Tattoo")
  police statement by, 83, 84
  at Velvet Room, 77–83
Drummond, Rashannibal ("Prince")
  friends of, 78
  murder of, 79–82, 224, 248
  partying by, 75
Drummond, Rasheym ("Sheym"), 77,
    249
"D-Shot." See Hall, Deron
dub, 76
Dupri, Jermaine, 56

"E." See Watkins, Ernest
E-40 (rapper), 61
ecstasy, 6, 67–68, 216
the Elevator, as stash house, 71, 114, 125,
    127, 191, 223, 225, 233, 264

Ellerbee, Demetrius ("Kinky B"),
    171–72, 176–77
Eminem (rapper), 8

Fabolous (rapper), 4, 61, 180–81
FBI. See Federal Bureau of Investigation
Federal Bureau of Investigation (FBI),
    214
Federation drug cartel, 266
Feinberg, James, 245, 263
"50 Cent" (rapper), 20, 43, 53. See also
    Guerville, Innocent
Findling, Drew, 227–28, 245, 263, 275
First Base, 100, 102, 150, 155, 156–57,
    192–93, 201–2
Fishman, Steve, 245
Flenory, Charles ("Pops"), 33–36, 55,
    96, 244–45, 267, 270, 276
Flenory, Demetrius ("Big Meech")
  aliases of, 13, 36, 51–52, 113–14, 229
  ankle monitor for, 64, 68, 228, 230
  appearance of, 6, 50
  arrests of, 1–4, 36, 51–52, 57, 64, 68,
    111–13, 124, 191, 215–17
  Babylon by, 131, 215
  billboards by, 71, 73, 162, 228, 264
  blunt use by, 16, 165, 215
  BMF Entertainment by, 61–65, 67,
    69, 71, 73, 84, 97, 162–67, 180, 213,
    227–29, 245, 264–65, 273
  bodyguards for, 5
  bond for, 124, 227–31
  Carothers as alias for, 51, 52, 113–14
  cars for, 29, 66, 215, 216, 220, 232
  cell phone violation by, 219
  Chaos shooting of, 8, 17–19, 24–25,
    64, 82, 162, 207, 215, 222, 246–48,
    264
  charges against, 217
  as cocaine boss, 191
  as Combs's friend, 44, 47, 207
  crew for, 2–3, 6, 8, 41–42, 49, 69, 70,
    272

Graham, Kai Franklin. *See also* Graham,
   Tremayne
  bankruptcy by, 152–53, 237, 259
  bond by, 103–5, 145–46, 153
  divorce by, 151, 237
  finances for, 95–96, 237, 255
  guilty plea by, 258–59
  job for, 95, 237
  "Kai phone" for, 146, 241
  as Kiki's girlfriend, 92
  Kiki's son and, 146, 149, 255
  lawsuit against, 259
  marriage to Kiki, 94
  search warrant for home of, 103–4
  tax evasion by, 258–59
Graham, Tremayne ("Kiki")
  arrest of, 200–201, 219
  bond for, 104–5, 145, 151, 153
  bounty hunter for, 146, 152, 192–98,
   236
  Demetrius Jr. and, 146, 149, 255, 272
  "E" as associate of, 105, 145
  federal drug trial for, 144–45
  404 Motorsports by, 23, 55–56, 57,
   94, 95–96, 207, 227, 244, 253
  as fugitive, 86–87, 145–47, 237, 253,
   255
  Graham Method by, 101–3, 105, 147,
   241–42
  guilty plea by, 236–39, 242, 251
  Hack as threat to, 106–7, 252
  house arrest for, 144–45, 254
  indictment of, 104, 201
  interrogation of, 236–37
  legal expenses for, 105–6
  legitimization by, 93–94
  Mookie and, 148, 155–56, 254
  police protection for, 143, 146
  polygraph test for, 239–40, 251
  search warrant for, 103–4
  sentencing for, 251, 257
  Sin City Mafia and, 90
  son of, 146, 149, 255

  stash house for, 88
  testimony by, 238–39, 256
  at Third Base, 145–46, 149, 196
  threat by, 254, 256
  wife of, 92, 94, 95–96, 103–5,
   145–46, 148, 149, 151–53, 237, 255
Graham Method, 101–3, 105, 147,
  241–42. *See also* Graham,
  Tremayne; transportation, of
  cocaine/money/bling
Green, Michael ("Freak"), 43, 55, 232
Greene, Jennifer, 152
"Gucci Mane." *See* Davis, Radric
Guerville, Innocent ("50 Cent"), 20,
  43, 53

"Hack." *See* Hackett, Ulysses
Hackett, Ulysses ("Hack"; "Stupid")
  as drug supplier, 88
  indictment of, 98, 201
  interrogation of, 236
  murder of, 109–10, 134, 143–44, 147,
   152, 205, 236, 238, 239, 241, 247,
   252–56, 260
  as threat, 106–7, 252
Hall, Cleveland, 181–84, 234
Hall, Deron ("D-Shot"), 82, 247, 264,
  272
Harris, Michael ("Playboy")
  D.C. shooting by, 91–92, 202
  murder by, 159
Harvey, Jack
  as DEA investigator, 11, 69, 73, 115,
   117, 159, 221, 227, 231, 241, 246,
   248
  search warrant for Kiki by, 103–4
  at Space Mountain, 141
  Stuckey arrest by, 14
  White House search by, 20
Hayes, Jabari
  drug arrest of, 29–30
  indictment of, 218
  police stop by, 26–29

Herlong, Henry, 254–57
Hewitt, Hamza, 113
HIDTA. *See* High Intensity Drug
    Trafficking Area task forces
High Intensity Drug Trafficking Area
    task forces (HIDTA)
    APD and, 122
    Burns and, 190
    Csehy and, 117, 120, 135–36
    equipment for, 115–16
    Leahr search warrant by, 140
    McCree search warrant by, 189–90
    responsibility of, 115
    Smurf investigation by, 117–19
    wiretap by, 123–24, 188
Hight, Ameen ("Bull"), 19, 42, 247
hip-hop
    in Atlanta, 49–50
    blame on, 7
    Chaos for, 8, 17
    Club 112 for, 23
    East *v.* West Coast, 8
    musical influences on, 76
    promotion of, 9
    Puritan Records for, 13
    stars in, 4
Hitsville USA, 33
the Horse Ranch, as stash house, 71
Hoskins, Charmela, 117, 118, 122, 188
Hoskins, Decarlo, 119–23, 129, 132–33,
    188
Houston, Whitney, 179
Howard, Paul, 72, 117

"Icy" (Gucci Mane, Jeezy), 170–71, 172,
    177
"Ill." *See* Daniels, Fleming
informant
    for federal government, 1
    information from, 1–3, 52
    on Meech, 12–13, 51–52, 225–26
    Omari as, 225–26
    relationship with, 12

on Smurf, 117
    Walker as, 52
inmate, privileges for, 1–2
Internal Revenue Service (IRS)
    BMF investigation by, 214, 226
    Form 8300 for, 45, 53–54, 210, 244
    investigation by, 98, 214
    Kai's evasion of, 258–59
    Terry's circumvention of, 226
IRS. *See* Internal Revenue Service
Ison, Dawn, 228–30, 269, 276
Iverson, Allen, 168
Ivory, Ronald. *See* Flenory, Demetrius

Jackson, Maynard, 93
Jacob & Co. *See also* Arabo, Jacob
    for celebrity jewelry, 53–54, 56, 172,
        208–9
    DEA visit to, 210–12, 243
    search warrant for, 242–44
"Jacob the Jeweler." *See* Arabo, Jacob
Jahmar (cousin of Prince)
    police statement by, 83, 84
    at Velvet Room, 78–83
Jameel (friend of Prince), 78–83
Jay-Z, 53
Jazzy T's (club), 113
"J-Bo." *See* Brown, Chad
jealousy
    between crews, 2, 3
    between Wolf and Meech, 10
Jeezy. *See* Jenkins, Jay
Jenkins, Jay ("Young Jeezy")
    "Air Forces" by, 66
    as authentic, 168–69
    Bad Boy Records signing of, 66, 207
    bling for video shoot for, 207–9
    Boyz N Da Hood and, 66
    car for, 127–28
    cocaine distribution by, 139, 274
    CTE by, 48–49, 65, 66, 171, 176–77
    Def Jam signing of, 66, 207
    ghetto life by, 170

racism, in Atlanta, 7

Racketeer Influenced and Corrupt Organizations (RICO), 217–18

Radio Monitor. *See Billboard*

Rajaee, Jay, 101, 103, 236–38, 241

"Ralphie." *See* Simms, Ralph

rap
    in Buckhead, 7, 49–50, 263–64
    lyrics for, 14
    mixtapes for, 48–49, 65, 66, 173
    superstars of, 1–2, 3

Rap City (BET), 177

reggae, 76

rep, street, 2

Rhodes, Carlos ("Low Down"), 174, 179

Rich, Gary. *See* Rivera, Eric

RICO. *See* Racketeer Influenced and Corrupt Organizations

"Ridin' High" (Loccish Lifestyle), 174–75

Rivera, Eric ("Mookie")
    alias of, 194, 197
    arrest of, 193, 237
    bounty hunter and, 156
    as courier, 102, 105, 144, 147, 193–94, 237, 254
    debt by, to J-Rock, 147–48
    J-Rock and, 147–48
    Kiki and, 148, 155–56, 254
    search warrant for, 194
    sentencing for, 251, 255
    testimony by, 237–38, 251, 256
    as working for Kiki, 148, 155–56

"Riz." *See* Girdy, Lamont

"Rosa Parks" (OutKast), 49

Rosales, Raul, 159

"Round 1" (Gucci), 173

Sadow, Steve, 231, 273

Santos, Ricardo, 113–14

Scarface, 20, 71, 142

Scheib, Dennis, 178

search warrant
    APD for, 260–61, 265–66
    for Doc's home, 22
    for Graham home, 103–4
    by HIDTA, 140, 189–90
    for Jacob & Co., 242–44
    for Mookie, 194
    for Space Mountain, 140–41, 161–62, 216
    for White House, 16, 20, 22, 57, 140, 222
    for XQuisite Empire, 22, 73

Seville, Rico. *See* Flenory, Demetrius ("Big Meech")

Shakur, Tupac, 20, 173

Shep (Terry's friend), 59

"Sheym." *See* Drummond, Rasheym

Short, Terrance ("Texas Cuz"), 43, 55, 226, 232

"Shyne." *See* Barrow, Jamal

silence, code of, 82, 115, 224, 228, 265, 268, 272

Simmons, Russell, 30. *See also* Def Jam

Simms, Ralph ("Ralphie"), 139–40, 141–42, 274

Simpson, Jessica, 53

Sin City Mafia
    BMF alliance with, 89
    crew of, 90
    defections from, to BMF, 90
    by J-Rock, 47–48, 89, 219
    Kiki and, 90
    King and, 90
    in Phenix City, Alabama, 88
    stash houses for, 89, 100, 145, 146, 149, 196–201, 219

Singer, Janice, 178

"Slick." *See* Darbins, Ricardo

Slick Pulla, 172

"Slim." *See* Bivens, Eric

Smack (magazine), 163, 168

Smith, Jason, 260–61

"Smurf." *See* Allison, Rafael

snitch. *See* informant

Snoop Dogg, 1–2

So So Def, billboard for, 73

SoBe Live (club), 168

SOHH.com (Web zine), 178

"Soul Survivor" (Jeezy), 213, 214

"Soup." *See* Ali, Jamad

The Source (magazine), 141, 162

"Southwest T." *See* Flenory, Terry

Space Mountain
  as distribution center, 191
  search warrant for, 140–41, 161–62, 216
  as stash house, 139–41, 161–62, 191, 216, 223, 232, 264, 274

Sparks, Calvin ("Playboy")
  cocaine transportation by, 29
  indictment of, 218

St. Clair County Detention and Intervention Center, 1–2

St. Louis, BMF cell in, 43, 57–58, 132, 217, 230, 264

stash house
  in Atlanta, 47, 50, 70–71, 114, 125, 127, 138, 139–41, 150–51, 161–62, 191–92, 216, 223, 225, 232, 233, 264, 267, 274
  drugs for, 30, 47–48
  the Elevator as, 71, 114, 125, 127, 191, 223, 225, 233, 264
  First/Second/Third Base as, 47–48, 100, 145–46, 149, 196–201
  the Gate as, 70–71, 138, 140, 191–92, 223, 225, 232, 264
  the Horse Ranch as, 71
  the Jump as, 47, 100, 150–51
  for Kiki/King partnership, 88
  for Sin City Mafia, 89, 100, 145, 146, 149, 196–201, 219

"Stay Strapped" (Jeezy), 173

Stevie Wonder, 33

Stuckey, Thelmon ("T-Stuck")
  arrest of, 14

audacity of, 13

as drug dealer/enforcer, 13

incarceration of, 15

Meech association with, 13–14, 17

murder by, 14

"Stupid." *See* Hackett, Ulysses

"Suge." *See* Knight, Marion

Supreme Team, 40–41

surveillance, of BMF, 11, 23, 100, 117–21, 124–26, 133–35, 138, 156, 159, 188, 192–93, 198–99, 203, 214

"Swift." *See* Whaley, Marc

tattoo
  on Bleu DaVinci/Baby Bleu, 235
  "BMF" as, 16, 45, 52–53, 275
  BMF motto as, 45, 235

"Tattoo." *See* Drummond, Raschaka

Taylor, Darryl ("Poppa")
  as Combs's cousin, 56, 264, 272–73
  as courier/distributor, 207, 264
  at 404 Motorsports, 57, 207
  as government witness, 272–73
  indictment of, 264

Teasers (club), 67, 164, 165

"Terry." *See* Flenory, Terry

"Texas Cruz." *See* Short, Terrance

Third Base, 100, 145–46, 149, 196–201

Thomas, Damon, 54, 208–12, 243–44

T.I. (rapper), 4, 49, 231

"Tito." *See* Byrth, Martez

Tobacco and Firearms, 214–15

Tongue & Groove (club), 263

transportation, of cocaine/money/bling, 26–30, 39–40, 101–3, 106, 147, 148, 207, 237, 254

trap, in vehicle, 39–40, 224, 274

Trap House (Gucci Mane), 177

Trap or Die (Jeezy), 66, 168, 169

traps, cars with, 39–40, 224

Trina, as "Diamond Princess," 168